LABORATORY MANUAL

for

Morphology and Syntax

Seventh Edition

William R. Merrifield
Constance M. Naish
Calvin R. Rensch
Gillian Story

SIL International
Dallas, Texas

Library of Congress No. 2003-112585
ISBN 1-55671-149-2

First edition 1960
Second edition, revised 1962
Third edition, revised 1965
Fourth edition, revised 1967
Fifth edition, revised 1974
Sixth edition, revised 1987
Seventh edition, 2003

Copies of this publication and other publications of SIL International may be obtained from:

International Academic Bookstore
SIL International
7500 W. Camp Wisdom Road
Dallas, TX 75236
Phone: 972-708-7404
Fax: 972-708-7363

Email: academic_books@sil.org
Internet: http://www.ethnologue.com

Laboratory Manual for Morphology and Syntax

Preface to the Seventh Edition

The promise of 'regular' upgrades of the sixth edition is now a beginning reality after a mere sixteen years, due, undoubtedly, to the wonders of 'electronic' storage. Actually, the electronic version of 1987 was helpful, but akin to a stone-age tool in 2003. This is not a major revision. A number of the datasets (née 'problems') are changed in minor ways; the typography is, I think, much improved; but none of the last-edition datasets has been deleted, nor have any new ones been added. IPA symbols have replaced Americanist symbols in some datasets; but not uniformly. Some datasets remain or have been recast in orthographies used by reading populations of certain languages where phonological issues are not in view. Thanks to you Instructors for continuing to find this manual useful for training.

Preface to the Sixth Edition

This is the sixth edition of the Laboratory Manual for Morphology and Syntax. A lot of water has gone under the bridge since its last revision in 1974. The first edition appeared in 1960, four years after attention began to shift from morphology to syntax in the introductory grammar courses offered by the Summer Institute of Linguistics. I believe it was in 1956 that Velma Pickett's first grammar textbook (1954) was introduced at the University of Oklahoma, marking a shift from an almost complete emphasis on morphology and morphophonemics, based on Nida (1949), to an increasing interest in structures larger than the word. Pickett's text was followed by Elson's first text (Elson 1958), which was first used at the SIL school at the University of Washington in 1958. These two early texts were subsequently combined in a joint text by Elson and Pickett (1960) which, along with the work of Longacre (1964), became the earliest sources of pedagogy within the tagmemic framework of Kenneth L. Pike.

It was in the context of the development of these textbooks that the 'Lab Manual' came into being at the University of Washington. Unfortunately, the team that created the early editions has not been able to work together for many years. Since the second edition, the responsibility for revision and update has been left to just one of the original authors. Now, after many years of not having taught introductory syntax, this author has had the enjoyable experience of returning to teaching it again. This sixth edition is the result.

This edition omits seven problems that were in the fifth edition and adds sixty-seven new ones. To aid instructors who have used the manual previously, the tables on the next two pages correlate problem numbers in the old and new editions.

This edition has been computerized in the hope that subsequent improvements can be made on a more regular basis. Such improvements include the modification of certain problems and the addition of problems suitable for use in the introductory syntax course. Suggestions for further improvement will be gratefully received.

William R. Merrifield
Dallas, Texas

Changes in the Seventh Edition

Apart from minor changes to some datasets, the following adjustments have been made: Eskimo is now listed as Inuit and Papago as O'odham. Some datasets have been rearranged and renumbered to accommodate new page layouts, namely:

25–26→26–27, 27→25; 79↔80; 149–153→150–154, 154→149; 162↔163; 184↔185; 197–198→198–199, 199→197; 209↔210; 216→221, 217–220→216–219, 221→222, 222→220; 237↔238; 240→242, 241–242→240–241; 265–266→266–267, 267→265; 270↔271; 272–273→274–275, 274→272; 275 –276→276–277, 277–278→279–280, 279→278, 280→273.

Acknowledgments

Over a number of years, a great many people, many of them unknown to the authors of this volume, have supplied data from their field notes or from languages of which they are native speakers, and have constructed problems for our use from these data. As the science of Linguistics has advanced and methods and procedures have shifted, these problems have been reworked and redesigned many times. This fact leaves us in heavy debt to a great number of people unknown to us, but to whom we wish to express our appreciation.

A partial acknowledgment concerning the various sources of data which we have been able to trace is made in the Language Index that follows. Where a particular speaker is known to have supplied data for a language, his/her name appears with that of the field linguist. If the language problem has been designed from a published source, rather than by personal communication, this source is footnoted to the problem.

Language Index

Laboratory Manual for Morphology and Syntax

Laboratory Manual for Morphology and Syntax

Dataset 1. Hyderabadi Telugu (India)

1.	pilla	'child'	8.	pillalu	'children'
2.	puwu	'flower'	9.	puwulu	'flowers'
3.	tʃiima	'ant'	10.	tʃiimalu	'ants'
4.	doma	'mosquito'	11.	domalu	'mosquitos'
5.	godugu	'elephant'	12.	godugulu	'elephants'
6.	tʃiire	'sari'	13.	tʃiirelu	'saris'
7.	annagaaru	'elder brother'	14.	annagaarulu	'elder brothers'

Dataset 2. Kewa (Papua New Guinea)

1.	ada	'house(s)'	5.	adanu	'group(s) of houses'
2.	pora	'path(s)'	6.	poranu	'group(s) of paths'
3.	yana	'dog(s)'	7.	yananu	'group(s) of dogs'
4.	nu	'net bag(s)'	8.	nunu	'group(s) of net bags'

Dataset 3. Southern Barasano (Colombia)

Phonemic stress is not indicated.

1.	kahea	'eye'	4.	kahe	'eyes'
2.	bitia	'bead'	5.	biti	'beads'
3.	kĩa	'cassava tuber'	6.	kĩ	'cassava tubers'

Dataset 4. Swahili (Uganda)

1.	mtoto	'child'	5.	watoto	'children'
2.	mtu	'person'	6.	watu	'people'
3.	mpiʃi	'cook'	7.	wapiʃi	'cooks'
4.	mgeni	'stranger'	8.	wageni	'strangers'

Laboratory Manual for Morphology and Syntax

Dataset 5. Palantla Chinantec (Mexico)

1. dsøi^2 'dog(s)'
2. lo^{12} 'pheasant(s)'
3. ŋié^{12} 'pig(s)'
4. tan^{12} 'bird(s)'

Dataset 6. Huixtec Tzotzil (Mexico)

Data from Marion M. Cowan 1969, Tzotzil Grammar, 67–70.

1. ná   'house(s)'
2. ʔánts   'woman, women'
3. vínik   'man, men'
4. ʔatséb   'girl(s)'

5. náetik   'houses'
6. ʔántsetik   'women'
7. víniketik   'men'
8. ʔatsébetik   'girls'

Dataset 7. Tepehua (Mexico)

1. kintʃʌqʌʔ   'my house'
2. mintʃʌqʌʔ   'your house'
3. iʃtʃʌqʌʔ   'his house'
4. kintʌntsʾ   'my stool'
5. mintʌntsʾ   'your stool'
6. iʃtʌntsʾ   'his stool'

7. kintʌpaqaʔut   'my name'
8. mintʌpaqaʔut   'your name'
9. iʃtʌpaqaʔut   'his name'
10. kintsʾʌpu   'my berries'
11. mintsʾʌpu   'your berries'
12. iʃtsʾʌpu   'his berries'

Dataset 8. Michoacán Nahuatl (Mexico)

1. nokali   'my house'
2. nokalimes   'my houses'
3. mokali   'your house'
4. ikali   'his house'
5. kali   'house'
6. kalimes   'houses'
7. nopelo   'my dog'
8. mopelo   'your dog'
9. mopelomes   'your dogs'
10. ipelo   'his dog'
11. pelo   'dog'
12. nokwahmili   'my cornfield'
13. mokwahmili   'your cornfield'
14. ikwahmili   'his cornfield'
15. ikwahmilimes   'his cornfields'
16. kwahmili   'cornfield'

Dataset 9. Isthmus Zapotec (Mexico)
Phonemic tone and stress not indicated.

1. ɲee   'foot'
2. kaɲee   'feet'
3. ɲeebe   'his foot'
4. kaɲeebe   'his feet'
5. ɲeeluʔ   'your foot'
6. kaɲeetu   'your (pl) feet'
7. kaɲeedu   'our feet'
8. ʒigi   'chin'
9. kaʒigi   'chins'
10. ʒigibe   'his chin'
11. ʒigiluʔ   'your chin'
12. kaʒigitu   'your (pl) chins'
13. kaʒigidu   'our chins'
14. ʒike   'shoulder'
15. ʒikebe   'his shoulder'
16. kaʒikeluʔ   'your shoulders'
17. diaga   'ear'
18. kadiagatu   'your (pl) ears'
19. kadiagadu   'our ears'
20. biʃozedu   'our father'
21. biʃozetu   'your (pl) father'
22. kabiʃozetu   'your (pl) fathers'

Dataset 10. Guaymí (Panama)

1. kuge	'burns	5. kugaba	'burned'
2. blite	'speaks'	6. blitaba	'spoke'
3. kite	'throws'	7. kitaba	'threw'
4. mete	'hits'	8. metaba	'hit'

Dataset 11. Tetelcingo Nahuatl (Mexico)

1. nikwika	'I sing.'	7. titʃuka	'You cry.'
2. tikwika	'You sing.'	8. titʃukataya	'You were crying.'
3. tikonik	'You drank.'	9. tikonitika	'You are drinking.'
4. nikonitika	'I am drinking.'	10. nikwikataya	'I was singing.'
5. tikwikas	'You will sing.'	11. nikonis	'I will drink.'
6. nitʃukatika	'I am crying.'	12. nitʃukak	'I cried.'

Dataset 12. Chiquihuitlán Mazatec (Mexico)

Phonemic tone is not indicated.'

1. faʔa	'takes'	7. tʃha	'speaks'
2. tifaʔa	'is taking'	8. titʃha	'is speaking'
3. kafaʔa	'took'	9. katʃha	'spoke'
4. sæ	'sings'	10. fi	'goes'
5. tisæ	'is singing'	11. tifi	'is going'
6. kasæ	'sang'	12. kafi	'went'

Dataset 13. Finnish

1. laulan	'I sing.'	7. yuon	'I drink.'
2. laulat	'You sing.'	8. yuot	'You drink.'
3. laulavi	'He sings.'	9. yuovi	'He drinks.'
4. laulamme	'We sing.	10. yuomme	'We drink.'
5. laulatte	'You (pl) sing.	11. yuotte	'You (pl) drink.'
6. laulavat	'They sing.	12. yuovat	'They drink.'

Dataset 14. Palantla Chinantec (Mexico)

1. cuú² jni	'I sneeze.'	7. júh² jni	'I cough.'
2. cuú² dsa	'He sneezes.'	8. júh³jni	'I'll cough.'
3. cuú³ jniang	'We'll sneeze.'	9. júh² dsa	'He coughs.'
4. hmíh³ jni	'I'll blink.'	10. ŋiú³ jni	'I'll vomit.'
5. hmíh² dsa	'He blinks.'	11. ŋiú² jniang	'We vomit.'
6. hmíh² jniang	'We blink.'	12. ŋiú³ jniang	'We'll vomit.'

Dataset 15. Mixtec of San Miguel (Mexico)

1. ʃítɨdē	'He is cutting.'	7. sāmātʃā	'It (water) will change.'
2. ʃítɨnā	'She is cutting.'	8. sāmāʒà	'He (god) will change.'
3. ʃɨtɨɲā	'She will cut.'	9. kǘṵdē	'He is descending.'
4. ʃɨtɨṵ́	'It (inan) will cut.'	10. kǘṵtʃā	'It is raining.'
5. sámātɨ̀	'It (an) is changing.'	11. kṵ̄ṵtɨ	'It (an) will descend.'
6. sámāṵ̀	'It (inan) is changing.'	12. kṵ̄ṵʒà	'He (god) will descend.'

Laboratory Manual for Morphology and Syntax

Dataset 16. Terêna (Brazil)
Phonemic stress is not indicated.

1.	ẽmõʔũ	'my word'	4.	ãyõ	'my brother'	7.	õwõkũ	'my house'
2.	yemoʔu	'your word'	5.	yayo	'your brother'	8.	yowoku	'your house'
3.	emoʔu	'his word'	6.	ayo	'his brother'	9.	owoku	'his house'

Dataset 17. Oaxaca Chontal (Mexico)
Phonemic stress is not indicated.

1.	tsetse	'squirrel'	9.	tseɬtse	'squirrels'
2.	tuwa	'foreigner'	10.	tuɬwa	'foreigners'
3.	teʔa	'elder'	11.	teɬʔa	'elders'
4.	akanʼoʔ	'woman'	12.	akaɬnʼoʔ	'women'
5.	konʼiʔ	'grandchild'	13.	koɬnʼiʔ	'grandchildren'
6.	ɬipo	'possum'	14.	ɬiɬpo	'possums'
7.	sewiʔ	'magpie'	15.	seɬwiʔ	'magpies'
8.	mekoʔ	'spoon'	16.	meɬkoʔ	'spoons'

Dataset 18. Agta (Philippines)

1.	gafutan	'grab'	5.	ginafut	'grabbed'
2.	dangagan	'hear'	6.	dinangag	'heard'
3.	hulutan	'follow'	7.	hinulut	'followed'
4.	paligatan	'hit (pres)'	8.	pinaligat	'hit (past)'

Dataset 19. Katu (Vietnam)

1.	gap	'to cut'	5.	ganap	'scissors'
2.	juut	'to rub'	6.	januut	'cloth'
3.	panh	'to shoot'	7.	pananh	'crossbow'
4.	piih	'to sweep'	8.	paniih	'broom'

Laboratory Manual for Morphology and Syntax

Dataset 20. Modern Hebrew

Data from Saad, George N. and Shmuel Bolozky. 1984. Causativization and Transitivization in Arabic and Modern Hebrew. Afroasiatic Linguistics 9:106.

1. naħal	'inherit'	6. hinħil	'bequest'
2. qaraʔ	'read'	7. hiqriʔ	'make read'
3. ṭaraf	'hire'	8. hiṭrif	'feed'
4. raqad	'dance'	9. hirqid	'make dance'
5. ʃaʔal	'borrow'	10. hiʃʔil	'lend'

Dataset 21. Arabic

Data from Saad, George N. and Shmuel Bolozky. 1984. Causativization and Transitivization in Arabic and Modern Hebrew. Afroasiatic Linguistics 9:105.

1. laqima	'gobble'	7. ʔalqama	'make gobble'
2. ʃariba	'drink'	8. ʔaʃraba	'make drink'
3. laʕiqa	'lick'	9. ʔalʕaqa	'make lick'
4. labisa	'wear'	10. ʔalbasa	'dress (someone)'
5. xasira	'lose'	11. ʔaxsara	'make lose'
6. samiʕa	'hear'	12. ʔasmaʕa	'make hear'

Dataset 22. Amharic (Ethiopia)

Phonemic stress is not indicated.

	'take'	'resemble'	'join'	'repeat'	'trade'	'get down'
1. 3S MASC PRF	wəssədə	məssələ	gəttəmə	dəggəmə	nəggədə	wərrədə
2. 3P PRF	wəssədu	məssəlu	gəttəmu	dəggəmu	nəggədu	wərrədu
3. 3S MASC IMPF	yɨwəsd	yɨməsl	yɨgətm	yɨdəgm	yɨnəgd	yɨwərd
4. 3P IMPF	yɨwəsdu	yɨməslu	yɨgətmu	yɨdəgmu	yɨnəgdu	yɨwərdu
5. 2S IMPV	wɨsəd	mɨsəl	gitəm	dɨgəm	nɨgəd	wɨrəd
6. 2P IMPV	wɨsədu	mɨsəlu	gitəmu	dɨgəmu	nɨgədu	wɨrədu
7. INFINITIVE	məwsəd	məmsəl	məgtəm	mədgəm	məngəd	məwrəd

Laboratory Manual for Morphology and Syntax

Dataset 23. Mezquital Otomí (Mexico)

Tones: ´ (high), ˘ (rising); low tone is unmarked.

1.	dímpení	'I launder.'	10.	bíntǐhi	'He hurries.'
2.	dántǐhi	'I hurried.'	11.	gimpení	'You will launder.'
3.	dampení	'He will launder.'	12.	gántǐhi	'You hurried.'
4.	díntǐhi	'I hurry.'	13.	bímpení	'He launders.'
5.	bimpení	'He laundered.'	14.	gantǐhi	'I will hurry.'
6.	bintǐhi	'He hurried.'	15.	gampení	'I will launder.'
7.	gintǐhi	'You will hurry.'	16.	dantǐhi	'He will hurry.'
8.	dámpení	'I laundered.'	17.	gámpení	'You laundered.'
9.	gímpení	'You launder.'	18.	gíntǐhi	'You hurry.'

Dataset 24. Pocomchí (Guatemala)

1.	qoril	'He sees us.'	8.	qoreht'al	'He recognizes us.'
2.	kiril	'He sees them.'	9.	kikeht'al	'They recognize them.'
3.	kiwil	'I see them.'	10.	kiweht'al	'I recognize them.'
4.	tiwil	'I see you (pl).'	11.	tireht'al	'He recognizes you (pl).'
5.	kiqil	'We see them.'	12.	kiqeht'al	'We recognize them.'
6.	qokil	'They see us.'	13.	tiqil	'We see you (pl).'
7.	tikeht'al	'They recognize you (pl).'	14.	tikil	'They see you (pl).'

Dataset 25. Huichol (Mexico)

Length, juncture, and tone not indicated.

1.	pepʌʔuki	'You are a man.'	6.	petinunutsi	'Are you a child?'
2.	nepʌʔuki	'I am a man.'	7.	pemʌnunutsi	'you who are a child'
3.	petiʔuki	'Are you a man?'	8.	netinunutsi	'Am I a child?'
4.	pemʌʔuki	'you who are a man'	9.	nemʌnunutsi	'I who am a child'
5.	pepʌnunutsi	'You are a child.'	10.	_____	'I am a child.'

Laboratory Manual for Morphology and Syntax

Dataset 26. Sierra Popoluca (Mexico)

1. miɲpa — 'He comes.'
2. miɲyahum — 'They came.'
3. miɲpanam — 'He still comes.'
4. miɲyahpatyim — 'They also come.'
5. se:tpa — 'He returns.'
6. se:tyahpa — 'They return.'
7. se:tyahumtyim — 'They also returned.'
8. se:tpatyim — 'He also returns.'
9. miɲyahpa — 'They come.'
10. miɲum — 'He came.'
11. miɲumtyim — 'He also came.'
12. miɲyahumtyim — 'They also came.'
13. se:tum — 'He returned.'
14. se:tyahpanam — 'They still return.'
15. se:tpanam — 'He still returns.'
16. se:tyahum — 'They returned.'

Dataset 27. Fore (Papua New Guinea)

Phonemic tone is not indicated.

1. natuwi — 'I ate yesterday.'
2. nagasuwi — 'I ate today.'
3. nakuwi — 'I will eat.'
4. nata:ni — 'You ate yesterday.'
5. nata:naw — 'You ate yesterday?'
6. nakiyi — 'He will eat.'
7. nakiyaw — 'He will eat?'
8. natuni — 'We ate yesterday.'
9. nagasuni — 'We ate today.'
10. nakuni — 'We will eat.'
11. nagasusi — 'We two ate today.'
12. nakusi — 'We two will eat.'
13. nata:wi — 'They ate yesterday.'
14. nata:si — 'They two ate yesterday.'

Dataset 28. Michoacán Nahuatl (Mexico)

1. nimoita — 'I see myself.'
2. nikita — 'I see him.'
3. timoita — 'You see yourself.'
4. nimoaniltia — 'I dirty myself.'
5. nikaniltia — 'I dirty him.'
6. timoaniltia — 'You dirty yourself.'
7. nimitsita — 'I see you.'
8. tinetʃita — 'You see me.'
9. tikita — 'You see him.'
10. nimitsaniltia — 'I dirty you.'
11. tinetʃaniltia — 'You dirty me.'
12. tikaniltia — 'You dirty him.'

Laboratory Manual for Morphology and Syntax

Dataset 29. Kikuyu (Kenya)

Phonemic tone is not indicated; Do not attempt to identify the meaning of ne-.

1. nenderadie — 'I am (already) going.'
2. neoradie — 'You are (already) going.'
3. nearadie — 'He is (already) going.'
4. neodiaga — 'You (usually) go.'
5. nemadiaga — 'They (usually) go.'
6. neogudie — 'You will go (immediately).'
7. nemogudie — 'You (pl) will go (immediately).'
8. nenderedie — 'I will go (today).'
9. nearedie — 'He will go (today).'
10. netogadie — 'We will go (after today).'
11. nemagadie — 'They will go (after today).'
12. neorediaga — 'You will (already) be going (today).'
13. nearediaga — 'He will (already) be going (today).'
14. nemogadiaga — 'You (pl) will (already) be going (after today).'
15. nemagadiaga — 'They will (already) be going (after today).'
16. neoadie — 'You have (just) gone.'
17. netoadie — 'We have (just) gone.'
18. neadiɛtɛ — 'He has gone (in the past).'
19. netodiɛtɛ — 'We have gone (in the past).'
20. nemadiɛtɛ — 'They have gone (in the past).'
21. netodire — 'We went (today).'
22. nemodire — 'You (pl) went (today).'
23. nenderadire — 'I went (yesterday).'
24. netoradire — 'We went (yesterday).'
25. netoadire — 'We went (day before yesterday).'
26. nemoadire — 'You (pl) went (day before yesterday).'
27. neogudiaga — 'You were (already) going (today).'
28. netogudiaga — 'We were (already) going (today).'
29. nenderadiaga — 'I was (already) going (yesterday).'
30. nemaradiaga — 'They were (already) going (yesterday).'
31. neoadiaga — 'You were (already) going (day before yesterday).'
32. nemoadiaga — 'You (pl) were (already) going (day before yesterday).'

Dataset 30. Sierra Popoluca (Mexico)

1. iko?tspa 'He is hitting him.'
2. aŋko?tspa 'I am hitting him.'
3. iŋwaspa 'You are biting him.'
4. iko?tsne 'He has hit him.'
5. ako?tsum 'He hit me.'
6. iwasneyahum 'He/they had bitten him/them.'
7. aŋko?tsta?mpa 'We are hitting him.'
8. miwasum 'He bit you.'
9. iwasyahpa 'He/they is/are biting him/them.'
10. awasneyahum 'They had bitten me.'
11. awasneta?mum 'He had bitten us.'
12. miko?tsta?mum 'He hit you (pl).'
13. iŋwasta?mpa 'You (pl) are biting him.'
14. aŋko?tsneum 'I had hit him.'
15. iŋko?tsne 'You have hit him.'
16. miwasneyah 'They have bitten you.'
17. iŋwasyahum 'You bit them.'
18. aŋwasneyah 'I have bitten them.'

Dataset 31. Sayula Popoluca (Mexico)

1. tʌtʃeʔmp   'I am seeking you.'

2. tʌntʃeʔmp   'I am seeking him/it.'

3. ʔintʃeʔmp   'You are seeking him/it.'

4. ʔitʃeʔmp   'He is seeking him/it.'

5. ʔiʃtʃeʔmp   'He is seeking you/you are seeking me.'

6. tʌʃtʃeʔmp   'He is seeking me.'

7. tʌʔeʔp   'I am looking at you.'

8. tʌnʔeʔp   'I am looking at him/it.'

9. ʔinʔeʔp   'You are looking at him/it.'

10. ʔiʔeʔp   'He is looking at him/it.'

11. ʔiʃʔeʔp   'He is looking at you/you are looking at me.'

12. tʌʃʔeʔp   'He is looking at me.'

13. tʌnhúyp   'I am buying it.'

14. ʔinhúyp   'You are buying it.'

15. ʔihúyp   'He is buying it.'

16. tʌnhúyhap   'I am buying it for him.'

17. ʔinhúyhap   'You are buying it for him.'

18. ʔihúyhap   'He is buying it for him.'

19. tʌhúyhap   'I am buying it for you.'

20. ʔiʃhúyhap   'He is buying it for you/you are buying it for me.'

21. tʌʃhúyhap   'He is buying it for me.'

22. tʌnhúyw   'I bought it.'

23. tʌʃhúyhaw   'He bought it for me.'

Dataset 32. Southern Barasano (Colombia)

Phonemic stress is not indicated.

1. wabõ   'She went.'
2. bĩdĩbĩ   'He went upstream.'
3. tɨdibɨ   'I/you returned.'
4. bĩdĩkoabĩ   'He really went upstream.'
5. tɨdiboabɨ   'I/you unexpectedly returned.'
6. wakoabɨ   'I/you really went.'
7. tɨdirũtũbĩ   'He continued to return.'
8. bĩdĩboabõ   'She unexpectedly went upstream.'
9. warũtũbĩ   'He continued going.'
10. tɨdikoabõ   'She really returned.'
11. bĩdĩrũtũbɨ   'I/you continued to go upstream.'
12. waboabõ   'She unexpectedly went.'

Dataset 33. Cheyenne (USA)

1. namesehe   'I eat.'
2. emesehe   'He eats.'
3. naeʃemesehe   'I already ate.'
4. esaamesehehe   'He doesn't eat.'
5. emeomesehe   'He ate this morning.'
6. eohkemesehe   'He always eats.'
7. epevemesehe   'He eats well.'
8. esaaeʃemesehehe   'He has not eaten yet.'
9. eohkesaapevemesehehe 'He never eats well.'
10. eohkepevemesehe   'He always eats well.'
11. nameoeʃemesehe   'I already ate this morning.'
12. naohkepevenemene   'I always sing well.'

Dataset 34. Huasteca Nahuatl (Mexico, Simplified)

Data from Elson and Pickett, 1983, Beginning Morphology and Syntax,
Dallas: Summer Institute of Linguistics, p.12.

1.	kikwa	'He eats it.'
2.	kitemo	'He hunts it.'
3.	kitemoh	'He hunted it.'
4.	kitemos	'He will hunt it.'
5.	kitemosok	'He will hunt it again.'
6.	kitemoltih	'He caused him to hunt it.'
7.	kitemoki	'He comes to hunt it.'
8.	kitemokiya	'He already comes to hunt it.'
9.	kitemokiok	'He comes to hunt it again.'
10.	kitemoltilih	'He caused him to hunt it for her.'
11.	kitemoltiki	'He causes him to come to hunt it.'
12.	kitemoltilis	'He will cause him to hunt it for her.'
13.	kitemoltiliki	'He causes him to come to hunt it for her.'
14.	kitemoskia	'He would hunt it.'
15.	kitemoskiaya	'Already (now) he would hunt it.'
16.	kitemoltiskia	'He would cause him to hunt it.'
17.	kitemoltiliskia	'He would cause him to hunt it for her.'
18.	kitemoskiaok	'He would hunt it again.'
19.	kitemokiyaok	'Already he comes to hunt it again.'
20.	kitemoskiayaok	'Already (now) he would hunt it again.'

Dataset 35. Sierra Nahuatl (Mexico)

1. nimitsita   'I see you.'

2. nikita   'I see him.'

3. tikmaka   'You give it to him.'

4. tinetʃita   'You see me.'

5. nannetʃmaka   'You (pl) give it to me.'

6. tikonmaka   'You give it to him, Sir.'

7. tikonitatihtsinoh   'You see him, most honored Sir.'

8. tikonmakatihtsinohtikah   'You give it to him, most very honored Sir.'

9. tinetʃonita   'You see me, Sir.'

10. tinetʃonmakatihtsinoh   'You give it to me, most honored Sir.'

11. nannetʃonmakatikah   'You (pl) give it to me, honored Sirs.'

12. nannetʃonitatihtsinohtikah   'You (pl) see me, most very honored Sirs.'

13. tinetʃonitatikah   'You see me, honored Sir.'

14. nannetʃonmakatihtsinoh   'You (pl) give it to me, most honored Sirs.'

Dataset 36. Cashinahua (Peru)

1. mĩ pikĩ	'You eat it.'	
2. ĩ pikĩ	'I eat it.'	
3. ĩ bɨkĩ	'I bring it.'	
4. ĩ bɨṣũ	'I brought it.'	
5. ĩ bɨṣũkĩ	'I bring it for him.'	
6. ĩ bɨbaiṣũ	'I brought it all day.'	
7. ĩ bɨtuṣirikĩ	'I suddenly bring it also.'	
8. ĩ bɨtuṣiṣṣũ	'I only brought it suddenly.'	
9. ĩ bɨṣũbidãṣũ	'I came and brought it for him.'	
10. ĩ bɨṣũskĩ	'I only bring it for him.'	
11. ĩ bɨyubãĩkĩ	'I first go and bring it.'	
12. ĩ bɨbaibãĩṣũ	'I went and brought it all day.'	
13. ĩ bɨbaibãũkĩ	'I bring it around all day.'	
14. ĩ bɨbaiyuṣũ	'I first brought it all day.'	
15. ĩ bɨribãĩkĩ	'I also go and bring it.'	
16. ĩ bɨsbãũṣũ	'I only brought it around.'	
17. ĩ bɨbãũkĩ	'I bring it around.'	
18. ĩ bɨmabidãkĩ	'I make him come and bring it.'	
19. ĩ bɨṣũtuṣiṣũ	'I suddenly brought it for him.'	
20. ĩ bɨmassũ	'I only made him bring it.'	
21. ĩ bɨmabaikĩ	'I make him bring it all day.'	
22. ĩ bɨyubidãṣũ	'I first came and brought it.'	
23. ĩ bɨbãĩṣũ	'I went and brought it.'	
24. ĩ bɨriṣũ	'I also brought it.'	
25. ĩ bɨmarikĩ	'I also make him bring it.'	

Dataset 37. Southern Barasano (Colombia)

Phonemic stress is not indicated.

1.	wabõ	'She went.'
2.	bãhãbĩ	'He ascended.'
3.	bɨdĩbã	'They went upstream.'
4.	warũgõbĩ	'He went on foot.'
5.	bãhãbetibã	'They did not ascend.'
6.	bɨdĩkoahɨ	'I/you went upstream there.'
7.	tɨdikudikoahɨ	'I/you stopped off while returning there.'
8.	bãhãbetiboabã	'Unexpectedly they did not ascend.'
9.	tɨdiboakoahɨ	'I/you returned there unexpectedly.'
10.	bãhãrũtũbãtsibĩ	'It seems he continued to ascend.'
11.	bɨdĩbãtsiboabõ	'It seems she went upstream unexpectedly.'
12.	wabetirũtũbĩ	'He continued not to go.'
13.	wabetibãtsibã	'It seems they did not go.'
14.	bãhãbãtsikoabã	'It seems they ascended there/really.'
15.	bɨdĩkoakoabõ	'She really went upstream there.'
16.	warũtũkoabĩ	'He continued to go there/really.'
17.	tɨdirũgõkoabõ	'She returned there/really on foot.'
18.	bãhãkudiboabã	'They stopped off while ascending unexpectedly.'
19.	warũgõboabĩ	'He went on foot unexpectedly.'
20.	bɨdĩbetikudibõ	'She did not stop off while going upstream.'
21.	tɨdibetirũgõbã	'They did not return on foot.'
22.	wabãtsikoahɨ	'It seems I/you went there.'
23.	tɨdirũgõbãtsibõ	'It seems she returned on foot.'
24.	bɨdĩkudibãtsibĩ	'It seems he stopped off while going upstream.'
25.	tɨdibetikoabõ	'She did not return there.'
26.	bɨdĩkudikoabĩ	'He stopped off while going upstream there/really.'

Dataset 38. Rotokas (Papua New Guinea)

1.	kareue	'You returned today.'
2.	ikaurae	'I hurried today.'
3.	ikauroei	'He hurries.'
4.	karerovere	'He will return.'
5.	ikaupaovere	'She will be hurrying.'
6.	kareragaoei	'She only returns.'
7.	ikauvirorae	'I hurried all the way today.'
8.	kareiraoroei	'He really returns.'
9.	ikaurovopaoe	'She began to be hurrying today.'
10.	kareviroparoe	'He was returning all the way today.'
11.	karerovorovere	'He will begin to return.'
12.	ikauragaparaei	'I am only hurrying.'
13.	kareragarovorae	'I began only to return today.'
14.	kareragaviroroe	'He only returned all the way today.'
15.	kareiraopauvere	'You really will be returning.'
16.	ikauiraovirouei	'You really hurry all the way.'
17.	ikauiraorovouvere	'You will begin really to hurry.'
18.	karerovoviroravere	'I will begin to return all the way.'

Dataset 39. Choctaw (USA, Regularized)

1.	pĩsalitok	'I saw.'	8.	iʃsapĩsatʃĩ	'You will see me.'
2.	tʃipĩsali	'I see you.'	9.	iʃsaso	'You hit me (pres)'
3.	tʃisoli	'I hit you (pres).'	10.	iʃsotok	'You hit (past).'
4.	solitʃĩ	'I will hit.'	11.	iʃpayatok	'You called.'
5.	tʃipayalitʃĩ	'I will call you.'	12.	iʃsapaya	'You call me.'
6.	tʃakmãnelitʃĩ	'I will like.'	13.	tʃitʃakmãnelitok	'I liked you.'
7.	iʃsatʃakmãne	'You like me.'	14.	iʃpĩsa	'You see.'

Dataset 40. Amuzgo (Mexico)

Phonemic tone and stress are not indicated.

1.	ndiya	'I hear.'	11.	hndæʔ	'You sell.'
2.	tyondiʔ	'You heard.'	12.	tyohndæya	'I sold.'
3.	nndiya	'I will hear.'	13.	nhndæʔ	'You will sell.'
4.	tandiʔ	'You no longer hear.'	14.	tahndæya	'I no longer sell.'
5.	tindiya	'I did not hear.'	15.	tihndæʔ	'You did not sell.'
6.	ʃondiʔ	'You will not hear.'	16.	ʃohndæya	'I will not sell.'
7.	leindiya	'I can't hear.'	17.	leihndæʔ	'You can't sell.'
8.	tatindiʔ	'You no longer heard.'	18.	tatihndæya	'I no longer sold.'
9.	taʃondiya	'I will no longer hear.'	19.	taʃohndæʔ	'You will no longer sell.'
10.	taleindiʔ	'You can no longer hear.'	20.	taleihndæya	'I can no longer sell.'

Laboratory Manual for Morphology and Syntax

Dataset 41. Khmu? (Laos, Regularized)

1.	siʔgii	'today'
2.	pmgii	'tomorrow'
3.	pmmuuy	'day after tomorrow'
4.	pmmaay	'day after day after tomorrow'
5.	pmmɪt	'the day after that'
6.	hnjəʔ	'yesterday'
7.	siʔmuuy	'day before yesterday'
8.	siʔmaay	'day before day before yesterday'
9.	siʔmɪt	'day before that'
10.	nɨmklaay	'last year'
11.	nɨmgii	'this year'
12.	nɨmmuuy	'year before last'
13.	nɨmmaay	'year before year before last'
14.	nɨmmɪt	'year before that'

Dataset 42. Isthmus Zapotec (Mexico)

Phonemic tone and stress are not indicated.

1.	bizaʔna Pedru	'Peter's sister'
2.	bizaʔna Maria	'Mary's brother'
3.	benda Maria	'Mary's sister'
4.	biʔtʃi Pedru	'Peter's brother'
5.	bizaʔnabe	'his sister, her brother'
6.	Rosa	'Rose'
7.		'Rose's brother'
8.		'Rose's sister'
9.		'her sister'
10.		'his brother'

Dataset 43. English

1. talk	5. talked	9. employ	13. employed
2. earn	6. earned	10. boil	14. boiled
3. laugh	7. laughed	11. play	15. played
4. go	8. went	12. am	16. was

Dataset 44. Palantla Chinantec (Mexico)

1. hløah^{12} jni	'I speak.'	7. hløah^{12} dsa	'He speaks.'
2. ho^{12} jni	'I cry.'	8. ho^{12} dsa	'He cries.'
3. júh^2 jni	'I cough.'	9. júh^2 dsa	'He coughs.'
4. nei^{12} jni	'I go.'	10. dság^{12} dsa	'He goes.'
5. gøh^{12} jni	'I drink.'	11. hónh^2 dsa	'He drinks.'
6. jmáh^{12} jni	'I grab.'	12. chiính^{12} dsa	'He grabs.'

Dataset 45. Palantla Chinantec (Mexico)

1. he^{12} jni	'I teach.'	9. tanh^2 jni	'I fall.'
2. he^{12} jniang	'We teach.'	10. tanh^2 dsa	'He/she falls.'
3. he^{12} dsa	'He/she/they teach.'	11. quian^2 jniang	'We fall.'
4. jmo^{12} jni	'I make.'	12. quian^2 dsa	'They fall.'
5. jmo^{12} jniang	'We make.'	13. jon^{12} jni	'I die.'
6. jmo^{12} dsa	'He/she/they make.'	14. jon^{12} dsa	'He/she dies.'
7. jái^{12} jni	'I see.'	15. dsan^{12} jniang	'We die.'
8. jái^{12} dsa	'He/she/they see.'	16. dsan^{12} dsa	'They die.'

Dataset 46. Kiowa (USA)

1. àbaːnma	'I go.'	16. yãtay	'I wake up.'
2. èmbaːnma	'You go.'	17. gyáttay	'You wake up.'
3. baːnma	'He goes.'	18. ãntay	'He wakes up.'
4. gyàtkhɔːmɔ	'I read.'	19. gyàthiːnmɔ	'I dig.'
5. bátkhɔːmɔ	'You read.'	20. báthiːnmɔ	'You dig.'
6. gyákhɔːmɔ	'He reads.'	21. gyáhiːnmɔ	'He digs.'
7. gyàtpiɔːmɔ	'I cook.'	22. yãyay	'I am busy.'
8. bátpiɔːmɔ	'You cook.'	23. gyátyay	'You are busy.'
9. gyápiɔːmɔ	'He cooks.	24. ányay	'He is busy.'
10. yãtõːzaːnma	'I talk.'	25. àpɔttɔ	'I eat.'
11. gyáttõːzaːnma	'You talk.'	26. èmpɔttɔ	'You eat.'
12. ántõːzáːnma	'He talks.'	27. pɔttɔ	'He eats.'
13. àphõ	'I stand up.'	28. gyàtguttɔ	'I write.'
14. èmphõ	'You stand up.'	29. bátguttɔ	'You write.'
15. phõ	'He stands up.'	30. gyáguttɔ	'He writes.'

Dataset 47. Isthmus Zapotec (Mexico)

Phonemic tone and stress are not indicated.

1.	rukaadu	'We write.'	18.	ruyubibe	'He looks for.'
2.	rukaabe	'He writes.'	19.	zuyubibe	'He will look for.'
3.	zukaabe	'He will write.'	20.	biyubibe	'He looked for.'
4.	bikaabe	'He wrote.'	21.	kuyubibe	'He is looking for.'
5.	kukaabe	'He is writing.'	22.	rireebe	'He goes out.'
6.	ruʒooɲebe	'He runs.'	23.	zareebe	'He will go out.'
7.	zuʒooɲebe	'He will run.'	24.	bireebe	'He went out.'
8.	biʒooɲebe	'He ran.'	25.	kareebe	'He is going out.'
9.	kuʒooɲebe	'He is running.'	26.	ribanibe	'He wakes up.'
10.	ridʒelabe	'He finds.'	27.	zabanibe	'He will wake up.'
11.	zadʒelabe	'He will find.'	28.	bibanibe	'He woke up.'
12.	bidʒelabe	'He found.'	29.	kabanibe	'He is waking up.'
13.	kadʒelabe	'He is finding.'	30.	kabanidu	'We are waking up.'
14.	rikabibe	'He answers.'	31.	rudʒiibabe	'He goes up.'
15.	zakabibe	'He will answer.'	32.	zudʒiibabe	'He will go up.'
16.	bikabibe	'He answered.'	33.	bidʒiibabe	'He went up.'
17.	kakabibe	'He is answering.'	34.	kudʒiibabe	'He is going up.'

Laboratory Manual for Morphology and Syntax

Dataset 48. Spanish
Phonemic stress not indicated.

	INFIN	1ST SG	3RD SG	1ST PL	PRTCPL
1. 'create'	crear	creo	crea	creamos	creado
2. 'stop'	parar	paro	para	paramos	parado
3. 'throw out'	botar	boto	bota	botamos	botado
4. 'burn'	quemar	quemo	quema	quemamos	quemado
5. 'believe'	creer	creo	cree	creemos	creido
6. 'insert'	meter	meto	mete	metemos	metido
7. 'eat'	comer	como	come	comemos	comido
8. 'drink'	beber	bebo	bebe	bebemos	bebido
9. 'depart'	partir	parto	parte	partimos	partido
10. 'stir	batir	bato	bate	batimos	batido
11. 'live'	vivir	vivo	vive	vivimos	vivido

Dataset 49. Lalana Chinantec (Mexico)

1. rɨ²ŋiːn³¹ — 'I will laugh.'
2. rɨ²ŋiːhn² — 'You will laugh.'
3. rɨ²³ŋiːh² — 'He will laugh.'
4. rɨ²ŋiː²³²ra² — 'We will laugh.'
5. rɨ²ŋiːh²raʔ³ — 'You (pl) will laugh.'
6. rɨ²ʔmeːn³¹ — 'I will press.'
7. rɨ²ʔmeːhn² — 'You will press.'
8. rɨ²³ʔmeːh² — 'He will press.'
9. mɨ³ʔmeːh² — 'He pressed.'
10. rɨ²ʔmeː²³²ra² — 'We will press.'
11. rɨ²ʔmeːh²raʔ³ — 'You (pl) will press.'
12. rɨ²hmeːn²³² — 'I will do.'
13. rɨ²hmeːhn² — 'You will do.'
14. rɨ²³hmeːh²³ — 'He will do.'
15. rɨ²hmeː²ra² — 'We will do.'
16. rɨ²hmeːh²raʔ³ — 'You (pl) will do.'
17. rɨ²kwẽn³¹ — 'I will sneeze.'
18. rɨ²kwẽhn² — 'You will sneeze.'
19. rɨ²³kwẽh² — 'He will sneeze.'
20. rɨ²kwẽ²³²ra² — 'We will sneeze.'
21. rɨ²kwẽh²raʔ³ — 'You (pl) will sneeze.'
22. rɨ²nöhn1 — 'I will knead.'
23. rɨ²nön³¹ — 'You will knead.'
24. rɨ²³nöh² — 'He will knead.'
25. rɨ²nö²³²ra² — 'We will knead.'
26. rɨ²nö³¹raʔ³ — 'You (pl) will knead.'
27. rɨ²ŋiːn²³² — 'I will ask.'
28. rɨ²ŋiːhn² — 'You will ask.'
29. rɨ²³ŋiːh²³ — 'He will ask.'
30. rɨ²ŋiː²ra² — 'We will ask.'
31. rɨ²ŋiːh²raʔ³ — 'You (pl) will ask.'
32. rɨ²hoːhn¹ — 'I will see.'
33. rɨ²hoːn³¹ — 'You will see.'
34. rɨ²³hoːh² — 'He will see.'
35. mɨ³hoːh² — 'He saw.'
36. rɨ²hoː²³²ra² — 'We will see.'
37. rɨ²hoː³¹raʔ³ — 'You (pl) will see.'
38. rɨ²ʃiːn³¹ — 'I will cut.'
39. rɨ²ʃiːhn² — 'You will cut.'
40. rɨ²³ʃiːh² — 'He will cut.'
41. rɨ²ʃiː²³²ra² — 'We will cut.'
42. rɨ²ʃiːh²raʔ³ — 'You (pl) will cut.'
43. rɨ²lön²³² — 'I will speak.'
44. rɨ²löhn² — 'You will speak.'
45. rɨ²³löh²³ — 'He will speak.'
46. rɨ²lö²ra² — 'We will speak.'
47. rɨ²löh²raʔ³ — 'You (pl) will speak.'
48. rɨ²hnɨhn1 — 'I will carry.'
49. rɨ²hnɨn³¹ — 'You will carry.'
50. rɨ²³hnɨh² — 'He will carry.'
51. rɨ²hnɨ²³²ra² — 'We will carry.'
52. rɨ²hnɨ³¹raʔ³ — 'You (pl) will carry.'

Laboratory Manual for Morphology and Syntax

Dataset 50. Rotokas (Papua New Guinea)

1. avaravere	'I'll go.'	25. puraavere	'I'll make (it).'
2. avauvere	'You'll go.'	26. purarivere	'You'll make (it).'
3. avarovere	'He'll go.'	27. purarevere	'He'll make (it).'
4. avaraepa	'I went.'	28. puraava	'I made (it).'
5. avauepa	'You went.'	29. purariva	'You made (it).'
6. avaroepa	'He went.'	30. purareva	'He made (it).'
7. puraravere	'I'll say (it).'	31. ruiparavere	'I'll want (it).'
8. purauvere	'You'll say (it).'	32. ruipauvere	'You'll want (it).'
9. purarovere	'He'll say (it).'	33. ruiparovere	'He'll want (it).'
10. puraraepa	'I said (it).'	34. ruiparaepa	'I wanted (it).'
11. purauepa	'You said (it).'	35. ruipauepa	'You wanted (it)'
12. puraroepa	'He said (it).'	36. ruiparoepa	'He wanted (it).'
13. pauavere	'I'll build (it).'	37. vokaavere	'I'll walk.'
14. paurivere	'You'll build (it).'	38. vokarivere	'You'll walk.'
15. paurevere	'He'll build (it).'	39. vokarevere	'He'll walk.'
16. pauava	'I built (it).'	40. vokaava	'I walked.'
17. pauriva	'You built (it).'	41. vokariva	'You walked.'
18. paureva	'He built (it).'	42. vokareva	'He walked.'
19. tapaavere	'I'll hit (it).'	43. pauravere	'I'll sit.'
20. taparivere	'You'll hit (it).'	44. pauuvere	'You'll sit.'
21. taparevere	'He'll hit (it).'	45. paurovere	'He'll sit.'
22. tapaava	'I hit (it).'	46. pauraepa	'I sat.'
23. tapariva	'You hit (it).'	47. pauuepa	'You sat.'
24. tapareva	'He hit (it).'	48. pauroepa	'He sat.'

Dataset 51. Mixtec of San Miguel (Mexico)

1.	kūnūrì	'I will weave.'	11.	t͡ʃāāī	'The child will load.'
2.	kúnūɲā	'She is weaving.'	12.	t͡ʃāāɲā	'She will load.'
3.	ká̰ʔa̰ī	'The child is speaking.'	13.	ʃítīdē	'He is cutting.'
4.	ká̰ʔàdē	'He is speaking.'	14.	ʃītīī	'The child will cut.'
5.	ka̰ʔàdē	'He will speak.'	15.	ká̰āī	'The child is adjusting.'
6.	kíbīrì	'I am entering.'	16.	kàāī	'The child will adjust.'
7.	kìbīɲā	'She will enter.'	17.	kḭ́ʔìrì	'I am going.'
8.	sḭ́hḭ̄ɲā	'She is sifting.'	18.	kḭ̄ʔìrì	'I will go.'
9.	sḭ̀hḭ̄rì	'I will sift.'	19.	t͡ʃāàrì	'I will come.'
10.	t͡ʃáādē	'He is loading.'	20.	t͡ʃáàɲā	'She is coming.'

Dataset 52. Rotokas (Papua New Guinea)

1.	kaakau	'dog'	13.	kaakaukare	'pack of dogs'
2.	avuka	'old woman'	14.	avukariako	'group of old women'
3.	avuru	'fly'	15.	avurupitu	'swarm of flies'
4.	koisi	'bee'	16.	koisipitu	'swarm of bees'
5.	atari	'fish'	17.	atarikare	'school of fish'
6.	isiso	'grass'	18.	isisokou	'bunch of grass'
7.	kokio	'bird'	19.	kokiokare	'flight of birds'
8.	aako	'mother'	20.	aakoriako	'group of mothers'
9.	kokopuo	'butterfly'	21.	kokopuopitu	'swarm of butterflies'
10.	toru	'wave'	22.	torukou	'series of waves'
11.	tavauru	'young girl'	23.	tavaururiako	'group of young girls'
12.	koie	'pig'	24.	koiekare	'herd of pigs'

Laboratory Manual for Morphology and Syntax

Dataset 53. Huichol (Mexico)

Length, juncture and tone are not indicated.

		SINGULAR	PLURAL	POSSESSED
1.	'fishhook'	qaitʃʌ	qaitʃʌte	qaitʃʌya
2.	'bead'	kuka	kukate	kukaya
3.	'tree'	kʌye	kʌyezi	kʌyeya
4.	'axe'	hatʃa	hatʃate	hatʃaya
5.	'candle'	hauri	haurite	yuhauri
6.	'road'	huye	huyete	yuhuye
7.	'pumpkin'	maku	makute	makuya
8.	'cat'	mitʃu	mitʃuri	yumitʃu
9.	'sheep'	muza	muzatʃi	muzaya
10.	'nit'	zʌnai	zʌnaitʃi	yuzʌnai

Dataset 54. Wali (Ghana)

1.	gbɛbiri	'toe'	17.	daa	'market'
2.	gbɛbiɛ	'toes'	18.	daahi	'markets'
3.	libiri	'coin'	19.	lumbiri	'orange'
4.	libiɛ	'coins'	20.	lumbiɛ	'oranges'
5.	nuɔ	'fowl'	21.	kpakpani	'arm'
6.	nuɔhi	'fowls'	22.	kpakpama	'arms'
7.	nɔgbani	'lip'	23.	wɔɔ	'yam'
8.	nɔgbama	'lips'	24.	wɔɔhi	'yams'
9.	ʤɛla	'egg'	25.	nubiri	'finger'
10.	ʤɛlii	'eggs'	26.	nubiɛ	'fingers'
11.	na	'cow'	27.	dau	'man'
12.	nii	'cows'	28.	dauba	'men'
13.	biɛ	'child'	29.	poga	'woman'
14.	biɛhi	'children'	30.	pogaba	'women'
15.	waʤɛ	'cloth'	31.	nimbiri	'eye'
16.	waʤɛhi	'cloths'	32.	nimbiɛ	'eyes'

Dataset 55. Kikuyu (Kenya)
Phonemic tone is not indicated.

		SG	PL			SG	PL
1.	teacher	murutani	arutani	21.	crocodile	kiɲaɲi	iɲaɲi
2.	old person	muduuri	aduuri	22.	sugar cane	kigoa	igoa
3.	girl	muiretu	airetu	23.	worm	kiŋguɲu	iŋguɲu
4.	woman	mutumia	atumia	24.	folk song	kibata	ibata
5.	parent	muʃiari	aʃiari	25.	flood	kiŋguo	iŋguo
6.	buyer	muguri	aguri	26.	steering wheel	kibara	ibara
7.	traveler	mugendi	agendi	27.	hiding place	kimamo	imamo
8.	politician	muteti	ateti	28.	spider	mbombue	mbombue
9.	root	muri	miri	29.	donkey	bunda	bunda
10.	tree	muti	miti	30.	cow	ŋɔmbe	ŋɔmbe
11.	lion	muroodi	miroodi	31.	pig	ŋgurue	ŋgurue
12.	gun	muʃiiŋga	miʃiiŋga	32.	stomach	nda	nda
13.	mattress	muuto	miuto	33.	house	ɲumba	ɲumba
14.	bottle	muʃuuba	miʃuuba	34.	mole	hukɔ	hukɔ
15.	comb	giʃanundi	iʃanundi	35.	wave	ikombi	makombi
16.	chair	geti	eti	36.	foot	ikiɲa	makiɲa
17.	cup	gikombɛ	ikombɛ	37.	tooth	igago	magago
18.	yam	gikoa	ikoa	38.	banana	irigu	marigu
19.	tray	gitaruru	itaruru	39.	cloud	itu	matu
20.	muscle	giʃoka	iʃoka	40.	stone	ihiga	mahiga

Dataset 56. Chiquihuitlán Mazatec (Mexico)

Phonemic tone is not indicated.

		1ST SG	1ST PL INCL	2ND SG	2ND PL
1.	'hand'	nca	ncã	nce	ncũ
2.	'receive'	faʔanca	faʔancã	faʔance	faʔancũ
3.	'tortilla'	niɲunaʔa	niɲunaha	niɲurihi	niɲunuhu
4.	'sister'	titʃha	titʃhã	titʃhe	titʃhũ
5.	'work'	ʃanaʔa	ʃanaha	ʃarihi	ʃanuhu
6.	'language'	ʔnenaʔa	ʔnenaha	ʔnerihi	ʔnenuhu
7.	'husk corn'	vithia	vithiã	vithie	vithiũ
8.	'father'	naʔminaʔa	naʔminaha	naʔmirihi	naʔminuhu

Dataset 57. Papago (USA)

Data from J. Mason

1.	hi	'go, walk'	7.	him	'is going'
2.	hɨo	'bloom'	8.	hɨos	'is blooming'
3.	kɨli	'shell corn'	9.	kɨlib	'is shelling corn'
4.	oʔo	'drip'	10.	oʔot	'is dripping'
5.	amo	'shout'	11.	amog	'is shouting'
6.	maa	'give'	12.	maak	'is giving'

Dataset 58. Saija (Colombia)

1.	waˈnu	'He/she goes.'	6.	ˈwaxi	'Go!'
2.	tʃeˈru	'He/she comes.'	7.	ˈtʃexi	'Come!'
3.	ˈkhode	'He/she eats.'	8.	ˈkhoxi	'Eat!'
4.	toˈna	'He/she drinks.'	9.	ˈtoxi	'Drink!'
5.	pedeeˈtho	'He/she talks.'	10.	peˈdeexi	'Talk!'

Dataset 59. Amuzgo (Mexico)

Data from Amy Bauernschmidt; phonemic tone is not indicated.

		SG	PL			SG	PL
1.	'paper'	com	nom	10.	'house'	wʔaa	lʔaa
2.	'mat'	cwe	lwe	11.	'scorpion'	kachɔ	kalhɔ
3.	'turtle'	cwi	lwi	12.	'turkey'	kachom	kanhom
4.	'hole'	cweʔ	lweʔ	13.	'pig'	kacku	kalku
5.	'bottle'	cyo	lyo	14.	'dog'	kacweʔ	kalweʔ
6.	'coal'	cyoom	nyoom	15.	'horse'	kaso	kaco
7.	'cat'	cymei	nymei	16.	'deer'	kasohndŋ	kacohndŋ
8.	'hand'	cʔɔɔ	lʔɔɔ	17.	'cow'	kasondye	kacondye
9.	'chili'	cʔa	lʔa	18.	'blanket'	lyaso	lyaco

Dataset 60. Oaxaca Chontal (Mexico)

Note: vertical bar marks following stressed syllable.

		SG	PL			SG	PL
1.	'bed'	kanaˈga	kanaˈgayʔ	10.	'monkey'	maˈtʃin	maˈtʃinʔ
2.	'firefly'	umˈma	umˈmayʔ	11.	'lizard'	kweˈpoʔ	kweɬpoʔ
3.	'butterfly'	paapaˈlo	paapaˈloʔ	12.	'grandchild'	koˈɲˈiʔ	koɬˈɲˈiʔ
4.	'wall'	ayˈtyaɬ	ayˈtyaɬʔ	13.	'woman'	akaˈnˈoʔ	akaɬˈnˈoʔ
5.	'squash'	ʔaˈwa	ʔaˈwaʔ	14.	'word'	aˈtaygiʔ	atayˈgiʔ
6.	'tortilla'	asˈkul	asˈkulʔ	15.	'basket'	anˈtʃupiʔ	antʃuˈpiʔ
7.	'fish'	atyú	atyúʔ	16.	'coyote'	aˈminko	aminˈko
8.	'cutter ant'	ampuˈlye	ampuˈlyeʔ	17.	'year'	aˈmatsʔ	aˈmaːtsʔ
9.	'wasp'	nanaˈra	nanaˈraʔ	18.	'lobster'	alaˈtʃʼuʔ	alaːˈtʃʼuʔ

Dataset 61. Tabasco Chontal (Mexico)

Phonemic stress is not indicated.

1.	kʌkolan	'I remain'	25.	kolon	'I remained'
2.	akolan	'you remain'	26.	kolet	'you remained'
3.	ukolan	'he remains'	27.	koli	'he remained'
4.	kʌyʌlo	'I fall'	28.	yʌlon	'I fell'
5.	ayʌlo	'you fall'	29.	yʌlet	'you fell'
6.	uyʌlo	'he falls'	30.	yʌli	'he fell'
7.	kʌkʼuʃnan	'I eat'	31.	kʼuʃnon	'I ate'
8.	akʼuʃnan	'you eat'	32.	kʼuʃnet	'you ate'
9.	ukʼuʃnan	'he eats'	33.	kʼuʃni	'he ate'
10.	kʌpʼiʃo	'I awake'	34.	pʼiʃon	'I awoke'
11.	apʼiʃo	'you awake'	35.	pʼiʃet	'you awoke'
12.	upʼiʃo	'he awakes'	36.	pʼiʃi	'he awoke'
13.	kʌhitsʼan	'I get hungry'	37.	hitsʼon	'I got hungry'
14.	ahitsʼan	'you get hungry'	38.	hitsʼet	'you got hungry'
15.	uhitsʼan	'he gets hungry'	39.	hitsʼi	'he got hungry'
16.	kʌtʼʌbo	'I climb up'	40.	tʼʌbon	'I climbed up'
17.	atʼʌbo	'you climb up'	41.	tʼʌbet	'you climbed up'
18.	utʼʌbo	'he climbs up'	42.	tʼʌbi	'he climbed up'
19.	kʌtʃʌmo	'I die'	43.	tʃʌmon	'I died'
20.	atʃʌmo	'you die'	44.	tʃʌmet	'you died'
21.	utʃʌmo	'he dies'	45.	tʃʌmi	'he died'
22.	kʌkuʃpan	'I revive'	46.	kuʃpon	'I revived'
23.	akuʃpan	'you revive'	47.	kuʃpet	'you revived'
24.	ukuʃpan	'he revives'	48.	kuʃpi	'he revived'

Dataset 62. Sierra Popoluca (Mexico)

1.	tʌk	'house'	21.	antʌk	'my house'
2.	petkuy	'broom'	22.	ampetkuy	'my broom'
3.	meːme	'butterfly'	23.	ammeːme	'my butterfly'
4.	tsoːgoy	'liver'	24.	antsoːgoy	'my liver'
5.	heːpe	'cup'	25.	anheːpe	'my cup'
6.	piyu	'hen'	26.	ampiyu	'my hen'
7.	kawah	'horse'	27.	aŋkawah	'my horse'
8.	yemkuy	'fan'	28.	aɲyemkuy	'my fan'
9.	nʌːyi	'name'	29.	annʌːyi	'my name'
10.	haːya	'husband'	30.	anhaːya	'my husband'
11.	tʃikʃi	'itch'	31.	aɲtʃikʃi	'my itch'
12.	wʌtʃoːmo	'wife'	32.	aŋwʌtʃoːmo	'my wife'
13.	suuŋ	'cooking pot'	33.	ansuuŋ	'my cooking pot'
14.	nʌts	'armadillo'	34.	annʌts	'my armadillo'
15.	ʃiʔmpa	'bamboo'	35.	aɲʃiʔmpa	'my bamboo'
16.	tyaka	'chick'	36.	aɲtyaka	'my chick'
17.	kʌːpi	'firewood'	37.	aŋkʌːpi	'my firewood'
18.	meːsah	'table'	38.	ammeːsah	'my table'
19.	ʃapun	'soap'	39.	aɲʃapun	'my soap'
20.	suskuy	'whistle'	40.	ansuskuy	'my whistle'

Dataset 63. Min Nan Chinese (Taiwan)

Phonemic tone is not indicated.

1.	cin ta	'very dry'	13.	sioŋ ta	'driest'
2.	cin sin	'very new'	14.	sioŋ sin	'newest'
3.	cin ho	'very good'	15.	sioŋ ho	'best'
4.	cin o	'very black'	16.	sioŋ o	'blackest'
5.	ciŋ kao	'very thick'	17.	sioŋ kao	'thickest'
6.	cin toa	'very big'	18.	sioŋ toa	'biggest'
7.	cin doa	'very hot'	19.	sioŋ doa	'hottest'
8.	cin sue	'very small'	20.	sioŋ sue	'smallest'
9.	cim pe	'very white'	21.	sioŋ pe	'whitest'
10.	cin əŋ	'very yellow'	22.	sioŋ əŋ	'yellowest'
11.	ciŋ kuã	'very cold'	23.	sioŋ kuã	'coldest'
12.	cim bai	'very ugly'	24.	sioŋ bai	'ugliest'

Dataset 64. Hausa (Nigeria)

1.	ʔyákkà	'your (m) sister'	8.	gídánkà	'your (m) house'
2.	ʔyákkì	'your (f) sister'	9.	gídánkì	'your (f) house'
3.	ʔyássà	'his sister'	10.	gídánsà	'his house'
4.	ʔyáttà	'her sister'	11.	gídántà	'her house'
5.	ʔyámmù	'our sister'	12.	gídámmù	'our house'
6.	ʔyákkù	'your (pl) sister'	13.	gídánkù	'your (pl) house'
7.	ʔyássù	'their sister'	14.	gídánsù	'their house'

Dataset 65. Xavánte (Brazil)

1.	du	'stomach'	10.	ʔaddu	'your stomach'
2.	ʔra	'child'	11.	ʔayʔra	'your child'
3.	hiʔrãti	'knee'	12.	ʔayhiʔrãti	'your knee'
4.	tɔ	'eye(s)'	13.	ʔattɔ	'your eye(s)'
5.	ʔwa	'tooth'	14.	ʔayʔwa	'your tooth'
6.	brɔ̃	'wife'	15.	ʔaybrɔ̃	'your wife'
7.	ʃɛːrɛ	'hair'	16.	ʔaʃʃɛːrɛ	'your hair'
8.	paːra	'foot'	17.	ʔaypaːra	'your foot'
9.	bã:bã	'father'	18.	ʔaybã:bã	'your father'

Dataset 66. San Miguel Mixtec (Mexico)
Phonemic tone is not indicated.

1.	kaka	'walk'	11.	skaka	'make walk'
2.	haa	'be frothy'	12.	shaa	'make frothy'
3.	dɨbɨ	'enter'	13.	ʃdɨbɨ	'make enter'
4.	taka	'assemble'	14.	staka	'make assemble'
5.	tʃaku	'live'	15.	stʃaku	'make live'
6.	lili	'be stiff'	16.	ʃlili	'make stiff'
7.	nɨ̰ʔɨ̰	'purr'	17.	ʃnɨ̰ʔɨ̰	'make purr'
8.	kunu	'run'	18.	skunu	'make run'
9.	data	'split'	19.	ʃdata	'make split'
10.	dʒaʔa	'landslide'	20.	ʃdʒaʔa	'make landslide'

Dataset 67. Copainalá Zoque (Mexico)

1.	kenu	'he looked'	8.	kenpa	'he looks'
2.	sihku	'he laughed'	9.	sikpa	'he laughs'
3.	wihtu	'he walked'	10.	witpa	'he walks'
4.	kaʔu	'he died'	11.	kaʔpa	'he dies'
5.	nahpu	'he kicked'	12.	nahpa	'he kicks'
6.	tsihtsu	'it tore'	13.	tsitspa	'it tears'
7.	sohsu	'it cooked'	14.	sospa	'it cooks'

Dataset 68. Usarufa (Papua New Guinea)

Phonemic tone is not indicated.

		1s	2s	3s MASC	2D
1.	'talk'	tune	tene	tiye	tekao
2.	'eat'	naune	naane	naiye	naakao
3.	'do'	une	one	iye	okao
4.	'give'	amune	amene	amiye	amekao
5.	'hear'	itaune	itaane	itaiye	itaakao
6.	'hit'	ikamune	ikamone	ikamiye	ikamokao

Dataset 69. Usarufa (Papua New Guinea)

Phonemic tone is not indicated.

		NOMINAL	VERBAL			NOMINAL	VERBAL
1.	'tree'	yaama	yaae	10.	'lid'	oma	oe
2.	'machete'	yaamma	yaane	11.	'pit pit'	omma	one
3.	'sugarcane'	yaaʔa	yaare	12.	'another'	oʔa	ore
4.	'sound'	aama	aae	13.	'queue'	araama	araae
5.	'path'	aamma	aane	14.	'mushroom'	araamma	araane
6.	'weather'	aaʔa	aare	15.	'offspring'	araaʔa	araare
7.	'housetop'	amuma	amue	16.	'man'	waama	waae
8.	'new growth'	amumma	amune	17.	'opossum'	waamma	waane
9.	'seed'	amuʔa	amure	18.	'noise'	waaʔa	waare

Dataset 70. Buang (Papua New Guinea)

		MY	YOUR	HIS
1.	'child'	naluɢ	nalʊm	nalu
2.	'knee'	luk	lup	lus
3.	'father'	amaɢ	amam	ama
4.	'tongue'	daɣɛɢ	daɣɛm	daɣɛn
5.	'head'	yuɢ	yum	yu
6.	'hand'	nmaɢ	nmam	nma
7.	'back'	kwbɛɢ	kwbɛm	kwbɛn
8.	'tail'	ʁuk	ʁup	ʁus
9.	'brother'	ariɢ	arim	ari
10.	'breath'	saʁɛɢ	saʁɛm	saʁɛn
11.	'name'	areɢ	arem	are
12.	'face'	malaɢ	malam	mala
13.	'cousin'	ɢadɛɢ	ɢadɛm	ɢadɛ
14.	'neck'	kwaɢ	kwam	kwa

Laboratory Manual for Morphology and Syntax

Dataset 71. San Miguel Mixtec (Mexico)

1.	bílóʒá	'god's lizard(s)'	10.	nūnìʒò	'our corn'
2.	tʃákáró	'your fish'	11.	lúsūrí	'my puppy/ies'
3.	ɲìtɨ́rí	'my sand'	12.	hā́ʔàʒò	'our feet'
4.	kwáɲūrō	'your squirrel(s)'	13.	ʃīnìrò	'your head'
5.	dā́ʔāʒá	'god's hands'	14.	nūnìrí	'my corn'
6.	ʃīnìʒá	'god's head'	15.	dā́ʔārō	'your hand(s)'
7.	lúsūʒō	'our puppy/ies'	16.	kwáɲūrí	'my squirrel(s)'
8.	tʃákárí	'my fish'	17.	ɲìtɨ́ʒó	'our sand'
9.	hā́ʔàʒá	'god's foot/feet'	18.	bílóʒó	'our lizard(s)'

Dataset 72. Isthmus Zapotec (Mexico)

Phonemic stress is not indicated; ` indicates high tone, ´indicates low tone, ˇ indicates rising tone.)

1.	tʃùpǎ	'two'	13.	tʃònnà bèúʔ	'three cherries'
2.	tʃònnǎ	'three'	14.	tʃònnà báʔdùʔ	'three children'
3.	tàpà	'four'	15.	tʃònnà gúnàà	'three women'
4.	nùú	'there are'	16.	tʃònnà dáà	'three mats'
5.	bèúʔ	'cherry'	17.	tàpà bèúʔ	'four cherries'
6.	bàʔdùʔ	'child'	18.	tàpà bàʔdùʔ	'four children'
7.	gùnàà	'woman'	19.	tàpà gùnàà	'four women'
8.	dàà	'mat'	20.	tàpà dàà	'four mats'
9.	tʃùpà bèúʔ	'two cherries'	21.	nùú bèúʔ	'there are cherries'
10.	tʃùpà báʔdùʔ	'two children'	22.	nùú báʔdùʔ	'there are children'
11.	tʃùpà gúnàà	'two women'	23.	nùú gúnàà	'there are women'
12.	tʃùpà dáà	'two mats'	24.	nùú dáà	'there are mats'

Dataset 73. Lalana Chinantec (Mexico)

1. zo:ʔn^{232} — 'I practice'
2. zo:ʔn^{232} — 'you practice'
3. zo:ʔ^{232}ra^{2} — 'we (in) practice'
4. zo:ʔ^{232}ra^{231} — 'we (ex) practice'
5. zo:ʔ^{232}ra^{23} — 'you (pl) practice'

6. ku^{3}ʤeʔn^{2}na^{23} — 'I send'
7. ku^{3}ʤeʔn^{2}nu^{3} — 'You send'
8. ku^{3}ʤeʔn^{2}na^{2} — 'We (in) send'
9. ku^{3}ʤeʔn^{2}na^{231} — 'We (ex) send'
10. ku^{3}ʤeʔn^{2}na^{23} — 'You (pl) send'

11. gwʌ:ʔn^{232}na^{1} — 'I change'
12. gwʌ:ʔn^{232}nu^{3} — 'You change'
13. gwʌ:ʔn^{232}na^{2} — 'We (in) change'
14. gwʌ:ʔn^{232}na^{231} — 'We (ex) change'
15. gwʌ:ʔn^{232}na^{23} — 'You (pl) change'

16. ʔmi:n^{232} — 'I mend'
17. ʔmi:n^{232} — 'You mend'
18. ʔmi:^{232}ra^{2} — 'We (in) mend'
19. ʔmi:^{232}ra^{231} — 'We (ex) mend'
20. ʔmi:^{232}ra^{23} — 'You (pl) mend'

21. ʔi:ʔn^{32} — 'I receive'
22. ʔi:ʔn^{32} — 'You receive'
23. ʔi:ʔ^{32}ra^{2} — 'We (in) receive'
24. ʔi:ʔ^{32}ra^{231} — 'We (ex) receive'
25. ʔi:ʔ^{32}ra^{23} — 'You (pl) receive'

26. ʔɲu:ʔn^{23}na^{23} — 'I tie him'
27. ʔɲu:ʔn^{23}nu^{3} — 'you tie him'
28. ʔɲu:ʔn^{23}na^{2} — 'we (in) tie him'
29. ʔɲu:ʔn^{23}na^{231} — 'we (ex) tie him'
30. ʔɲu:ʔn^{23}na^{23} — 'you (pl) tie him'

31. ʔu:n^{232}na^{1} — 'I pour on him'
32. ʔu:n^{232}nu^{3} — 'You pour on him'
33. ʔu:n^{232}na^{2} — 'We (in) pour on him'
34. ʔu:n^{232}na^{231} — 'We (ex) pour on him'
35. ʔu:n^{232}na^{23} — 'You (pl) pour on him'

36. ʔĩhn^{2}na^{23} — 'I answer'
37. ʔĩhn^{2}nu^{3} — 'You answer'
38. ʔĩhn^{2}na^{2} — 'We (in) answer'
39. ʔĩhn^{2}na^{231} — 'We (ex) answer'
40. ʔĩhn^{2}na^{23} — 'You (pl) answer'

41. hnɨ:n^{32}na^{23} — 'I am in the way'
42. hnɨ:n^{32}nu^{3} — 'You are in the way'
43. hnɨ:n^{32}na^{2} — 'We (in) are in the way'
44. hnɨ:n^{32}na^{231} — 'We (ex) are in the way'
45. hnɨ:n^{32}na^{23} — 'You (pl) are in the way'

46. zuʔn^{232}na^{1} — 'I fold over'
47. zuʔn^{232}nu^{3} — 'You fold over'
48. zuʔn^{232}na^{2} — 'We (in) fold over'
49. zuʔn^{232}na^{231} — 'We (ex) fold over'
50. zuʔn^{232}na^{23} — 'You (pl) fold over'

Dataset 74. Pitjantjatjara--Warburton Ranges (Australia)

		DESIDERATIVE	CONT IMPV	IMPV	PAST	FUTURE
1.	'listen'	kuliɭṭaku	kulinma	kulila	kulinu	kulilku
2.	'hide'	kumpilṭaku	kumpinma	kumpila	kumpinu	kumpilku
3.	'sing'	yinkaṭaku	yinkama	yinka	yinkaŋu	yinkaku
4.	'hurry'	warpuŋkuṭaku	warpuŋama	warpuwa	warpuŋu	warpuŋku
5.	'get it'	manṭilṭaku	manṭinma	manṭila	manṭinu	manṭilku
6.	'put it'	ṭunkuṭaku	ṭunama	ṭura	ṭunu	ṭunku
7.	'cry'	yulaṭaku	yulama	yula	yulaŋu	yulaku
8.	'hit it'	puŋkuṭaku	puŋama	puwa	puŋu	puŋku
9.	'rejoice'	pukuʎariṭaku	pukuʎarima	pukuʎari	pukuʎariŋu	pukuʎariku
10.	'learn'	ŋintiriŋkuṭaku	ŋintiriŋama	ŋintiriwa	ŋintiriŋu	ŋintiriŋku
11.	'climb'	ṭatilṭaku	ṭatinma	ṭatila	ṭatinu	ṭatilku
12.	'talk'	waŋkaṭaku	waŋkama	waŋka	waŋkaŋu	waŋkaku
13.	'breathe'	ŋa:ʎmankuṭaku	ŋa:ʎmanama	ŋa:ʎmara	ŋa:ʎmanu	ŋa:ʎmanku
14.	'arise'	katuriŋkuṭaku	katuriŋama	katuriwa	katuriŋu	katuriŋku
15.	'give it'	ɲintilṭaku	ɲintinma	ɲintila	ɲintinu	ɲintilku
16.	'run'	kukuralṭaku	kukuranma	kukurala	kukuranu	kukuralku
17.	'hide'	kumpiṭunkuṭaku	kumpiṭunama	kumpiṭura	kumpiṭunu	kumpiṭunku
18.	'carry it'	katiṭaku	katima	kati	katiŋu	katiku

Dataset 75. Kasem (Ghana)

		SG	PL			SG	PL
1.	'dry season'	kwɪa	kwɪ	16.	'back'	kɔga	kʊɛ
2.	'truth'	tʃɪga	tʃɪ	17.	'bowstring'	miə	mi
3.	'hand'	jĩŋa	jĩ	18.	'medicine'	lidə	lidi
4.	'finger'	nʊa	nʊɪ	19.	'room'	digə	di
5.	'fishnet'	bʊda	bʊdɪ	20.	'bone'	kuə	kui
6.	'bile'	lũŋa	lũɪ	21.	'funeral'	luə	lui
7.	'calabash'	zũŋa	zũɪ	22.	'river'	bugə	bui
8.	'knife'	fana	fanɪ	23.	'shea-nut oil'	nugə	nui
9.	'farm'	kada	kadɪ	24.	'granary'	tulə	tuli
10.	'type of pot'	kala	kalɪ	25.	'white person'	fələ	fəli
11.	'bee'	tʊa	tʊɪ	26.	'shelter'	poŋə	pue
12.	'stick'	daa	dɛ	27.	'path'	tʃoŋə	tʃue
13.	'market'	yaga	yɛ	28.	'place'	z̧əgə	z̧e
14.	'leg'	naga	nɛ	29.	'roof beam'	bəŋə	be
15.	'bow'	taŋa	tɛ	30.	'song'	ləŋə	le

Dataset 76. Hungarian

		SG	PL			SG	PL
1.	'door'	aytoo	aytook	16.	'horse'	loo	lovak
2.	'woman'	nöö	nöök	17.	'red'	piroʃ	piroʃak
3.	'pupil'	tanuloo	tanulook	18.	'iron'	vaʃ	vaʃak
4.	'salt'	ʃoo	ʃook	19.	'wall'	fal	falak
5.	'boy'	fiuu	fiuuk	20.	'tooth'	fog	fogak
6.	'hour'	oora	ooraak	21.	'gentleman'	uur	urak
7.	'tree'	fa	faak	22.	'spoon'	kanaal	kanalak
8.	'brown'	barna	barnaak	23.	'bird'	madaar	madarak
9.	'pear'	körte	körteek	24.	'summer'	ɲaar	ɲarak
10.	'camel'	teve	teveek	25.	'noise'	zörey	zöreyek
11.	'brush'	kefe	kefeek	26.	'water'	viiz	vizek
12.	'tube'	tʃöö	tʃövek	27.	'fire'	tüüz	tüzek
13.	'stone'	köö	kövek	28.	'name'	neev	nevek
14.	'juice'	lee	levek	29.	'book'	köɲv	köɲvek
15.	'art'	müu	müvek	30.	'heart'	siiv	sivek

Dataset 77. Tetelcingo Nahuatl (Mexico)

		PRESENT	PAST	FUTURE
1.	'know'	kɪmati	okɪmat	kɪmatis
2.	'go out'	kisa	okis	kisas
3.	'stop'	moketsa	omokets	moketsas
4.	'sleep'	kotʃɪ	okotʃ	kotʃɪs
5.	'die'	mɪki	omɪk	mɪkis
6.	'seem'	niesi	onies	niesis

Dataset 78. Wantoat (Papua New Guinea)

	MY	YOUR	HIS	OUR
1. hand	katakŋa	katakga	katakŋʌ	katakŋin
2. foot	kepina	kepika	kepinʌ	kepinin
3. house	yotna	yotda	yotnʌ	yotnin

Dataset 79. Isthmus Zapotec (Mexico)

Phonemic tone and stress are not indicated.

1.	taburete	'chair'	19.	mani?	'horse'
2.	ʃtaburetebe	'his chair'	20.	hmanibe	'his horse'
3.	ʃtaburetedu	'our chair'	21.	diidʒa?	'word'
4.	tanguyu	'clay doll'	22.	ʃtiidʒabe	'his word'
5.	ʃtanguyube	'her clay doll'	23.	daa	'mat'
6.	patʃeeza?	'meeting place'	24.	ʃtaabe	'his mat'
7.	ʃpatʃeezadu	'our meeting place'	25	doo	'rope'
8.	pan	'bread'	26.	ʃtoobe	'his rope'
9.	ʃpanbe	'her bread'	27.	geta	'tortilla'
10.	ʃpandu	'our bread'	28.	ʃketabe	'her tortilla'
11.	kuba	'dough'	29.	giɲa	'trunk'
12.	ʃkubabe	'her dough'	30.	ʃkiɲabe	'his trunk'
13.	kuananaʃi	'fruit'	31.	gamidʒa?	'shirt'
14.	ʃkuananaʃibe	'his fruit'	32.	ʃkamidʒabe	'his shirt'
15.	luuna?	'bed'	33.	bere	'chicken'
16.	hluunabe	'his bed'	34.	ʃperebe	'her chicken'
17.	neza	'road'	35.	biuuza?	'guest'
18.	hnezabe	'his road'	36.	ʃpiuuzabe	'his guest'

Laboratory Manual for Morphology and Syntax

Dataset 80. Xavánte (Brazil; Regularized)

		3ʀᴅ Sɢ	2ɴᴅ Sɢ	3ʀᴅ Sɢ Nᴇɢ	2ɴᴅ Sɢ Nᴇɢ	Iᴍᴘᴠ
1.	run	waːra	ʔaywa	waraʔɔ̃di	ʔaywaraʔɔ̃di	ʔaywaːra
2.	lie down	dɔ̃ːbrɔ̃	ʔaddɔ̃	dɔ̃brɔ̃ʔɔ̃di	ʔaddɔ̃brɔ̃ʔɔ̃di	ʔaddɔ̃ːbrɔ̃
3.	sleep	ʃɔ̃ːtɔ̃	ʔaʃʃɔ̃	ʃɔ̃tɔ̃ʔɔ̃di	ʔaʃʃɔ̃tɔ̃ʔɔ̃di	ʔaʃʃɔ̃ːtɔ̃
4.	go	bɔ̃ːri	ʔaybɔ̃	bɔ̃riʔɔ̃di	ʔaybɔ̃riʔɔ̃di	ʔaybɔ̃ːri

Dataset 81. Koiné Greek
Phonemic stress is not indicated.

		Nᴏᴍ Sɢ	Gᴇɴ Sɢ	Aᴄᴄ Sɢ
1.	'Ethiopian'	aiθiops	aiθiopos	aiθiopa
2.	'Arab'	araps	arabos	araba
3.	'stake'	skolops	skolopos	skolopa
4.	'southwest'	lips	libos	liba
5.	'vein'	fleps	flebos	fleba
6.	'date palm'	foiniks	foinikos	foinika
7.	'flame'	floks	flogos	floga
8.	'throat'	larugks	laruggos	larugga
9.	'flesh'	sarks	sarkos	sarka
10.	'trumpet'	salpigks	salpiggos	salpigga
11.	'lash'	mastiks	mastigos	mastiga
12.	'hope'	ɛlpis	ɛlpidos	ɛlpida
13.	'key'	kleːs	kleːdos	kleːda
14.	'favor'	xaris	xaritos	xarita
15.	'night'	nuks	nuktos	nukta
16.	'ear'	oːs	oːtos	oːta
17.	'witness'	martus	marturos	martura
18.	'bird'	ornis	orniθos	orniθa
19.	'nose'	hris	hrinos	hrina
20.	'thong'	himas	himantos	himanta

Dataset 82. Polish

		SG	PL			SG	PL
1.	'wife'	ʒona	ʒonɪ	18.	'leg'	noga	nogi
2.	'train'	potʃõk	potʃõgi	19.	'pear tree'	gruʃa	gruʃe
3.	'horse'	koɲ	koɲe	20.	'country'	kraʲ	kraʲe
4.	'neck'	ʃrʲa	ʃrʲe	21.	'shore'	bʒek	bʒegi
5.	'house'	dom	domɪ	22.	'bread'	xlep	xlebɪ
6.	'nose'	nos	nosɪ	23.	'fish'	rɪba	rɪbɪ
7.	'cow'	krova	krovɪ	24.	'mother'	matka	matki
8.	'river'	ʒeka	ʒeki	25.	'bear'	ɲedʒvʲetʃ	ɲedʒvʲedʒe
9.	'storm'	buʒa	buʒe	26.	'cheese'	ser	serɪ
10.	'rose'	ruʒa	ruʒe	27.	'cloud'	xmura	xmurɪ
11.	'shadow'	tʃeɲ	tʃeɲe	28.	'bird'	ptak	ptaki
12.	'shoe'	but	butɪ	29.	'road'	droga	drogi
13.	'person'	osoba	osobɪ	30.	'dress'	sukɲa	sukɲe
14.	'winter'	ʒima	ʒimɪ	31.	'kitchen'	kuxɲa	kuxɲe
15.	'elephant'	swoɲ	swoɲe	32.	'thief'	zwodʒeʲ	zwodʒeʲe
16.	'guest'	goʃtʃ	goʃtʃe	33.	'physician'	lekaʃ	lekaʒe
17.	'book'	kʃõʃka	kʃõʃki	34.	'shop'	sklep	sklepɪ

Laboratory Manual for Morphology and Syntax

Dataset 83. Cocama (Peru)

			MY	YOUR
1.	'arm'	iwa	tiwa	niwa
2.	'heart'	ia	tia	nia
3.	'head'	dakɨ	tiakɨ	niakɨ
4.	'nose'	ti	tati	nati
5.	'farm'	ka	taka	naka
6.	'cassava'	dawidi	tiawidi	niawidi
7.	'hand'	pua	tapua	napua
8.	'house'	uka	tuka	nuka

Dataset 84. Kamano (Papua New Guinea)

		IT IS	IN	ON		DUAL
1.	'house'	no	nona	nompi	nonteʔ	nontere
2.	'my hand'	naza	nazana	nazampi	nazanteʔ	nazantere
3.	'water'	ti	tina	timpi	tinteʔ	
4.	'bamboo'	tfe	tfena	tfempi	tfenteʔ	tfentere
5.	'plaited wall'	pra	prana	prampi	pranteʔ	prantere
6.	'pig'	afuʔ	afura	afuʔpi	afuʔteʔ	afuʔtere
7.	'string'	nofiʔ	nofira	nofiʔpi	nofiʔteʔ	
8.	'man'	vheʔ	vhera	vheʔpi	vheʔteʔ	vheʔtere
9.	'dog'	maʔmaʔ	maʔmara	maʔmaʔpi	maʔmaʔteʔ	maʔmaʔtere
10.	'grass'	hofa	hofa	hofafi	hofareʔ	
11.	'earth'	mopa	mopa	mopafi	mopareʔ	
12.	'skirt'	kena	kena	kenafi	kenareʔ	kenarere
13.	'sky'	mona	mona	monafi	monareʔ	
14.	'rat'	kfa	kfa			kfarere
15.	'bow'	ati	atia		atireʔ	atirere
16.	'mist'	hmpo	hmpoa	hmpofi	hmporeʔ	

Dataset 85. Ixtlahuaca Mazahua (Mexico)

Tone only partially indicated.

Partial pardigm of the Mazahua verb 'go':

		PRF	FUT	PROG	IMPRF	HABIT	PSTPRF
1.	1s	ɾómagɔ	ɾámagɔ	ɾámagɔ	mímagɔ	ɾípagɔ	mípagɔ
2.	2s	ímage	ɾímage	nímage	mímage	ípage	mípage
3.	3s	óma	ɾama	níma	míma	pa	mípa
4.	1dx	ɾómægɔbe	ɾámægɔbe	ɾámægɔbe	mímægɔbe	ɾípægɔbe	mípægɔbe
5.	1di	ɾómægɔvi	ɾámægɔvi	ɾámægɔvi	mímægɔvi	ɾípægɔvi	mípægɔvi
6.	2d	ímægevi	ɾímægevi	nímægevi	mímægevi	ípægevi	mípægevi
7.	3d	ómævi	ɾamævi	nímævi	mímævi	pævi	mípævi
8.	1px	ɾómɔkʰɔhme	ɾámɔkʰɔhme	ɾámɔkʰɔhme	mímɔkʰɔhme	ɾípɔkʰɔhme	mípɔkʰɔhme
9.	1pi	ɾómɔkʰɔhi	ɾámɔkʰɔhi	ɾámɔkʰɔhi	mímɔkʰɔhi	ɾípɔkʰɔhi	mípɔkʰɔhi
10.	2p	ímɔkʰehi	ɾímɔkʰehi	nímɔkʰehi	mímɔkʰehi	ípɔkʰehi	mípɔkʰehi
11.	3p	ómɔhi	ɾamɔhi	nímɔhi	mímɔhi	pɔhi	mípɔhi

Laboratory Manual for Morphology and Syntax

Dataset 86. North Pame (Mexico)

		SG	DU	PL
1.	'bed'	ŋgobé	ŋgobé	mbé
2.	'bean'	ŋgokhwèʔ	ŋgokhwèʔ	ŋkhwèʔ
3.	'dog'	nadò	nadòi	ladòt
4.	'hummingbird'	nilyè	nilyè	rilyèt
5.	'locust'	tʃíkhiʃ	tʃíkhiʃ	ʃíkhiʃt
6.	'basket'	mancáʔ	mancáʔ	wancáʔ
7.	'manure'	ŋgophói	ŋgophói	mphói
8.	'coyote'	nanʔò	nanʔòi	lanʔòt
9.	'night'	ŋgosậoŋ	ŋgosậoŋ	nsậoŋ
10.	'frog'	ŋgowòʔ	ŋgowòiʔ	wòʔt
11.	'cat'	nimìʃ	nimìʃ	rimìʃt
12.	'grass'	tʃíʃʃi	tʃíʃʃi	ʃíʃʃi
13.	'paper'	ŋgokʔwéʃ	ŋgokʔwéʃ	ŋgʔwéʃ
14.	'century plant'	ŋgodôa	ŋgodôa	ndôa
15.	'arroyo'	nanhá	nanhá	lanhá
16.	'flower'	ŋgotógŋ	ŋgotógŋ	ndógŋ
17.	'mouse'	niŋgyào	niŋgyàoi	riŋgyàot
18.	'fish'	tʃikyáo	tʃikyáoi	ʃikyáot
19.	'moon, month'	ŋgomʔậoʔ	ŋgomʔậoʔ	mʔậoʔ
20.	'chair'	ŋgopʔóho	ŋgopʔóho	mbʔóho
21.	'adult'	tʃikèʔ	tʃikèʔ	ʃikèʔt
22.	'path'	nanʔɛ́hɛʔ	nanʔɛ́hɛʔ	lanʔɛ́hɛʔ
23.	'corn'	ŋgolhwá̧	ŋgolhwá̧	nlhwá̧
24.	'lion'	máncweʔ	máncwiʔ	wáncweʔt
25.	'tree, stick'	ŋgokwá̧ŋ	ŋgokwá̧ŋ	ŋgwá̧ŋ
26.	'thunder'	ŋgonwɛ́	ŋgonwɛ́i	nwɛ́t
27.	'leaf'	niʃʃi	niʃʃi	riʃʃi
28.	'monkey'	ŋgokhwèʔ	ŋgokhwèiʔ	ŋkhwèʔt

Dataset 87. Koiné Greek

1.	luo:	'I loose'	10.	leluka	'I have loosed '
2.	pisteuo:	'I believe'	11.	pepisteuka	'I have believed'
3.	kapiao:	'I toil'	12.	kekapiaka	'I have toiled'
4.	paideuo:	'I teach'	13.	pepaideuka	'I have taught '
5.	mageuo:	'I practice magic'	14.	memageuka	'I have practiced magic'
6.	teleo:	'I finish'	15.	teteleka	'I have finished '
7.	geuo:	'I eat'	16.	gegeuka	'I have eaten'
8.	saleuo:	'I shake'	17.	sesaleuka	'I have shaken'
9.	deo:	'I tie'	18.	dedeka	'I have tied'

Dataset 88. Lyele (Burkina Faso)

1.	kúmí	'bird'	8.	kúmíí	'the bird'
2.	yálá	'millet'	9.	yáláá	'the millet'
3.	nà	'foot'	10.	nàá	'the foot'
4.	yijì	'church'	11.	yijìí	'the church'
5.	ya	'market'	12.	yaá	'the market'
6.	cèlé	'parrot'	13.	cèléé	'the parrot'
7.	kùlí	'dog'	14.	kùlíí	'the dog'

Dataset 89. Pocomchí (Guatemala)

1.	q'an	'ripe'	8.	q'anq'an	'rotten'
2.	suk	'good'	9.	suksuk	'delicious'
3.	raʃ	'green'	10.	raʃraʃ	'very green'
4.	qʔeq	'black'	11.	qʔeqqʔeq	'jet black'
5.	nim	'big'	12.	nimnim	'very big'
6.	kaq	'red'	13.	kaqkaq	'very red'
7.	saq	'white'	14.	saqsaq	'very white'

Laboratory Manual for Morphology and Syntax

Dataset 90. Amharic (Ethiopia)

Record all stems in lexicon as strings of simple consonants;
account for vowels and geminate consonants by grammatical or phonological rule.

1. gəṭṭəmə
   'he joined, vt'

2. məssələ
   'he resembled, vt'

3. məkkərə
   'he counselled, vt'

4. məlləsə
   'he returned, vt'

5. kəffələ
   'he divided, vt'

6. gələbbəṭə
   'he turned over, vt'

7. gəṭṭəmu
   'they joined, vt'

8. məssəlu
   'they resembled, vt'

9. məkkəru
   'they counselled, vt'

10. məlləsu
    'they returned, vt'

11. kəffəlu
    'they divided, vt'

12. gələbbəṭu
    'they turned over, vt'

13. təgaṭṭəmə
    'it was joined together, vi'

14. təmassəlu
    'they resembled each other, vi'

15. təmakkərə
    'he was counselled, vi'

16. təmalləsə
    'he returned, vi'

17. təkaffəlu
    'they were divided, vi'

18. təgəlabbəṭu
    'they were turned over, vi'

19. təgəṭaṭṭəmu
    'they were joined together repeatedly, vi'

20. təməsassəlu
    'they resembled each other very much, vi'

21. təməkakkəru
    'they counselled together repeatedly, vi'

22. təməlalləsu
    'they returned repeatedly, vi'

23. təkəfaffələ
    'it was divided completely , vi'

24. təgələbabbəṭə
    'it was turned over repeatedly, vi'

Dataset 91. Tabasco Chontal (Mexico)

1. untu bekʔet   'one cow'
2. untuntu bekʔet   'only one cow'
3. unʃe   'one side'
4. unʃenʃe   'only one side'
5. umpʔe otot   'one house'
6. umpʔempʔe otot   'only one house'
7. unkʔe pop   'one sleeping mat'
8. unkʔenkʔe pop   'only one sleeping mat'

Dataset 92. Sierra Popoluca (Mexico)

1. pet   'He swept.'
2. miɲ   'He came.'
3. wiʔk   'He ate.'
4. nʌk   'He went.'
5. hoks   'He hoed.'
6. miɲɲeʔ   'He has come.'
7. wiʔkneʔ   'He has eaten.'
8. hoksneʔ   'He has hoed.'
9. pedoʔy   'He swept here and there.'
10. hoksoʔy   'He hoed here and there.'
11. petpetneʔ   'He kept sweeping over and over.'
12. wiʔkwikneʔ   'He kept eating over and over.'
13. nʌknʌkneʔ   'He kept going over and over.'
14. hokshoksneʔ   'He kept hoeing over and over.'
15. petpedoʔy   'He kept sweeping here and there.'
16. hokshoksoʔy   'He kept hoeing here and there.'

Laboratory Manual for Morphology and Syntax

Dataset 93. Turkish

1.	enli	'broad'	31.	epenli	'very broad'
2.	soguk	'cold'	32.	sopsoguk	'very cold'
3.	tamam	'correct'	33.	tastamam	'exactly correct'
4.	boʃ	'empty'	34.	bomboʃ	'completely empty'
5.	ʤavlak	'bald'	35.	ʤasʤavlak	'completely bald'
6.	paslɨ	'stained'	36.	pampaslɨ	'very stained'
7.	yaltʃin	'steep'	37.	yapyaltʃin	'very steep'
8.	toparlak	'round'	38.	tostoparlak	'perfectly round'
9.	ulu	'great'	39.	upulu	'very great'
10.	buz	'ice cold'	40.	bumbuz	'extremely cold'
11.	pembe	'pink'	41.	pespembe	'very pink'
12.	besli	'fat'	42.	bembesli	'very fat'
13.	dolu	'full'	43.	dopdolu	'chock full'
14.	yaʃ	'wet'	44.	yamyaʃ	'all wet'
15.	yamuk	'uneven'	45.	yasyamuk	'shapeless'
16.	yoz	'wild'	46.	yomyoz	'extremely wild'
17.	kara	'black'	47.	kapkara	'jet black'
18.	ölgün	'faded'	48.	öpölgün	'completely faded'
19.	diri	'vigorous'	49.	dipdiri	'extremely vigorous'
20.	piʃkin	'mature'	50.	pimpiʃkin	'very mature'
21.	düz	'smooth'	51.	dümdüz	'perfectly smooth'
22.	dintʃ	'healthy'	52.	dipdintʃ	'very healthy'
23.	yassɨ	'flat'	53.	yamyassɨ	'perfectly flat'
24.	kaba	'coarse'	54.	kaskaba	'very coarse'
25.	köpüklü	'foamy'	55.	kösköpüklü	'very foamy'
26.	kalɨn	'thick'	56.	kapkalɨn	'very thick'
27.	mavi	'blue'	57.	masmavi	'very blue'
28.	kɨvrak	'supple'	58.	kɨskɨvrak	'very supple'
29.	babaʤan	'good-natured'	59.	basbabaʤan	'very good-natured'
30.	oyuk	'hollow'	60.	opoyuk	'completely hollow'

Laboratory Manual for Morphology and Syntax

Dataset 94. Agta (Philippines)

Phonemic stress is not indicated; data from Phyllis M. Healey,
1960, An Agta Grammar, Manila: Bureau of Printing)

1.	assaŋ	'small'	11.	alaʔassaŋ	'very small'
2.	wer	'creek'	12.	walawer	'small creek'
3.	talobag	'beetle'	13.	talatalobag	'lady-bird'
4.	bakbakat	'granny'	14.	balabakbakat	'little granny'
5.	bag	'g-string'	15.	balabag	'small g-string'
6.	kʷak	'mine'	16.	kʷalakʷak	'my small thing'
7.	pirak	'money'	17.	palapirak	'a little money'
8.	abbiŋ	'child'	18.	alaʔabbiŋ	'a little child'
9.	bahuy	'pig'	19.	balabahuy	'a little pig'
10.	pesuk	'peso'	20.	palapesuk	'a mere peso'

Dataset 95. Agta (Philippines)

Phonemic stress is not indicated; data from Phyllis M. Healey,
1960, An Agta Grammar, Manila: Bureau of Printing)

1.	adanuk	'long'	13.	adadanuk	'very long'
2.	addu	'many'	14.	adaddu	'very many'
3.	apisi	'small'	15.	apapisi	'very small'
4.	abikan	'near'	16.	ababikan	'very near'
5.	uffu	'thigh'	17.	ufuffu	'thighs'
6.	takki	'leg'	18.	taktakki	'legs'
7.	labaŋ	'patch'	19.	lablabaŋ	'patches'
8.	dakal	'big'	20.	dadakal	'very big'
9.	dana	'old'	21.	dadana	'very old'
10.	ŋaŋay	'months'	22.	ŋaŋaŋay	'years'
11.	furab	'afternoon'	23.	fufurab	'late afternoon'
12.	laʔwat	'tomorrow'	24.	lalaʔwat	'morning'

Laboratory Manual for Morphology and Syntax

Dataset 96. Afar (Ethiopia)

Phonemic stress is not indicated.

		SG	PL			SG	PL
1.	'fire'	gira	girari	11.	'week'	ayyam	ayyamite
2.	'sore'	dale	dalela	12.	'face'	nabsi	nabsite
3.	'debt'	mago	magoga	13.	'baby'	alʔi	alʔite
4.	'head'	amo	amoma	14.	'fingernail'	lifiʔ	lifiʔa
5.	'police cap'	torbus	torabus	15.	'knee'	gulub	guluba
6.	'picture'	taswir	tasawir	16.	'ox'	aʔur	aʔura
7.	'canvas'	torbal	torabil	17.	'fellow'	wakali	wakalwa
8.	'pants'	sirwal	sirawil	18.	'brain'	hangala	hangalwa
9.	'nail'	bismar	bisamir	19.	'sieve'	manfio	manfiwa
10.	'nose'	san	sanite	20.	'log'	gurumuda	gurumudwa

Dataset 97. Northern Tepehuán (Mexico)

Phonemic tone is not indicated.

		SG	PL			SG	PL
1.	'rabbit'	toʃi	totoʃi	11.	'turkey'	tova	totova
2.	'man'	kʌli	kʌkʌli	12.	'older brother'	ʃiʌgi	ʃiʃiʌgi
3.	'foreigner'	obai	obai	13.	'wool thread'	avoxadai	apoxadai
4.	'tree'	uʃi	uʃi	14.	'kind of bird'	adatomali	aadatomali
5.	'son'	mara	mamara	15.	'needle'	oyi	oxoyi
6.	'aunt'	vovoita	vopoita	16.	'y. brother'	sukuli	susukuli
7.	'cliff'	vavoi	vapavoi	17.	'kind of fish'	aaʃi	aaʃi
8.	'stone'	odai	oxodai	18.	'rat'	dʌgi	dʌdʌgi
9.	'kinsman'	aduɲi	aaduɲi	19.	'eye'	vuxi	vupuxi
10.	'arrow'	uyi	uxuyi	20.	'water jar'	ayi	axayi

Dataset 98. Turkish

		SG	PL			SG	PL
1.	'candle'	mum	mumlar	17.	'your candle'	mumun	mumlarɨn
2.	'match'	kibrit	kibritler	18.	'your match'	kibritin	kibritlerin
3.	'grape'	üzüm	üzümler	19.	'your grape'	üzümün	üzümlerin
4.	'class'	sɨnɨf	sɨnɨflar	20.	'your class'	sɨnɨfɨn	sɨnɨflarɨn
5.	'lesson'	ders	dersler	21.	'your lesson'	dersin	derslerin
6.	'hair'	satʃ	satʃlar	22.	'your hair'	satʃin	satʃlarɨn
7.	'eye'	göz	gözler	23.	'your eye'	gözün	gözlerin
8.	'gun'	top	toplar	24.	'your gun'	topun	toplarɨn
9.	'bird'	kuʃ	kuʃlar	25.	'your bird'	kuʃun	kuʃlarɨn
10.	'tooth'	diʃ	diʃler	26.	'your tooth'	diʃin	diʃlerin
11.	'day'	gün	günler	27.	'your day'	günün	günlerin
12.	'girl'	kɨz	kɨzlar	28.	'your daughter'	kɨzɨn	kɨzlarɨn
13.	'hand'	el	eller	29.	'your hand'	elin	ellerin
14.	'horse'	at	atlar	30.	'your horse'	atɨn	atlarɨn
15.	'arrow'	ok	oklar	31.	'your arrow'	okun	oklarɨn
16.	'root'	kök	kökler	32.	'your root'	kökün	köklerin

Laboratory Manual for Morphology and Syntax

Dataset 99. Turkish

1.	gördü	'He saw.'		21.	yetti	'He reached it.'
2.	görüldü	'He was seen.'		22.	yetmeliydim	'I should have reached it.'
3.	görülmedi	'He was not seen.'		23.	yeteʤekmiyiz	'Will we reach it?'
4.	görüyordu	'He was seeing.'		24.	yetmemeli	'He should not reach it.'
5.	görmedimi	'Didn't he see?'		25.	yetmiʃti	'He has reached it.'
6.	görülmüyoruz	'We are not being seen.'		26.	yetiyoruz	'We are reaching it.'
7.	görmeyeʤekmi	'Won't he see?'		27.	kɨrdɨ	'He broke it.'
8.	göreʤektim	'I was going to see.'		28.	kɨrɨyorum	'I am breaking it.'
9.	göreʤekler	'They will see.'		29.	kɨrɨlmiʃti	'It has been broken.'
10.	görmüʃtü	'He has seen.'		30.	kɨrmayaʤakmɨyɨm	'Won't I break it?'
11.	görmemiʃti	'He has not seen.'		31.	kɨrɨlmayaʤakmɨ	'Won't it be broken?'
12.	atʃtɨ	'He opened it.'		32.	kɨrmamalɨyɨz	'We should not break it.'
13.	atʃmiʃlardɨ	'They have opened it.'		33.	kɨraʤaktɨm	'I was going to break it.'
14.	atʃaʤaklar	'They will open it. '		34.	yazɨyorlar	'They are writing.'
15.	atʃaʤakmiʃim	'I will have opened it.'		35.	yazmalɨymiʃim	'I should have written.'
16.	atʃtimɨ	'Did he open it?'		36.	yazɨlmamiʃti	'It has not been written.'
17.	atʃmalɨydɨm	'I should have opened it.'	37.	yazaʤakmɨ	'Will he write?'
18.	atʃɨyormu	'Is he opening it?'		38.	yazaʤakmɨyɨz	'Will we write?'
19.	atʃmadɨm	'I did not open it.'		39.	yazmɨyordu	'He was not writing.'
20.	yetmedimi	'Didn't he reach it?'		40.	yazaʤakmiʃiz	'We will have written.'

Laboratory Manual for Morphology and Syntax

Dataset 100. Finnish

		INF 1	INF 1 INTERROG	INF 2 INSTR
1.	'sleep'	nukkua	nukkuako	nukkuen
2.	'succeed'	onnistua	onnistuako	onnistuen
3.	'get'	saada	saadako	saaden
4.	'read'	lukea	lukeako	lukien
5.	'sell'	müüdö	müüdökä	müüden
6.	'drink'	yuoda	yuodako	yuoden
7.	'scare'	pelyöttöö	pelyöttöökä	pelyöttöen
8.	'live'	elöö	elöökä	elöen
9.	'sing'	laulaa	laulaako	laulaen
10.	'seek'	etsiö	etsiökä	etsien
11.	'look'	katsoa	katsoako	katsoen
12.	'swim'	uida	uidako	uiden
13.	'eat'	süädö	süädökä	süäden
14.	'walk'	köüdö	köüdökä	köüden
15.	'take'	viedö	viedökä	vieden
16.	'hit'	lüädö	lüädökä	lüäden

	INF 3	INF 4 NOMSG	PST PRTCPL NOMSG	PST PRTCPL PARTPL
1.	nukkuma	nukkuminen	nukkunut	nukkuneita
2.	onnistuma	onnistuminen	onnistunut	onnistuneita
3.	saama	saaminen	saanut	saaneita
4.	lukema	lukeminen	lukenut	lukeneita
5.	müümö	müüminen	müünüt	müüneitö
6.	yuoma	yuominen	yuonut	yuoneita
7.	pelyöttömö	pelyöttöminen	pelyöttönüt	pelyöttöneitö
8.	elömö	elöminen	elönüt	elöneitö
9.	laulama	laulaminen	laulanut	laulaneita
10.	etsimö	etsiminen	etsinüt	etsineitö
11.	katsoma	katsominen	katsonut	katsoneita
12.	uima	uiminen	uinut	uineita
13.	süämö	süäminen	süänüt	süäneitö
14.	köümö	köüminen	köünüt	köüneitö
15.	viemö	vieminen	vienüt	vieneitö
16.	lüämö	lüäminen	lüänüt	lüäneitö

Dataset 101. Hungarian

Consider each form below to be a stem followed by a single suffix.

		INFINITIVE	1S SUBJN	3S SUBJN	1P SUBJN
1.	'scold'	rooni	rooyak	rooyon	rooyunk
2.	'shoot'	lööni	lööyek	lööyön	lööyünk
3.	'obtain'	kapni	kapyak	kapyon	kapyunk
4.	'put'	tenni	tedyek	tedyen	tedyünk
5.	'carry'	vinni	vidyek	vidyen	vidyünk
6.	'ask'	keerni	keeryek	keeryen	keeryünk
7.	'dine'	ebeedelni	ebeedelyek	ebeedelyen	ebeedelyünk
8.	'lead'	vezetni	vezeʃʃek	vezeʃʃen	vezeʃʃünk
9.	'listen'	hallgatni	hallgaʃʃak	hallgaʃʃon	hallgaʃʃunk
10.	'love'	seretni	sereʃʃek	sereʃʃen	sereʃʃünk
11.	'recline'	feküdni	feküdyek	feküdyön	feküdyünk
12.	'know'	tudni	tudyak	tudyon	tudyunk
13.	'perish'	vesni	vessek	vessen	vessünk
14.	'fish'	halaasni	halaassak	halaasson	halaassunk
15.	'crawl'	maasni	maassak	maasson	maassunk
16.	'cook'	föözni	föözzek	föözzön	föözzünk
17.	'pull'	huuzni	huuzzak	huuzzon	huuzzunk
18.	'look at'	neezni	neezzek	neezzen	neezzünk
19.	'wash'	moʃni	moʃʃak	moʃʃon	moʃʃunk
20.	'dig'	aaʃni	aaʃʃak	aaʃʃon	aaʃʃunk

Dataset 102. Upper Asaro (Papua New Guinea)

1.	embeʔ	'village'	13. nosolotiʔ	'from on the water'
2.	geheni	'stone'	14. nosoloʔ	'on the water'
3.	gesi	'fence'	15. nosouʔ	'in the water'
4.	kali	'car'	16. numudoʔ	'on the house'
5.	noso	'water'	17. numugutiʔ	'from in the house'
6.	numuno	'house'	18. numuguʔ	'in the house'
7.	oloʔ	'fire'	19. numuʔveloʔ	'on his house'
8.	embekutiʔ	'from in the village'	20. numuʔveuʔ	'in his house'
9.	gehedoʔ	'on the stone'	21. olokuʔ	'in the fire'
10.	geheguʔ	'in the stone'	22. olotoʔ	'on the fire'
11.	gesiloʔ	'on the fence'	23. oloʔveloʔ	'on his fire'
12.	kaliuʔ	'in the car'		

Dataset 103. Southern Barasano (Colombia)
Phonemic stress is not indicated.

		SG	PL	DIMIN
1.	'deer'	yãbã	yãbã	yãbãka
2.	'fish'	wai	waia	waiaka
3.	'parrot'	weko	wekoa	wekoaka
4.	'toucan'	ratse	ratsea	ratseaka
5.	'turtle'	gu	gua	guaka
6.	'snake'	ãya	ãya	ãyaka
7.	'eagle'	ga	ga	gaka
8.	'hummingbird'	bĩbĩ	bĩbĩa	bĩbĩaka
9.	'armadillo'	habõ	habõa	habõaka
10.	'bird'	bĩdĩ	bĩdĩa	bĩdĩaka
11.	'quacamayo'	bãha	bãha	bãhaka
12.	'peccary'	yetse	yetsea	yetseaka
13.	'crab'	kawia	kawia	kawiaka
14.	'tiger'	yai	yaia	yaiaka

Laboratory Manual for Morphology and Syntax

Dataset 104. Southern Barasano (Colombia)
Phonemic stress is not indicated.

The verb ending -bĩ means 'he'.

1.	wabĩ	'He went.'
2.	wabetibĩ	'He did not go.'
3.	waro	'when (he) went'
4.	wabeto	'when (he) did not go'
5.	wadibĩ	'He came.'
6.	wadibetibĩ	'He did not come.'
7.	wado	'when (he) came'
8.	wadibeto	'when (he) did not come'
9.	bahibĩ	'He was.'
10.	bahibetibĩ	'He was not.'
11.	bahiro	'when (he) was'
12.	bahibeto	'when (he) was not'
13.	yibĩ	'He did (it) .'
14.	yibetibĩ	'He did not do (it).'
15.	yiro	'when (he) did (it)'
16.	yibeto	'when (he) did not do (it)'
17.	kɨtibĩ	'He had (it).'
18.	kɨtibetibĩ	'He did not have (it).'
19.	kɨto	'when (he) had (it)'
20.	kɨtibeto	'when (he) did not have (it)'
21.	budibĩ	'He left.'
22.	budibetibĩ	'He did not leave.'
23.	budiro	'when (he) left'
24.	budibeto	'when (he) did not leave'

Laboratory Manual for Morphology and Syntax

Dataset 105. Barrow Eskimo

		1s Pres Decl	1s Past Decl	1d Fut Decl
1.	come	qairuŋa	qaiɲaruŋa	qaiɲiaqtuguk
2.	fly	tiŋmiruŋa	tiŋmiɲaruŋa	tiŋmiɲiaqtuguk
3.	eat	niɢiruŋa	niɢiɲaruŋa	niɢiɲiaqtuguk
4.	sick	naŋittuŋa	naŋinŋaruŋa	naŋinniaqtuguk
5.	stand	makittuŋa	makinŋaruŋa	makinniaqtuguk
6.	sit	aquvittuŋa	aquvinŋaruŋa	aquvinniaqtuguk
7.	depart	aullaqtuŋa	aullaŋaruŋa	aullaɢniaqtuguk
8.	enter	isiqtuŋa	isiŋaruŋa	isiɢniaqtuguk
9.	walk	pisuaqtuŋa	pisuaŋaruŋa	pisuaɢniaqtuguk
10.	never come	qaiʎaittʃuŋa	qaiʎaiɲŋaruŋa	qaiʎaiɲɲiaqtuguk
11.	never fly	tiŋmiɭaittʃuŋa	tiŋmiɭaiɲŋaruŋa	tiŋmiɭaiɲɲiaqtuguk
12.	never eat	niɢiɭaittʃuŋa	niɢiɭaiɲŋaruŋa	niɢiɭaiɲɲiaqtuguk
13.	never sick	naŋilaittʃuŋa	naŋilaiɲŋaruŋa	naŋilaiɲɲiaqtuguk
14.	never stand	makilaittʃuŋa	makilaiɲŋaruŋa	makilaiɲɲiaqtuguk
15.	never sit	aquvilaittʃuŋa	aquvilaiɲŋaruŋa	aquvilaiɲɲiaqtuguk
16.	never depart	aullalaittʃuŋa	aullalaiɲŋaruŋa	aullalaiɲɲiaqtuguk
17.	never enter	isilaittʃuŋa	isilaiɲŋaruŋa	isilaiɲɲiaqtuguk
18.	never walk	pisualaittʃuŋa	pisualaiɲŋaruŋa	pisualaiɲɲiaqtuguk

		1d Pres Interr	2p Past Interr	2p Fut Interr
1.	come	qaiviɲuk	qaiɲavisi	qaiɲiaqpisi
2.	fly	tiŋmiviɲuk	tiŋmiɲavisi	tiŋmiɲiaqpisi
3.	eat	niɢiviɲuk	niɢiɲavisi	niɢiɲiaqpisi
4.	sick	naŋitpiɲuk	naŋinŋavisi	naŋinniaqpisi
5.	stand	makitpiɲuk	makinŋavisi	makinniaqpisi
6.	sit	aquvitpiɲuk	aquvinŋavisi	aquvinniaqpisi
7.	depart	aullaqpiɲuk	aullaŋavisi	aullaɢniaqpisi
8.	enter	isiqpiɲuk	isiŋavisi	isiɢniaqpisi
9.	walk	pisuaqpiɲuk	pisuaŋavisi	pisuaɢniaqpisi
10.	never come	qaiʎaitpiɲuk	qaiʎaiɲŋavisi	qaiʎaiɲɲiaqpisi
11.	never fly	tiŋmiɭaitpiɲuk	tiŋmiɭaiɲŋavisi	tiŋmiɭaiɲɲiaqpisi
12.	never eat	niɢiɭaitpiɲuk	niɢiɭaiɲŋavisi	niɢiɭaiɲɲiaqpisi
13.	never sick	naŋilaitpiɲuk	naŋilaiɲŋavisi	naŋilaiɲɲiaqpisi
14.	never stand	makilaitpiɲuk	makilaiɲŋavisi	makilaiɲɲiaqpisi
15.	never sit	aquvilaitpiɲuk	aquvilaiɲŋavisi	aquvilaiɲɲiaqpisi
16.	never depart	aullalaitpiɲuk	aullalaiɲŋavisi	aullalaiɲɲiaqpisi
17.	never enter	isilaitpiɲuk	isilaiɲŋavisi	isilaiɲɲiaqpisi
18.	never walk	pisualaitpiɲuk	pisualaiɲŋavisi	pisualaiɲɲiaqpisi

Dataset 106. Northern Puebla Totonac (Mexico)

1. liːmin — 'He brings it/him.'
2. laqtsiːʔn — 'He sees it/him.'
3. ʧiʔpa — 'He seizes it/him.'
4. maːwiːʔ — 'He feeds it/him.'
5. liːmil — 'He brought it/him.'
6. ʧiʔpal — 'He seized it/him.'
7. laqtsiːʔl — 'He saw it/him.'
8. maːwiːʔkuʔtun — 'He wants to feed it/him.'
9. laqtsiːʔnkuʔtun — 'He wants to see it/him.'
10. liːminkuʔtun — 'He wants to bring it/him.'
11. laqtsiːʔniʔ — 'He sees it/him for him.'
12. liːminqoːʔ — 'He brings it all.'
13. laqtsiːʔnkuʔtul — 'He wanted to see it/him.'
14. laqtsiːʔnqoːʔ — 'He sees it all.'
15. liːminiʔl — 'He brought it/him for him.'
16. ʧiʔpaniʔkuʔtul — 'He wanted to seize it/him for him.'
17. kaːkiːʧiʔpaniʔqoːʔl — 'He went to seize all of them for him' or
    'He went to seize it/him for all of them.'

18. naʧiʔpa — 'He will seize it/him.'
19. nakaːkiːʧiʔpakuʔtunqoːʔ — 'He will want to go seize them all.'
20. kinʧiʔpal — 'He seized me.'
21. kaːʧiʔpaqoːʔ — 'He seizes them all.'
22. kilaqtsiːʔnkuʔtul — 'He wanted to see me.'
23. namaːwiːʔ — 'He will feed it/him.'
24. nakiːmaːwiːʔ — 'He will go feed it/him.'
25. kilaqtsiːʔn — 'He sees me.'
26. nakiːtaːʔʧiʔpa — 'He will go with him to grab it/him.'
27. kimaːwiːʔniʔl — 'He fed it/him for me' or 'He fed me for him.'
28. kinkiːʧiʔpaniʔl — 'He went to grab it/him for me' or
    'He went to grab me for him.'

29. nakaːʧiʔpa — 'He will seize them.'
30. kiːtaːʔlaqtsiːʔnkuʔtun — 'He wants to go with him to see it/him.'

Dataset 107. Southern Barasano (Colombia)
Phonemic stress is not indicated.

		SG	PL	SG DIMIN	PL DIMIN
1.	'house'	wi	wiri	wiaka	wiriaka
2.	'cassava'	kĩa	kĩ	kĩaka	kĩaka
3.	'louse'	gia	gi	giaka	giaka
4.	'eagle'	ga	ga	gaka	gaka
5.	'snake'	ãya	ãya	ãyaka	ãyaka
6.	'banana'	ohoro	oho	ohoroaka	ohoaka
7.	'turtle'	gu	gua	guaka	guaka
8.	'hair'	hoabã	hoa	hoabãka	hoaka
9.	'bone'	gõaro	gõa	gõaroaka	gõaka
10.	'pot'	tsotɨ	tsotɨri	tsotɨaka	tsotɨriaka
11.	'vine'	bĩtsibã	bĩtsi	bĩtsibãka	bĩtsiaka
12.	'pile'	widiro	widi	widiroaka	widiaka
13.	'armadillo'	habõ	habõa	habõaka	habõaka
14.	'eye'	kahea	kahe	kaheaka	kaheaka
15.	'platform'	katsabo	katsabori	katsaboaka	katsaboriaka
16.	'bench'	kubôro	kubô	kubôroaka	kubôaka
17.	'shelter'	wihãi	wihãiri	wihãiaka	wihãiriaka
18.	'toucan'	ratse	ratsea	ratseaka	ratseaka
19.	'bead'	bitia	biti	bitiaka	bitiaka
20.	'tiger'	yai	yaia	yaiaka	yaiaka

Dataset 108. Isthmus Zapotec (Mexico)

Phonemic tone is not indicated.

All Zapotec verbforms below are in the habitual aspect, indicated by the prefix ri-, ru-, or r-. Zapotec laryngeal vowels are always stressed. Indicated elsewhere in the manual as doubled vowels (VV), laryngeal vowels are here indicated by an apostrophe centered over a single vowel, as in v̌, to facilitate a simpler statement of the phonological processes found in the data.

		2ND SG	3RD SG	1ST SG
1.	'glean'	ribáguluʔ	ribágube	ribágʷaʔ
2.	'put in'	rigu̇luʔ	rigu̇be	regʷa̓ʔ
3.	'sell'	ruto̓luʔ	rutóbe	rutʷa̓ʔ
4.	'sleep'	rásiluʔ	rásibe	ráseʔ
5.	'sit'	ribíluʔ	ribíbe	ribʸéʔ
6.	'scrape'	rura̓luʔ	rura̓be	rura̓ʔ
7.	'fall'	riábaluʔ	riábabe	riábaʔ
8.	'cover'	rutʃiluʔ	rutʃibe	rutʃʸe̓ʔ
9.	'get fat'	riro̓luʔ	riróbe	rirʷa̓ʔ
10.	'bathe'	rázeluʔ	rázebe	rázeʔ
11.	'pinch'	rigʸéluʔ	rigʸébe	rigʸéʔ
12.	'walk'	rizáluʔ	rizábe	rizáʸaʔ
13.	'put on'	rákuluʔ	rákube	rákʷaʔ
14.	'err'	rutʃe̓luʔ	rutʃe̓be	rutʃe̓ʔ
15.	'get old'	rio̓ʃoluʔ	rio̓ʃobe	rio̓ʃʷaʔ
16.	'cough'	rurúluʔ	rurúbe	rurʷáʔ
17.	'enter'	riu̓luʔ	riu̓be	riʷa̓ʔ
18.	'take out'	ribe̓luʔ	ribe̓be	ribe̓ʔ
19.	'say'	rábiluʔ	rábibe	rábeʔ
20.	'get up'	riásaluʔ	riásabe	riásaʔ
21.	'give'	rudi̓luʔ	rudi̓be	rudʸe̓ʔ
22.	'faint'	rie̓guluʔ	rie̓gube	rie̓gʷaʔ
23.	'suppose'	ruzulúluʔ	ruzulúbe	ruzulʷáʔ
24.	'hunt'	rukʷa̓guluʔ	rukʷa̓gube	rukʷa̓gʷaʔ
25.	'save'	ruláluʔ	rulábe	ruláʸaʔ

Laboratory Manual for Morphology and Syntax

Dataset 109. Alekano (Papua New Guinea)
Phonemic tone is not indicated.

1. nonepelene — 'You are striking me.'
2. nogupuluve — 'I am striking you.'
3. napuluve — 'I am striking him.'
4. napelene — 'You are striking him.'
5. nonipilive — 'He is striking me.'
6. ninepeleve — 'They are striking me.'
7. nogipilive — 'He is striking you.'
8. nigepeleve — 'They are striking you.'
9. ninepelesive — 'You two are striking me.'
10. nolukupuluve — 'I am striking you two.'
11. nokupuluve — 'I am striking them.'
12. nokepelene — 'You are striking them.'
13. napelesive — 'You two are striking him.'
14. napeleve — 'They are striking him.'
15. nikepeleve — 'They are striking them.'
16. nolikipilive — 'He is striking you two.'
17. apuluve — 'I struck him.'
18. kepeleve — 'They struck them.'
19. nepelene — 'You struck me.'

Dataset 110. Sierra Nahuatl (Mexico)

		SG	PL			SG	PL
1.	'egg'	piotet	piotemeh	8.	'cat'	miston	mistomeh
2.	'fire'	tit	timeh	9.	'star'	sitalin	sitalimeh
3.	'skunk'	epat	epameh	10.	'rat'	minitʃin	kimitʃimeh
4.	'man'	takat	takah	11.	'grasshopper'	tʃapolin	tʃapolimeh
5.	'deer'	masat	masameh	12.	'rock'	tet	temeh
6.	'ant'	askat	askameh	13.	'day'	mosta	mostah
7.	'rabbit'	totʃin	totʃimeh	14.	'chicken	pio	piomeh

Dataset 111. Kaiwá (Brazil)

1. idʸavati — 'his corn'
2. idʸape — 'his shell'
3. inãmbi — 'his ear'
4. iɲãkã — 'his head'
5. iɲãpẽkũ — 'his tongue'
6. ikɨse — 'his knife'
7. hẽmbireko — 'his wife'
8. hẽĩndɨrɨ — 'his sister'
9. hape — 'his track'
10. hupa — 'his lying place'
11. oavati — 'his own corn'
12. oape — 'his own shell'
13. onãmbi — 'his own ear'
14. oãkã — 'his own head'
15. oãpẽkũ — 'his own tongue'
16. okɨse — 'his own knife'
17. ŋʷẽmbireko — 'his own wife'
18. ŋʷẽĩndɨrɨ — 'his own sister'
19. gʷape — 'his own track'
20. gʷupa — 'his own lying place'

Laboratory Manual for Morphology and Syntax

Dataset 112. Spanish

Stress explicitly marked beyond normal orthographic convention. Ignore orthographic variation between 'gu' and 'g' in verb meaning 'follow'.

		INF	PRESINDIC	PRESSUBJN	IMPRFINDIC	PSTPRTCPL
1.	'speak'	hablár	hábla	háble	hablába	habládo
2.	'cite'	citár	cíta	cíte	citába	citádo
3.	'doubt'	dudár	dúda	dúde	dudába	dudádo
4.	'burn'	quemár	quéma	quéme	quemába	quemádo
5.	'think'	pensár	piénsa	piénse	pensába	pensádo
6.	'steal'	robár	róba	róbe	robába	robádo
7.	'cost'	costár	cuésta	cuéste	costába	costádo
8.	'sweep'	barrér	bárre	bárra	barría	barrído
9.	'sell'	vendér	vénde	vénda	vendía	vendído
10.	'lose'	perdér	piérde	piérda	perdía	perdído
11.	'eat'	comér	cóme	cóma	comía	comído
12.	'move'	movér	muéve	muéva	movía	movído
13.	'yelp'	gañír	gáñe	gáña	gañía	gañído
14.	'suggest'	sugerír	sugiére	sugiéra	sugería	sugerído
15.	'feel'	sentír	siénte	siénta	sentía	sentído
16.	'ask for'	pedír	píde	pída	pedía	pedído
17.	'sleep'	dormír	duérme	duérma	dormía	dormído
18.	'burnish'	bruñír	brúñe	brúña	bruñía	bruñído
19.	'follow'	seguír	sígue	síga	seguía	seguído

Laboratory Manual for Morphology and Syntax

Dataset 113. German

		NOM SG	GEN SG	NOM PL
1.	'light'	liçt	liçtes	liçter
2.	'egg'	ai	aies	aier
3.	'song'	liːt	liːdes	liːder
4.	'nest'	nest	nestes	nester
5.	'ox'	rint	rindes	rinder
6.	'log'	ʃait	ʃaites	ʃaiter
7.	'evening'	aːbent	aːbents	aːbende
8.	'maple'	aːhorn	aːhorns	aːhorne
9.	'paper'	papiːr	papiːrs	papiːre
10.	'flour'	meːl	meːls	meːle
11.	'swamp'	moːr	moːrs	moːre
12.	'oil'	öːl	öːls	öːle
13.	'cloud'	volke	volke	volken
14.	'woman'	frau	frau	frauen
15.	'toad'	kröːte	kröːte	kröːten
16.	'cure'	kur	kur	kuren
17.	'muse'	muːze	muːze	muːzen
18.	'coal'	koːle	koːle	koːlen
19.	'beast'	tiːr	tiːres	tiːre
20.	'hoof'	huːf	huːfes	huːfe
21.	'dog'	hunt	hundes	hunde
22.	'shoe'	ʃuː	ʃuːes	ʃuːe
23.	'spear'	ʃpiːs	ʃpiːses	ʃpiːse
24.	'murder'	mort	mordes	morde
25.	'jam'	muːs	muːzes	muːze
26.	'residue'	rest	restes	reste
27.	'sprout'	triːp	triːbes	triːbe
28.	'war'	kriːk	kriːges	kriːge
29.	'cabbage'	koːl	koːles	koːle
30.	'lion'	löːve	löːven	löːven
31.	'layman'	laie	laien	laien
32.	'comet'	komeːt	komeːten	komeːten
33.	'boy'	knaːbe	knaːben	knaːben
34.	'parrot'	papagai	papagaien	papagaien
35.	'paragraph'	paragraːf	paragraːfen	paragraːfen
36.	'ox'	okse	oksen	oksen

Laboratory Manual for Morphology and Syntax

Dataset 114. Palantla Chinantec (Mexico)

'qu' and 'c' are orthographic variants of the same sound (k), following the Spanish convention.

		1ST SG	1ST PL	2ND
1.	'scratch'	tsá^{12}	tsá^{2}	tsáh^{2}
2.	'extract'	li^{12}	li^{2}	lih^{2}
3.	'step on'	høa^{12}	høa^{2}	høah^{2}
4.	'set'	hai^{12}	hei^{2}	høih^{2}
5.	'pay'	cǿ^{12}	quií^{2}	cǿh^{2}
6.	'sell'	hnai^{12}	hnøi^{2}	hnøih^{2}
7.	'chew'	juøin^{12}	juøin^{2}	juøinh^{2}
8.	'compete'	co^{12}	cøg^{2}	cøgh^{2}
9.	'dream'	cø^{12}	cø^{2}	cøh^{2}
10.	'strike'	quieng^{12}	quieng^{2}	quiengh^{2}
11.	'slap'	jnáng^{12}	jnáng^{2}	jnángh^{2}
12.	'do'	jmo^{12}	jmo^{2}	jmoh^{2}
13.	'cry'	ho^{12}	høg^{2}	høgh^{2}
14.	'jear'	nang^{12}	neng^{2}	nøngh^{2}
15.	'catch'	hiéih^{12}	hiéih^{2}	hiéih^{2}
16.	'raise'	chio^{12}	chieg^{2}	chiegh^{2}
17.	'tie'	cøin^{12}	quiing^{2}	cøinh^{2}
18.	'dig'	guiég^{12}	guiég^{2}	guiégh^{2}
19.	'rub'	tsí^{12}	tsí^{2}	tsíh^{2}
20.	'roast'	to^{12}	teg^{2}	tigh^{2}
21.	'accept'	hiei^{12}	hiig^{2}	hiigh^{2}
22.	'clear'	jai^{12}	jei^{2}	jøih^{2}
23.	'grind'	ieih^{12}	iigh^{2}	iigh^{2}
24.	'recite'	høa^{12}	hig^{2}	høah^{2}
25.	'hand over'	jáinh^{12}	jáinh^{2}	jáinh^{2}
26.	'inhale'	jøn^{12}	jin^{2}	jønh^{2}
27.	'shave'	tei^{12}	tig^{2}	tigh^{2}
28.	'earn'	hno^{12}	hneng^{2}	hnøngh^{2}

Laboratory Manual for Morphology and Syntax

Dataset 115. Huixtec Tzotzil (Mexico)

The possessive is not specifically masculine, but rather general third-person 'his/her/its' in all forms given here.

1.	abtel	'work'	18.	yabtel	'his work'
2.	ats'am	'salt'	19.	yats'am	'his salt'
3.	itʃ	'chili'	20.	yitʃ	'her chili'
4.	its'inal	'younger brother'	21.	yits'in	'his younger brother'
5.	bankilal	'older brother'	22.	sbankil	'his older brother'
6.	tʃ'ulelal	'soul'	23.	stʃ'ulel	'his soul'
7.	tʃenek'	'beans'	24.	stʃenek'	'his beans'
8.	kerem	'boy'	25.	skerem	'his boy'
9.	lum	'land'	26.	slum	'his land'
10.	motʃ	'basket'	27.	smotʃ	'her basket'
11.	motonil	'gift'	28.	smoton	'his gift'
12.	mulil	'sin'	29.	smul	'his sin'
13.	nitʃ'onil	'son'	30.	snitʃ'on	'his son'
14.	sempatil	'sandal'	31.	sempat	'his sandal'
15.	ton	'stone'	32.	ston	'its egg'
16.	totil	'male'	33.	stot	'his father'
17.	vakaʃ	'bull'	34.	svakaʃ	'his bull'

Dataset 116. Huastec (Mexico)

1. unuhpiy — 'I hurriedly sold it.'

2. anuhtʃal — 'You sell it to him.'

3. anuhuwits — 'You already sold it.'

4. unuhpiyal — 'I hurriedly sell it.'

5. unuhpintʃi — 'I hurriedly sold it to him.'

6. unuhuwtʃik — 'I sold them.'

7. unuhtʃamal — 'I have sold it to him.'

8. anuhtʃintʃi — 'You sold it to him for someone.'

9. unuhuwalits — 'I already sell it.'

10. unuhuwamal — 'I have sold it.'

11. anuhuwamal — 'You have sold it.'

12. anuhuwalak — 'You would sell it.'

13. unuhpiyamal — 'I hurriedly have sold it.'

14. anuhuwictʃik — 'You already sold them.'

15. unuhpiyalak — 'I hurriedly would sell it.'

16. unuhuwaltʃik — 'I sell them.'

17. anuhuwalakits — 'You already would sell it.'

18. anuhtʃintʃalak — 'You would sell it to him for someone.'

19. unuhuwamaltʃik — 'I have sold them.'

20. unuhpintʃintʃal — 'I hurriedly sell it to him for someone.'

Dataset 117. Highland Tzeltal (Mexico)

		1 SG FUT	2 SG FUT	1 SG PERF	2 SG PERF
1.	'die'	yaʃtʃamon	yaʃtʃamat	tʃamenon	tʃamenat
2.	'fall'	yaʃyahlon	yaʃyahlat	yahlemon	yahlemat
3.	'recover'	yaʃkolon	yaʃkolat	kolemon	kolemat
4.	'burst'	yaʃtʼohmon	yaʃtʼohmat	tʼohmenon	tʼohmenat
5.	'increase'	yaʃpʼohlon	yaʃpʼohlat	pʼohlemon	pʼohlemat
6.	'return'	yasuhton	yasuhtat	suhtemon	suhtemat
7.	'stop'	yaʃkohmon	yaʃkohmat	kohmenon	kohmenat
8.	'be hindered'	yaʃmahkon	yaʃmahkat	mahkemon	mahkemat
9.	'get separated'	yaʃpihton	yaʃpihtat	pihtemon	pihtemat
10.	'be cut open'	yaʃxuhtʼon	yaʃxuhtʼat	xuhtʼemon	xuhtʼemat
11.	'make it wilt'	yaxtʃamtes	yakatʃamtes	xtʃamtesex	atʃamtesex
12.	'drop it'	yaxyaltes	yakayaltes	xyaltesex	ayaltesex
13.	'raise it'	yaxkoltes	yakakoltes	xkoltesex	akoltesex
14.	'burst it'	yaxtʼomtes	yakatʼomtes	xtʼomtesex	atʼomtesex
15.	'make it increase'	yaxpʼoltes	yakapʼoltes	xpʼoltesex	apʼoltesex
16.	'return it'	yaxsutes	yakasutes	xsutesex	asutesex
17.	'stop it'	yaxkom	yakakom	xkomox	akomox
18.	'close it'	yaxmak	yakamak	xmakox	amakox
19.	'separate it'	yaxpit	yakapit	xpitox	apitox
20.	'cut it open'	yaxutʼ	yakaxutʼ	xutʼox	axutʼox

Dataset 118. Ocotepec Zoque (Mexico)

1.	kobahk	'head'	11.	kyobahk	'his head'
2.	atsi	'brother'	12.	yatsi	'his brother'
3.	ane	'tortilla'	13.	yane	'his tortilla'
4.	tuwi	'dog'	14.	tyuwi	'his dog'
5.	aŋbʌhk	'beard'	15.	yaŋbʌhk	'his beard'
6.	eme	'aunt'	16.	yeme	'his aunt'
7.	otsi	'tobacco'	17.	yotsi	'his tobacco'
8.	une	'child'	18.	yune	'his child'
9.	ʌŋguy	'bed'	19.	yʌŋguy	'his bed'
10.	kama	'cornfield'	20.	kyama	'his cornfield'

Dataset 119. Yagua (Peru)

			HER	MY
1.	'man'	wanũ	cawanų	rawyanũ
2.	'bread'	pã́ã	capã́ã	rapyã́ã
3.	'poison'	rã́ã́wã́ã́	carã́ã́wã́ã́	raryã́ã́wã́ã́
4.	'grub fat'	nií	canií	ranyií
5.	'wild fruit'	ní̃yã́ã́	caní̃yã́ã́	ranyí̃yã́ã́
6.	'fishhook'	tóóya	catóóya	ratyóóya
7.	'bug'	tootóo	catootóo	ratyootóo
8.	'snack'	kõkṍő	cakõkṍő	rakyõkṍő
9.	'bottle'	puutíya	capuutíya	rapyuutíya
10.	'table'	mĩ́ĩca	camĩ́ĩca	ramyĩ́ĩca

Dataset 120. Biblical Hebrew

		3RD SG IMPRF INTENSIVE	3RD SG PRF REFLEXIVE
1.	'kill'	yqaṭṭel	hitqaṭṭel
2.	'unite'	ydabbeq	hidabbeq
3.	'frighten'	yyareʔ	hityareʔ
4.	'warm'	yħammem	hitħammem
5.	'slap'	ysappeq	histappeq
6.	'make despicable'	ybazze	hitbazze
7.	'justify'	ytsaddeq	hitstaddeq
8.	'equip'	yʔazzer	hitʔazzer
9.	'watch'	yʃammer	hiʃtammer
10.	'steal'	ygannev	hitgannev
11.	'honor'	yhadder	hithadder
12.	'purify'	yzakkex	hizdakkex
13.	'stupify'	yṭamṭem	hiṭamṭem
14.	'mark'	ytsayyen	hitstayyen
15.	'prove perjury'	yzammem	hizdammem
16.	'compare'	ydamme	hidamme
17.	'mock'	ytaʕateaʕ	hitaʕateaʕ

Laboratory Manual for Morphology and Syntax

Dataset 121. Fore (Papua New Guinea)
Phonemic tone is not indicated.

		1s	2s	3s	1p
1.	'axe'	tunte	tuka	tunkwa	tute
2.	'clothes'	kayne	kayga	kaywa	kayre
3.	'one (thing)'	kaːʔne	kaːka	kaːʔwa	kaːte
4.	'liver'	awnte	awka	awnkwa	awte
5.	'knot'	awʔne	awka	awʔwa	awte
6.	'eye'	awne	awga	awwa	awre
7.	'shell'	pine	piga	piwa	pire
8.	'snake'	maːʔne	maːka	maːʔwa	maːte
9.	'trap'	kone	koga	kowa	kore
10.	'skin'	awʔne	awka	awʔwa	awte
11.	'bee'	inte	ika	inkwa	ite
12.	'house'	naːnte	naːka	naːnkwa	naːte
13.	'name'	agene	agega	agewa	agere
14.	'bag'	koʔne	koka	koʔwa	kote
15.	'vomit'	mune	muga	muwa	mure
16.	'kneecap'	arawnte	arawka	arawnkwa	arawte
17.	'ginger'	kaynte	kayka	kaynkwa	kayte
18.	'navel'	abeʔne	abeka	abeʔwa	abete

Dataset 122. Totontepec Mixe (Mexico)

		1s	2s	3s
1.	'see'	nʔiʃ	mʔiʃ	yʔiʃ
2.	'play'	nkoːʔya	mkoːʔya	kyoːʔya
3.	'plow'	nyuʔu	myuʔu	yuʔu
4.	'get angry'	nʔekhʌ	mʔekhʌ	yʔekhʌ
5.	'sneeze'	nhaʔanʤa	mhaʔanʤa	hyaʔanʤa
6.	'laugh'	nʒiʔik	mʒiʔik	ʃyiʔik

Laboratory Manual for Morphology and Syntax

Dataset 123. Khmu? (Laos)

VERBS

1.	kap	'grasp with tongs'	
2.	poot	'walk on'	
3.	toh	'chisel'	
4.	see	'drill'	
5.	pəəy	'fan'	
6.	hoom	'tie'	
7.	hiip	'eat with spoon'	
8.	cok	'gouge'	
9.	teh	'kick backwards'	
10.	tiap	'fold as package'	
11.	sal	'place in earlobe'	

NOUNS

1a.	krnap	'tongs'	
2a.	prnoot	'platform around house'	
3a.	trnoh	'chisel'	
4a.	srnee	'drill'	
5a.	prnəəy	'fan'	
6a.	hrnoom	'something to tie with'	
7a.	hrniip	'spoon'	
8a.	crnok	'gouging instrument'	
9a.	trneh	'match'	
10a.	trniap	'small package'	
11a.	srnal	'ear ornament'	

Dataset 124. Huixtec Tzotzil (Mexico)

1.	nibát	'I went'		13.	nabát	'you went'
2.	nikóm	'I stayed'		14.	nakóm	'you stayed'
3.	nivé?	'I ate'		15.	navé?	'you ate'
4.	nitál	'I came'		16.	natál	'you came'
5.	tʃibát	'I will go'		17.	tʃabát	'you will go'
6.	tʃikóm	'I will stay'		18.	tʃakóm	'you will stay'
7.	tʃivé?	'I will eat'		19.	tʃavé?	'you will eat'
8.	tʃitál	'I will come'		20.	tʃatál	'you will come'
9.	bátemun	'I have gone'		21.	bátemot	'you have gone'
10.	kómenun	'I have stayed'		22.	kómeɲot	'you have stayed'
11.	vé?emun	'I have eaten'		23.	vé?emot	'you have eaten'
12.	tálemun	'I have come'		24.	tálemot	'you have come'

Laboratory Manual for Morphology and Syntax

Dataset 125. French

1.	ʒömölüiprezãt	'I present myself to him.'
2.	ilmölüiprezãt	'He presents me to him.'
3.	ilmölöprezãt	'He presents him to me.'
4.	ʒölölüiprezãt	'I present him to him.'
5.	illölüiprezãt	'He presents him to him.'
6.	ʒömölöprezãt	'I present him to myself.'
7.	ʒönömölüiprezãtpa	'I don't present myself to him.'
8.	ilnömölüiprezãtpa	'He doesn't present me to him.'
9.	ilnömölöprezãtpa	'He doesn't present him to me.'
10.	ʒömölüieprezãte	'I presented myself to him.'
11.	ilmölüiaprezãte	'He presented me to him.'
12.	ilmölaprezãte	'He presented him to me.'
13.	ʒölölüieprezãte	'I presented him to him.'
14.	ʒömöleprezãte	'I presented him to myself.'
15.	ilnömölüiapaprezãte	'He didn't present me to him.'
16.	ilnömölapaprezãte	'He didn't present him to me.'

Dataset 126. Waorani (Ecuador)

1.	abo	'I see.'	13.	kækãta	'He did.'
2.	ãmo	'I say.'	14.	kæmõ	'We (incl) do.'
3.	ãŋã	'He says.'	15.	kækĩŋã	'He will do.'
4.	kǽnã	'She eats.'	16.	kǽŋãta	'He ate.'
5.	adãta	'She saw.'	17.	kǽŋĩnã	'She will eat.'
6.	ǽŋĩŋã	'He will take.'	18.	kækã	'He does.'
7.	akĩmo	'I shall see.'	19.	ǽnãta	'She took.'
8.	kætamõ	'We (incl) did.'	20.	ǽŋĩmõ	'We (incl) shall take.'
9.	adã	'She sees.'	21.	ǽtabo	'I took.'
10.	ãtabo	'I said.'	22.	kǽŋĩmo	'I shall eat.'
11.	kækĩmõ	'We (incl) shall do.'	23.	amõ	'We (incl) see.'
12.	akĩnã	'She will see.'	24.	ǽŋĩmo	'I shall take.'

Laboratory Manual for Morphology and Syntax

Dataset 127. Huixtec Tzotzil (Mexico)

These data are presented in a morphophonemic orthography with morpheme boundaries indicated by hyphen (-) to expedite the analysis. Assume the following structure for the verb: tns + pn + vs + pl + pn + pl. Describe when, where, and how plural is marked in Tzotzil.

1. láx-k-ʔíl-ot	'I saw you.'		17. láx-k-ʔíl-tutik-ot	'We (excl) saw you.'
2. láx-k-ʔíl	'I saw him.'		18. láx-k-ʔíl-tutik	'We (excl) saw him.'
3. láx-av-ʔíl-un	'You saw me.'		19. láx-av-ʔíl-Uk-un	'You (pl) saw me.'
4. láx-av-ʔíl	'You saw him.'		20. láx-av-ʔíl-Uk	'You (pl) saw him.'
5. láx-y-ʔíl-un	'He saw me.'		21. láx-y-ʔíl-Uk-un	'They saw me.'
6. láx-y-ʔíl-ot	'He saw you.'		22. láx-y-ʔíl-Uk-ot	'They saw you.'
7. láx-y-ʔíl	'He saw him.'		23. láx-y-ʔíl-Uk	'They saw him.'
8. láx-k-ʔíl-ot-Uk	'I saw you (pl).'		24. láx-k-ʔíl-tik	'We (incl) saw them.'
9. láx-k-ʔíl-Uk	'I saw them.'		25. láx-k-ʔíl-ot-Uk	'We (excl) saw you (pl).'
10. láx-av-ʔíl-un-tutik	'You saw us.'		26. láx-k-ʔíl-tutik	'We (excl) saw them.'
11. láx-av-ʔíl	'You saw them.'		27. láx-av-ʔíl-un-tutik	'You (pl) saw us.'
12. láx-y-ʔíl-ukutik	'He saw us (incl).'		28. láx-av-ʔíl-Uk	'You (pl) saw them.'
13. láx-y-ʔíl-un-tutik	'He saw us (excl).'		29. láx-y-ʔíl-ukutik	'They saw us (incl).'
14. láx-y-ʔíl-ot-Uk	'He saw you (pl).'		30. láx-y-ʔíl-un-tutik	'They saw us (excl).'
15. láx-y-ʔíl	'He saw them.'		31. láx-y-ʔíl-ot-Uk	'They saw you (pl).'
16. láx-k-ʔíl-tik	'We (incl) saw him.'		32. láx-y-ʔíl-Uk	'They saw them.'

Dataset 128. English

1. Mary went.
2. John came.
3. Judy fell.
4. Ralph swam.

Dataset 129. San Miguel Mixtec (Mexico)

1. Kēē ʔīsò.   'The rabbit will go away.'
2. Kēē kōò.   'The snake will go away.'
3. Kēē sùtʃí.   'The child will go away.'
4. Kēē sáná.   'The turkey will go away.'
5. Dòō kōò.   'The snake will stay.'
6. Doō sùtʃí.   'The child will stay.'
7. ʒéē ʔīsò.   'The rabbit is eating.'
8. ʒéē sáná.   'The turkey is eating.'

Dataset 130. Awa (Papua New Guinea)

1. Wæ tópa næʔ.   'The man is eating sweet potatoes.'
2. Ibaní tópa uwí.   'The woman is planting sweet potatoes.'
3. Arʌri kʌripe tídíʔ.   'The girl is cooking peanuts.'
4. Wæ kʌripe uwí.   'The man is planting peanuts.'
5. Mabi aŋko næʔ.   'The young man is eating taro.'
6. Ibaní tópa tídíʔ.   'The woman is cooking sweet potatoes.'
7. Ibaní aŋko uwí.   'The woman is planting taro.'
8. Arʌri ca uwí.   'The girl is planting sugar cane.'
9. Mabi aŋko tídíʔ.   'The young man is cooking taro.'
10. Ibaní ca næʔ.   'The woman is eating sugar cane.'

Dataset 131. Lotuko (The Sudan)

1. Idulak atulo ema.   'The man is planting grain.'
2. Idulak atulo aful.   'The man is planting peanuts.'
3. Abak atulo ezok.   'The man hit the dog.'
4. Ohonya eito erizo.   'The child is eating meat.'
5. Amata eito aari.   'The child is drinking water.'
6. Amata odwoti aari.   'The girl is drinking water.'
7. Ohonya odwoti erizo.   'The girl is eating meat.'
8. Ohonya ezok erizo.   'The dog is eating meat.'

Dataset 132. Hixkaryána (Brazil)

1. Toto yahosɨye kamara.   'The jaguar grabbed the man.'

2. Bɨryekomo yahosɨye toto.   'The man grabbed the boy.'

3. Waywɨ yeryeye bɨryekomo.   'The boy put the arrow down.'

4. Yawaka yeryeye wosɨ.   'The woman put the axe down.'

5. Kamara yotahano toto.   'The man hit the jaguar.'

6. Wosɨ yotahano bɨryekomo.   'The boy hit the woman.'

Dataset 133. Mono (Democratic Republic of Congo)

1. Àbá dá mì.   'Father spanked me.'

2. Àbá dà mì.   'Father will spank me.'

3. Gbòlò lú màngè.   'The child planted corn.'

4. Gbòlò ú lù màngè.   'The child will plant corn.'

5. Kòmbá zɨ́ gbàgà.   'The bird ate the peanut.'

6. Kòmbá zɨ̀ gbàgà.   'The bird will eat the peanut.'

7. Kapítà ʃó kɨ̀ndɨ̀.   'The chief burned the field.'

8. Kapítà ó ʃò kɨ̀ndɨ̀.   'The chief will burn the field.'

9. Yàsè zɨ́ gbàgà.   'The woman ate the peanut.'

10. Yàsè ɨ́ zɨ̀ gbàgà.   'The woman will eat the peanut.'

11. Múrú wó ʃè.   'The leopard killed him.'

12. Múrú wò ʃè.   'The leopard will kill him.'

13. Àbá dá ʃè.   'Father spanked him.'

14. Àbá dà ʃè.   'Father will spank him.'

Dataset 134. Palantla Chinantec (Mexico)

1. Hma^{12} jni cuøi^2.   'I'm hiding corn.'

2. Hma^{13} jni høng^2.   'I'll hide the peppers.'

3. Hma^{12} dsa sei^3.   'He's hiding the cassava.'

4. Hma^1 dsa jneng^2.   'He'll hide the beans.'

5. Ranh^{13} jni cuøi^2.   'I'm/I'll wash the corn.'

6. Ranh^{12} dsa høng^2.   'He's washing the peppers.'

7. Ranh^1 dsa jneng^2.   'He'll wash the beans.'

8. Dsǿh^{12} jni sei^3.   'I'm burning up the cassava.'

9. Dsǿh^{13} jni høng^2.   'I'll burn up the peppers.'

10. Dsǿh^2 dsa cuøi^2.   'He's/He'll burn up the corn.'

11. Høa^{12} jni cuøi^2.   'I'm counting the ears of corn.'

12. Høa^{13} jni høng^2.   'I'll count the peppers.'

13. Høa^{12} dsa sei^3.   'He's counting the cassava.'

14. Høa^1 dsa jneng^2.   'He'll count the beans.'

15. Juu^3 jni sei^3.   'I'm/I'll stack the cassava'

16. Juu^{12} dsa cuøi^2.   'He's stacking the corn.'

17. Juu^1 dsa cuøi^2.   'He'll stack the corn.'

18. Hnai^{12} jni cuøi^2.   'I'm selling the corn.'

19. Hnai^{13} jni høng^2.   'I'll sell the peppers.'

20. Hnai^{12} dsa sei^3.   'He's selling the cassava.'

21. Hnai^1 dsa jneng^2.   'He'll sell the beans.'

(continued)

Dataset 134 continued:

22. Jŋiángh^3 jni høng^2.　　　'I'm/I'll move the peppers.'

23. Jŋiángh^{12} dsa jneng^2.　　'He's moving the beans.'

24. Jŋiángh^1 dsa sei^3.　　　'He'll move the cassava.'

25. Jló̷^{12} jni høng^2.　　　　'I'm covering the peppers.'

26. Jló̷^{13} jni cuøi^2.　　　　'I'll cover the corn.'

27. Jló̷^{2} dsa jneng^2.　　　'He's/He'll cover the beans.'

28. Dsióh^{13} jni sei^3.　　　'I'm/I'll distribute the cassava.'

29. Dsióh^{12} dsa cuøi^2.　　'He's distributing the corn.'

30. Dsióh^1 dsa høng^2.　　'He'll distribute the peppers.'

31. Guieh^{12} jni jneng^2.　　'I'm throwing away the beans.'

32. Guieh^{13} jni cuøi^2.　　'I'll throw away the corn.'

33. Guieh^{12} dsa høng^2.　　'He's throwing away the peppers.'

34. Guieh^1 dsa sei^3.　　　'He'll throw away the cassava.'

35. Huan^3 jni jneng^2.　　'I'm/I'll sort out the bad beans.'

36. Huan^{12} dsa høng^2.　　'He's sorting out the bad peppers.'

37. Huan^1 dsa sei^3.　　　'He'll sort out the bad cassava.'

38. Jŋiíh^{12} jni cuøi^2.　　'I'm removing the corn.'

39. Jŋiíh^{13} jni jneng^2.　　'I'll remove the beans.'

40. Jŋiíh^2 dsa høng^2.　　'He's/He'll remove the peppers.'

41. Ten^{13} jni cuøi^2.　　'I'm/I'll let down the corn.'

42. Ten^{12} dsa sei^3.　　　'He's letting down the cassava.'

43. Ten^1 dsa jneng^2.　　　'He'll let down the beans.'

Dataset 135. Palantla Chinantec (Mexico)

1. Jáinh^{12} hio^{13} cog^{3}.   'The woman hands over the money.'

2. Jáinh^{12} guiuh^{13} si^{2}.   'The man hands over the paper.'

3. Jáinh^{12} tsih^{2}.   'The child hands it over.'

4. Jŋiíh^{2} tsih^{2} si^{2}.   'The child removes the paper.'

5. Jŋiíh^{2} guiuh^{13} cog^{3}.   'The man removes the money.'

6. Jŋiíh^{2} hio^{13}.   'The woman removes it.'

7. He^{12} tsih^{2} cog^{3}.   'The child shows the money.'

8. He^{12} hio^{13} si^{2}.   'The woman shows the paper.'

9. He^{12} guiuh^{13}.   'The man shows it.'

Dataset 136. Mezquital Otomí (Mexico)
Phonemic tone is not indicate

1. Bi-kuwi   ri   t'aʃa   miʃi   ma   tsatyo.
3s.PST-chase   2s   white   cat   my   dog
'My dog chased your white cat'

2. Da-tæni   ra   tsatyo   ri   miʃi.
3s.FUT-follow   DEF   dog   2s   cat
'Your cat will follow the dog.'

3. Da-kuwi   ma   tsatyo   ri   t'ika   fani.
3s.FUT-chase   1s   dog   2s   little   horse
'Your little horse will chase my dog.'

4. Bi-pëhë   ma   t'aʃa   tsatyo   ra   dạta   miʃi.
3s.PST-rescue   1s   white   dog   DEF   big   cat
'The big cat rescued my white dog.'

5. Da-pëhë   ra   t'ika   tsatyo   ra   fani.
3s.FUT-rescue   DEF   little   dog   DEF   horse
'The horse will rescue the little dog.'

6. Bi-tæni   ri   fani   ma   dạta   fani.
3s.PST-follow   2s   horse   1s   big   horse
'My big horse followed your horse.'

Dataset 137. Palantla Chinantec (Mexico)

1. Sen¹ mǿ² banh² tsih².   'The chubby woman will bathe the child.'
2. Jën¹² cuø³ mǿ² pan¹³.   'The horse will see the fat woman.'
3. Dsianh¹² guiuh¹³ tsih².   'The gentleman will find the child.'
4. Jën¹² cuø³ guiuh¹³.   'The horse will see the gentleman.'
5. Dsianh¹² cuø³ banh² tsih².   'The stocky horse will find the child.'
6. Sen¹ tsih² cuø³ píh³.   'The child will bathe the little horse.'
7. Jën¹² mǿ² tsih² banh².   'The woman will see the chubby child.'
8. Dsianh¹² tsih² píh³ cuø³ banh².   'The little child will find the stocky horse.'
9. Jën¹² guiuh¹³ pan¹³ mǿ².   'The fat gentleman will see the woman.'
10. Jën¹² tsih² ten² guiuh¹³.   'The skinny child will see the gentleman.'
11. Sen¹ guiuh¹³ píh³ cuø³ ten².   'The little gentleman will bathe the skinny horse.'
12. Dsianh¹² mǿ² guiuh¹³.   'The woman will find the gentleman.'

Dataset 138. Vietnamese
Phonemic tone is not indicated.

1. ʧɔ sem ʧim tɔ.   'The dog sees the big bird.'
2. ʧɔ tɔ xʌwŋ sem ʧɔ ɲɔ.   'The big dog does not see the little dog.'
3. Thʌy ʧim ɲɔ.   'Someone perceives the little bird.'
4. ʧim kuʔŋ sem ʧɔ.   'The bird also sees the dog.'
5. ʧim kuʔŋ thʌy.   'The bird also perceives.'
6. Xʌwŋ thʌy.   'Someone does not perceive.'
7. ʧɔ thʌy ʧim.   'The dog perceives the bird.'
8. Sem.   'Someone sees.'
9. ʧim tɔ thʌy ʧɔ tɔ.   'The big bird perceives the big dog.'
10. ʧim ɲɔ kuʔŋ thʌy ʧim tɔ.   'The little bird also perceives the big bird.'

Laboratory Manual for Morphology and Syntax

Dataset 139. Apinayé (Brazil)

1. Kukrẽ kokoi.   'The monkey eats.'

2. Kukrẽ kra.   'The child eats.'

3. Ape kra.   'The child works.'

4. Kukrẽ kokoi ratʃ.   'The big monkey eats.'

5. Ape kra mɛtʃ.   'The good child works.'

6. Ape mɛtʃ kra.   'The child works well.'

7. Ape ratʃ mɨ mɛtʃ.   'The good man works a lot.'

8. Kukrẽ ratʃ kokoi punui.   'The bad monkey eats a lot.'

9. Ape ŋre mɨ punui.   'The bad man works a little.'

10. Ape punui mɨ.   'The man works badly.'

Dataset 140. Oaxaca Chontal (Mexico)
Regularized; Phonological stress is not indicated.

1. ʃimpa nulyi lawʔa nulyi lapanla.   'One child sees one duck.'

2. ʃimpa lapanla lawʔa.   'The duck sees the child.'

3. Xoyʔpa lawʔa lapanla.   'The child calls the duck.'

4. Xanaxpa lapanla tige lawʔa.   'The duck likes that child.'

5. Xoyʔpaʔ lapanla piɬki lapanlayʔ.   'The duck called all the ducks.'

6. Xanaxpaʔ piɬki lapanlayʔ tige lawʔa.   'All the ducks liked that child.'

7. Xoyʔpaʔ tige lawʔa ataxu lawʔayʔ.   'That child called many children.'

8. ʃimpaʔ lawʔayʔ piɬki lapanlayʔ.   'The children saw all the ducks.'

9. Xanaxpaʔ piɬki lawʔayʔ piɬki lapanlayʔ.   'All the children liked all the ducks.'

10. Xanaxpaʔ piɬki lapanlayʔ piɬki lawʔayʔ.   'All the ducks liked all the children.'

Dataset 141. Michoacán Nahuatl (Mexico)

1. Mayanak inpelo we.   'The big dog hungered.'

2. Mayanaya imula we.   'His big mule was hungry.'

3. Mayanas noʃolul.   'My child will be hungry.'

4. Mayana intuntʃi tomawak.   'The/their fat cat is hungry.'

5. Mayana nomula.   'My mule is hungry.'

6. Molaluk inmula tomawak.   'The/their fat mule ran.'

7. Molaluk ituntʃi we.   'His big cat ran.'

8. Molaluaya nopelo tomawak.   'My fat dog was running.'

9. Molalus inʃolul we.   'The/their big child will run.'

10. Molalua impitʃo.   'Their turkey is running.'

11. Nehnemik ipitʃo we.   'His big turkey walked.'

12. Nehnemiaya notuntʃi.   'My cat was walking.'

13. Nehnemis impelo.   'Their dog will walk.'

14. Nehnemis inpitʃo tomawak.   'The fat turkey will walk.'

15. Nehnemi iʃolul tomawak.   'His fat child is walking.'

Dataset 142. Bahnar (Vietnam)

Data from Elizabeth M. Banker, 1964, "Bahnar Reduplication,"
Mon-Khmer Studies 1, Publication 1 of the Linguistic Circle of Saigon.

1. kɔ́   'dog'

2. ʼdák   'water'

3. bʌnɔ́t   'dam'

4. pʌnái   'stirring stick'

5. kɔ́ kɛ́l kɔ́ kɛ́t   'disgusting dog'

6. ʼdák ʼdɛ́l ʼdák ʼdɛ́t   'disgusting water'

7. bʌnɔ́t bʌnɛ́l bʌnɔ́t bʌnɛ́t   'disgusting dam'

8. pʌnái pʌnɛ́l pʌnái pʌnɛ́t   'disgusting stirring stick'

Laboratory Manual for Morphology and Syntax

Dataset 143. Bahnar (Vietnam)
Data from Elizabeth M. Banker, 1964, "Bahnar Reduplication,"
Mon-Khmer Studies 1, Publication 1 of the Linguistic Circle of Saigon.

1.	gó	'Wait!'
2.	tɔ́k	'Go up!'
3.	sá	'Eat it!'
4.	pʌhrúk	'Dress him!'
5.	tʌtón	'Hit each other!'
6.	gó géh	'Don't wait! What are you waiting for?'
7.	tɔ́k téh	'Don't go up! Why are you going up?'
8.	sá séh	'Don't eat it! It isn't worth eating!'
9.	pʌhrúk hréh	'Don't dress him! Why are you doing that?'
10.	tʌtón téh	'Don't hit each other! That's not good!'

Dataset 144. Bahnar (Vietnam)
Data from Elizabeth M. Banker, 1964, "Bahnar Reduplication,"
Mon-Khmer Studies 1, Publication 1 of the Linguistic Circle of Saigon.

1.	hʌɲír	'sweaty person'
2.	bʌbrɔ́k	'noise of people talking'
3.	tʌbúl	'person to sleep curled up'
4.	sʌlwé	'evil looking face'
5.	'bʌ'blɔ́	'lazy person'
6.	hʌháh	'girls laughing and giggling'
7.	mʌlwéŋ	'drunk person'
8.	hʌɲír hʌɲóɲ móɲ	'each of many sweaty people'
9.	bʌbrɔ́k bʌbróɲ móɲ	'noise of each group of many people talking'
10.	tʌbúl tʌbóɲ móɲ	'each of many people to sleep curled up'
11.	sʌlwé sʌlwóɲ móɲ	'each of many evil looking faces'
12.	'bʌ'blɔ́ 'bʌ'blóɲ móɲ	'each of many lazy people'
13.	hʌháh hʌhóɲ móɲ	'each of many girls laughing and giggling'
14.	mʌlwéŋ mʌlwóɲ móɲ	'each of many drunk people'

Dataset 145. Northern Puebla Totonac (Mexico)

1. Wan ʧiʔʃkuʔ puʔʃa kafe palaʔ.
   the man is.picking coffee energetically
   'The man is energetically picking coffee.'

2. Qałatin puskaːt waʔ laːʃaʃ wampala.
   one woman is.eating oranges again
   'A woman is eating oranges again.'

3. Waʔma qaʔwaːʔʧu staːʔ stapuːn lakatsuku.
   this boy is.selling beans slowly
   'This boy is slowly selling beans.'

4. Qałatin qaʔwaːʔʧu puʔʃa laːʃaʃ pałaʔ.
   one boy is.picking oranges energetically
   'A boy is energetically picking oranges.'

5. Waʔma ʧiʔʃkuʔ staːʔ kafe lakatsuku.
   this man is.selling coffee slowly
   'This man is slowly selling coffee.'

6. Wan puskaːt staːʔ stapuːn wampala.
   the woman is.selling beans again
   'The woman is selling beans again.'

7. Wan qaʔwaːʔʧu waʔ stapuːn pałaʔ.
   the boy is.eating beans energetically
   'The boy is eating beans energetically.'

8. Qałatin ʧiʔʃkuʔ waʔ laːʃaʃ.
   one man is.eating oranges
   'A man is eating oranges.'

9. Waʔma puskaːt puʔʃa kafe lakatsuku.
   this woman is.picking coffee slowly
   'This woman is picking coffee slowly.'

10. Waʔma qaʔwaːʔʧu staːʔ stapuːn.
    this boy is.selling beans
    'This boy is selling beans.'

Laboratory Manual for Morphology and Syntax

Dataset 146. Coatlán Mixe (Mexico)

1. He   tsuːk   tsuk   tiʔiʃ.
   that   rat   ant   saw
   'That rat saw the ant.'

2. He   muts   tsuːk   tugʌːk   tsuk   tiʔiʃ.
   that   little   rat   three   ant   saw
   'That little rat saw three ants.'

3. He   tsuːtʃ   poːp   tsuːk   tiʔiʃ.
   that   horsefly   white   rat   saw
   'That horsefly saw the white rat.'

4. ʔuk   mets   tsuk   tiʔiʃ.
   dog   two   ant   saw
   'The dog saw two ants.'

5. Tugʌːk   tsuk   mets   poːʃ   tiʔiʃ.
   three   ant   two   spider   saw
   'Three ants saw two spiders.'

6. tsuːk   poːp   tsuːtʃ   tiʔiʃ.
   rat   white   horsefly   saw
   'The rat saw the white horsefly.'

7. tʃiːt   muts   tsuːk   tikoʃ.
   cat   little   rat   hit
   'The cat hit the little rat.'

8. Mʌk   tʃiːt   he   muts   tsuːk   tikoʃ.
   strong   cat   that   little   rat   hit
   'The strong cat hit that little rat.'

9. He   kaː   muts   wah   tiyahʔoʔok.
   that   tiger   little   calf   killed
   'That tiger killed the little calf.'

10. Mʌh   kaː   mets   wah   tiyahʔoʔok.
    big   tiger   two   calf   killed
    'The big tiger killed two calves.'

(continued)

Dataset 146 continued:

11. He   mʌh   tsuːk   tsahkaːyk   tikaːy.
    that   big   rat   bread   ate
    'That big rat ate the bread.'

12. ʔuk   he   mʌk   kaː   tiʔiʃ.
    dog   that strong   tiger   saw
    'The dog saw that strong tiger.'

13. He   mets   poːp   tsuːk   tsahkaːyk   kaːyɨp.
    that two   white   rat   bread   will.eat
    'Those two white rats will eat the bread.'

14. Tugʌːk   mʌk   kaː   he   muts   wah   kaːyɨp.
    three   strong   tiger   that   little   calf   will.eat
    'Three strong tigers will eat that little calf.'

15. Mʌh   tsuːʧ   he   tugʌːk   muts   tsuk   ʔiʃp.
    big   horsefly   that   three   little   ant   sees
    'The big horsefly sees those three little ants.'

16. He   tugʌːk   ʧiːt   ʔuk   yahʔoʔokp.
    that three   cat   dog   kill
    'Those three cats kill the dog.'

17. Poːp   ʔuk   tsuk   yahʔoʔokɨp.
    white   dog   ant   will.kill
    'The white dog will kill the ant.'

18. Mʌh   wah   he   tsahkaːyk   ʔiʃɨp.
    big   calf   that   bread   will.see
    'The big calf will see that bread.'

19. Poːʃ   tsuːʧ   kaːyp.
    spider   horsefly   eats
    'The spider eats the horsefly.'

20. He   poːp   ʧiːt   mets   mʌh   tsuːk   koʃɨp.
    that white   cat   two   big   rat   will.hit
    'That white cat will hit the two big rats.'

Dataset 147. Waorani (Ecuador)

1. Mãἐpo õmædẽ go.   'Daddy goes to the jungle.'

2. Gĩta go.   'Doggie goes along.'

3. Mãἐpo taadõ go.   'Daddy goes along the trail.'

4. Gĩta wĩi taadõ go.   'Doggie doesn't go along the trail.'

5. Õnõke õmædẽ go.   'He just goes in the jungle.'

6. Wĩi kĩŋἐ go.   'He doesn't go fast.'

7. Gõŋa põ.   'A red monkey comes.'

8. Kĩŋἐ go.   'He goes fast.'

9. Mãἐpo ayἐ õõ.   'Then daddy shoots (his blowgun).'

10. Gõŋa ayἐ õmædẽ wἐ.   'The red monkey then falls in the jungle.'

11. Wĩi taadõ wἐ.   'He doesn't fall on the trail.'

12. Gĩta ayἐ kĩŋἐ õmædẽ go.   'Doggie then goes fast through the jungle.'

13. ἐ.   'He takes it.'

14. Wĩi kἐ.   'He doesn't eat it.'

15. Õnõke kĩŋἐ ἐ.   'He just takes it fast.'

16. Mãἐpo ayἐ ἐ.   'Daddy then takes it.'

17. Wĩi õmædẽ kἐ.   'He doesn't eat it in the jungle.'

18. Õnõke õkõnẽ põ.   'He just comes home.'

19. Põ.   'He comes.'

20. Ayἐ kἐ.   'Then he eats.'

21. Kĩŋἐ kἐ.   'He eats fast.'

22. Gĩta ayἐ õkõnẽ kἐ.   'Doggie then eats at home.'

Dataset 148. Hausa (Nigeria)

1. Ná tàfĩ.   'I went away.'
2. Ná fìtá gídánsà.   'I went out of his house.'
3. Ná ʃìgá gídánkù.   'I went into your (pl) house.'
4. Ná dáwó jíyà.   'I returned here yesterday.'
5. Zân tàfĩ gòbé.   'I'll go away tomorrow.'
6. Ká ʃìgá gídánsà.   'You (masc) went into his house.'
7. Kín dáwó.   'You (fem) returned here.'
8. Zân fìtá gídámmù gòbé.   'I'll go out of our house tomorrow.'
9. Kín tàfĩ gídánsù.   'You (fem) went away to their house.'
10. Ná ʃìgá gídàjénsà.   'I went into his houses.'
11. Zân dáwó.   'I'll return here.'
12. Ká dáwó gídàjénsù jíyà.   'You (masc) returned here to their houses yesterday.'

Dataset 149. Apinayé (Brazil)

1. Mrɨ mɛtʃ.   'The meat is good.'
2. Pitʃo mɛtʃ.   'The bananas are good.'
3. Pitʃo punui.   'The bananas are bad.'
4. Mrɨ mɛtʃ kumrẽtʃ.   'The meat is very good.'
5. Mrɨ mɛtʃ kenʌ̃.   'The meat is definitely good.'
6. Pitʃo mɛtʃ ʒape.   'The bananas may be good.'
7. Pitʃo punui kenʌ̃.   'The bananas are definitely bad.'
8. Mrɨ ʒa mɛtʃ.   'This meat is good.'
9. Pitʃo mũi mɛtʃ kumrẽtʃ.   'Those bananas are very good.'
10. Pitʃo ʒa ʒar mɛtʃ.   'These bananas here are good.'
11. Mrɨ mũi atar punui.   'That meat there is bad.'
12. Mrɨ ʒa ʒar mɛtʃ.   'This meat here is good.'
13. Pitʃo mũi atar mɛtʃ ʒape.   'Those bananas there may be good.'
14. Mrɨ ʒa ʒar punui kenʌ̃.   'This meat here is definitely bad.'

Laboratory Manual for Morphology and Syntax

Dataset 150. State of Mexico Otomí (Mexico)
Phonemic tone is only partially indicated.

1. Bihyoni karphani karʔɲëhë.   'The man hunted for the horse.'

2. Bihohki karhɲuni karʔbæhɲã.   'The woman fixed the meal.'

3. Biʔini karphani karʔɲëhë.   'The man hurt the horse.'

4. Biza karʔɲëhë karphani.   'The horse bit the man.'

5. Bime karbayo karʔbæhɲã ranoho.   'The big woman wove the shawl.'

6. Bimeni karbayo ranoho karʔbæhɲã.   'The woman washed the big shawl.'

7. Biʔini karphani ranthæni karbãhci.   'The child hurt the red horse.'

8. Bihohki karhɲuni karʔbæhɲã tʃitʃʔï.   'The little woman fixed the meal.'

9. Bihyoni kárphani karʔɲëhë.   'The man hunted for his horse.'

10. Dahyoni kïphani nurʔɲëhë.   'This man will hunt for the horses.'

11. Damɔʔti nurbãhci karʔyo ranthæni.   'The red dog will kill this child.'

12. Daʔïni kárʔyo nurʔɲëhë.   'This man will hurt his dog.'

13. Daza kïbãhci nurʔyo ranoho.   'This big dog will bite the children.'

14. Bimɔʔti kiʔyo tʃitʃʔï nurphani ranoho.   'This big horse killed the little dogs.'

15. Biza kïʔɲëhë nurʔyo tʃitʃʔï.   'This little dog bit the men.'

16. Dameni kïbayo nurʔbæhɲã.   'This woman will wash the shawls.'

17. Dahohki kárhɲuni kárʔbæhɲã.   'His wife will fix his meal.'

18. Dame nurbayo nurʔbæhɲã.   'This woman will weave this shawl.'

Dataset 151. Min Nan Chinese (Taiwan)

Phonemic tone is not indicated.

1. I t'at tsu.
   3s read book
   'He reads a book.'

2. Gua k'uã tsu.
   'I see a book.'

3. Gua t'at tsu.
   'I read a book.'

4. Gua t'it t'at tsu.
   'I am reading a book.'

5. Gua be t'at tsu.
   'I shall read a book.'

6. Gua e sai t'at tsu.
   'I am permitted to read a book.'

7. Gua e hiaŋ t'at tsu.
   'I am able to read a book.'

8. Gua be t'it t'at tsu.
   'I shall be reading a book.'

9. Gua tio si t'it t'at tsu.
   'I am reading a book.'

10. Gua bo e hiaŋ t'at tsu.
    'I am not able to read a book.'

11. Gua bo e hiaŋ be t'at tsu.
    'I shall not be able to read a book.'

12. Gua e sai be k'i t'at tsu.
    'I shall be permitted to go read a book.'

13. Gua e sai k'i t'at tsu.
    'I am permitted to go read a book.'

14. Gua bo e sai k'i t'at tsu.
    'I am not permitted to go read a book.'

15. Gua e hiaŋ k'i t'at tsu.
    'I am able to go read a book.'

16. Gua e hiaŋ be t'it t'at tsu.
    'I shall be able to read a book.'

17. Gua bo e hiaŋ be t'it t'at tsu.
    'I shall not be able to read a book.'

18. Gua be k'i t'at tsu.
    'I shall go read a book.'

19. Gua bo t'it t'at tsu.
    'I am not reading a book.'

20. Gua tio si bo be t'at tsu.
    'I shall not read a book.'

Dataset 152. Pitjantjatjara—Warburton Ranges (Australia)

1. Ṭiṭi yulaŋu.
   'The child cried.'

2. Kuŋka yulaŋu.
   'The girl cried.'

3. Ṭiṭi kuṭara yulaŋu.
   'The two children cried.'

4. Ṭiṭi ŋariŋu.
   'The child lay down.'

5. Kuŋka waʎkumunu yikariŋu.
   'The good girl laughed.'

6. Kuŋka pukuḷariŋu.
   'The girl rejoiced.'

7. Ṭiṭi waʎkumunu yikariŋu.
   'The good child laughed.'

8. Kuŋka puḷka kuṭara yulaŋu.
   'The two big girls cried.'

9. Ṭiṭi waʎkumunu kuṭara yulaŋu.
   'The two good children cried.'

10. Wati puḷka kuṭu ŋaṛaŋu.
    'One big man stood up.'

11. Ṭiṭi maṇkurpa ŋuḷuriŋu.
    'The three children became afraid.'

12. Wati yikariŋu.
    'The man laughed.'

13. Ṭiṭi waʎkumunu maṇkurpa pukuḷariŋu.
    'The three good children rejoiced.'

14. Wati ŋa:ɲa ɲinaŋu.
    'This man sat down.'

(Continued)

Dataset 152 continued:

15. Ṭiṭi kuṯu kutipiṯaŋu.
    'One child went away.'

16. Wati kuṯu ŋa:ɲa katuriŋu.
    'This one man arose.'

17. Ŋankuku ṭiṭi ŋariŋu.
    'My child lay down.'

18. Ṭiṭi waʎkumunu kuṯu ɲaraɲa yulaŋu.
    'That (distant) one good child cried.'

19. Wati puḻka kuṯu palaɲa ŋalturiŋu.
    'That (mid-distant) one big man became sorry.'

20. Palaku ṭiṭi yikariŋu.
    'His child laughed.'

21. Ṭiṭi palaɲa miririŋu.
    'That (mid-distant) child died.'

22. Miɲma maŋkurpa yulaŋu.
    'Three women cried.'

23. Ŋankuku ṭiṭi ŋa:ɲaya pukuḻariŋu.
    'These children of mine rejoiced.'

24. Ɲuntuku kuŋka puḻka kuṯara kutipiṯaŋu.
    'Your two big girls went away.'

25. Palaku yuṇṭalpa kuṯara ŋa:ɲaya yikariŋu.
    'These two daughters of his laughed.'

26. Ŋankuku ṭiṭi pika kuṯara ɲaraɲaya kuḻiriŋu.
    'Yonder two sick children of mine became hot.'

27. Ɲuntuku kuŋka pika maŋkurpa palaɲaya palyaṛuŋuriŋu.
    'Those (mid-distant) three sick girls of yours have become better.'

28. Palaku wati waʎkumunu maŋkurpa ɲaraɲaya kutipiṯaŋu.
    'Yonder three good men of his went away.'

Dataset 153. Rotokas (Papua New Guinea)

1. Kareaera.   'They returned.'

2. Pouviroaepa.   'They arrived.'

3. Tuariri kareaera.   'They returned long ago.'

4. Voea pouviroaepa.   'The people arrived.'

5. Vairo rutu kareaera.   'All the women returned.'

6. Vairo rutu pouviroaepa.   'All the women arrived.'

7. Ikauvira raga pouviroaepa.   'They arrived only momentarily.'

8. Voea ikauvira pouviroaepa.   'The people arrived quickly.'

9. Vairo raga tuariri kareaera.   'Only the women returned long ago.'

10. Vairo tuariri rutu kareaera.   'The women returned very long ago.'

11. Voea rutu tuariri raga kareaera.   'All the people returned only long ago.'

12. Voea raga ikauvira rutu pouviroaepa.   'Only the people arrived very quickly.'

Dataset 154. Pocomchí (Guatemala)

1. Kinwirik.   'I sleep.'

2. Tiqʼehb.   'You fall down.'

3. Intʃal.   'He comes.'

4. Nimeʃ intʃal.   'My cat comes.'

5. Acʼiʔ inqʼehb.   'Your dog falls down.'

6. Ihin kinqʼehb.   'I fall down.'

7. Rimeʃ inqʼehb.   'His cat falls down.'

8. Nicʼiʔ inwirik. 'My dog sleeps.'

9. Hat titʃal.   'You come.'

10. Ameʃ inwirik.   'Your cat sleeps.'

11. Ricʼiʔ intʃal. 'His dog comes.'

12. Reʔ inwirik.   'He sleeps.'

13. Reʔ intʃal.   'He comes.'

14. Ihin kinwirik. 'I sleep.'

Dataset 155. Rotokas (Papua New Guinea)

1. Ragai uusiraepa tuariri.   'I slept long ago (remote).'

2. Vii uriouepa rovopakekiraia.   'You came in January (remote).'

3. Rera uusiroera rovopakekiraia.   'He slept in January.'

4. Oira uriooera tuariri.   'She came long ago.'

5. Ragai urioraerao rovopakekiraia.   'I came in January (near).'

6. Vii uusiuerao aruvea.   'You slept yesterday.'

7. Rera urioroe vovokio.   'He came today.'

8. Oira uusioe rovopakekiraia.   'She slept in January (today).'

9. Ragai uusiraei vovokio.   'I sleep today (now).'

10. Vii uriouei vaviopavira.   'You come now.'

11. Rera uusiroei rovopakekiraia.   'He sleeps in January (now).'

12. Oira urioovere vovokio.   'She will come today.'

13. Ragai urioravere vokipavira.   'I will come tomorrow.'

14. Vii uusiuvere rovopakekiraia.   'You will sleep in January (near).'

15. Rera uriorovere utupaiva.   'He will come next year (near).'

16. Oira uusioverea utupaiva.   'She will sleep next year (remote).'

17. Ragai urioraverea rovopakekiraia.   'I will come in January (remote).'

Dataset 156. Lalana Chinantec (Mexico)

1. Ka^{23}gwɨːn^3 ʃiːʔ^3 mɨ^{3}hoːh^2.
   slept   boy   day.before.yesterday
   'The boy slept day before yesterday.'

2. Ka^{23}naːʔn^{23} dzɨː^3 dʒoːh^3.
   got.up   dog   yesterday
   'The dog got up yesterday.'

3. Mɨ^{3}naːʔn^{23} ʃiːʔ^3 ʔmɨːh^3.
   got.up   boy   earlier.today
   'The boy got up earlier today.'

4. Mɨ^{3}gwɨːn^3 dzɨː^3 rɨ^{3}nɨ^{23}.
   slept   dog   today
   'The dog slept today.'

5. Rɨ^{23}naːʔn^{23} ʃiːʔ^3 rɨ^{3}nɨ^{23}.
   will.get.up   boy   today
   'The boy will get up today.'

6. Rɨ^{23}gwɨːn^3 ʃiːʔ^3 ʔäːh^{23}.
   will.sleep   boy   tomorrow
   'The boy will sleep tomorrow.'

7. Rɨ^{23}naːʔn^{23} dzɨː^3 ʔyoːh^2.
   will.get.up   dog   day.after.tomorrow
   'The dog will get up day after tomorrow.'

Dataset 157. Palantla Chinantec (Mexico)

Do not attempt to analyze tone-accent distinctions on verbs.

1. Ca^{1}lán^2 jní^2 dsøi^2. 'I bought the dog(s).'

2. Bán^2 dsa^2 ŋié^{12}. 'He strikes/will strike the pig(s).'

3. Ca^{1}lá^2 jní^2 hma^2. 'I bought the wood.'

4. Bá^2 dsa^2 ŋií^3. 'He strikes/will strike the metal object(s).'

5. Ca^{1}liánh^1 hning^2 ŋié^{12} pan^{13}. 'You bought the fat pig(s).'

6. Bánh^3 hning^2 og^1 ŋié^{12}. 'You will strike two pigs.'

7. Ca^{1}bá^2 dsa^2 cøng^2 hma^2. 'He struck one piece of wood.'

8. Bánh^3 hning^2 úg^2 dsøi^2. 'You will strike three dogs.'

9. Bán^3 jní^2 dsøi^2 tsánh^2. 'I will strike the dirty dog(s).'

10. Ca^{1}liáh^1 hning^2 ŋií^3 pa^3. 'You bought the big metal object(s).'

11. Ca^{1}báh^1 hning^2 ton^1 ŋií^3. 'You struck two metal objects.'

12. Lá^3 jní^2 hma^2 tsáh^2. 'I will buy the dirty wood.'

13. Bá^3 jní^2 hnøa^{12} ŋií^3 tsáh^2. 'I will strike three dirty metal objects.'

14. Lán^3 jní^2 og^1 dsøi^2 tsánh^2. 'I will buy two dirty dogs.'

15. Ca^{1}liáh^1 hning^2 hnøa^{12} hma^2 pa^3. 'You bought three big pieces of wood.'

16. Lá^3 jní^2 cøng^2 ŋií^3 tsáh^2. 'I will buy one dirty metal object.'

17. Ca^{1}lán^2 jní^2 jan^2 ŋié^{12} tsánh^2. 'I bought one dirty pig.'

18. Ca^{1}bán^2 dsa^2 jan^2 dsøi^2 pan^{13}. 'He struck one fat dog.'

Dataset 158. Spanish

1.	Yo llegé.	'I arrived.'
2.	Tú llegaste.	'You arrived.'
3.	Él llegó.	'He arrived.'
4.	Ellos llegaron.	'They arrived.'
5.	Yo miré.	'I looked.'
6.	Tú miraste.	'You looked.'
7.	Él miró.	'He looked.'
8.	Ellos miraron.	'They looked.'
9.	El león miró.	'The lion looked.'
10.	Los hombres llegaron.	'The men arrived.'
11.	Las mujeres llegaron.	'The women arrived.'
12.	La yegua llegó.	'The mare arrived.'
13.	El león hermoso llegó.	'The handsome lion arrived.'
14.	El hombre chico miró.	'The small man looked.'
15.	La mujer chica llegó.	'The small woman arrived.'
16.	La mujer hermosa miró.	'The beautiful woman looked.'
17.	Las yeguas chicas miraron.	'The small mares looked.'
18.	Las yeguas hermosas llegaron.	'The handsome mares arrived.'
19.	Los leones chicos miraron.	'The small lions looked.'
20.	Los hombres hermosos miraron.	'The handsome men looked.'

Dataset 159. Hyderabadi Telugu (India)

1. Waaɖu mantʃiwaaɖu.   'He is good.'
2. Atanu peddawaaɖu.   'He (respect) is big.'
3. Adi peddadi.   'She/it is big.'
4. Aame mantʃidi.   'She (respect) is good.'
5. Naanna mantʃiwaaɖu.   'Father is good.'
6. Anna peddawaaɖu.   'Older brother is big.'
7. Pilla mantʃidi.   'The child is good.'
8. Akka peddadi.   'Older sister is big.'
9. Amma mantʃidi.   'Mother is good.'
10. Godugu peddadi.   'The elephant is big.'
11. tʃiire mantʃidi.   'The sari is good.'
12. Puwu peddadi.   'The flower is big.'
13. Waaɭɭu peddawaaɭɭu.   'They (human) are big.'
14. Awi mantʃiwi.   'They (nonhuman) are good.'
15. Naannalu peddawaaɭɭu.   'The fathers are big.'
16. Annalu mantʃiwaaɭɭu.   'The older brothers are good.'
17. Pillalu peddawaaɭɭu.   'The children are big.'
18. Akkalu mantʃiwaaɭɭu.   'The older sisters are good.'
19. Ammalu peddawaaɭɭu.   'The mothers are big.'
20. Godugulu mantʃiwi.   'The elephants are good.'
21. tʃiirelu peddawi.   'The saris are big.'
22. Puwulu mantʃiwi.   'The flowers are good.'

Dataset 160. Tsonga (South Africa)
Regularized; phonemic tone is not indicated.

1. Mufana watlaŋga.   'The boy plays.'

2. Mufana loŋkulu watirha.   'The big boy works.'

3. Mufana waɬɛka.   'The boy laughs.'

4. Mufana watsutsuma.   'The boy runs.'

5. Mufana wadya.   'The boy eats.'

6. Vafana vatlaŋga.   'The boys play.'

7. Vafana lavakulu vatirha.   'The big boys work.'

8. Vafana vaɬɛka.   'The boys laugh.'

9. Vafana vatsutsuma.   'The boys run.'

10. Vafana vadya.   'The boys eat.'

11. ʃihari ʃatsutsuma.   'The animal runs.'

12. ʃihari leʃikulu ʃabaleka.   'The big animal runs away.'

13. ʃiluva leʃitsoŋgo ʃanuhela.   'The small flower smells nice.'

14. Sihari satsutsuma.   'The animals run.'

15. Sihari lesikulu sabaleka.   'The big animals run away.'

Laboratory Manual for Morphology and Syntax

Dataset 161. Turkish

1. Bu kütʃük kedi buradadɨr.	'This little cat is here.'
2. O kara köpek buradadɨr.	'That black dog is here.'
3. O hoʤa oradadɨr.	'That teacher is there.'
4. Kütʃük kedi buradadɨr.	'The little cat is here.'
5. Bu kediler buradadɨr.	'These cats are here.'
6. Kütʃük arkadaʃ buradadɨr.	'The little friend is here.'
7. Kütʃük arkadaʃlarɨ buradadɨr.	'His little friends are here.'
8. O hoʤalar buradaydɨ.	'Those teachers were here.'
9. Iki hoʤa buradaydɨ.	'Two teachers were here.'
10. Hoʤasɨ oradadɨr.	'His teacher is there.'
11. Kara kedi buradadɨr.	'The black cat is here.'
12. Köpeklerim oradaydɨ.	'My dogs were there.'
13. Kara kedim buradadɨr.	'My black cat is here.'
14. O ütʃ kütʃük kɨz buradadɨr.	'Those three little girls are here.'
15. Iki büyük köpek buradadɨr.	'Two big dogs are here.'
16. Hoʤamɨn kütʃük kɨzɨ oradadɨr.	'My teacher's little girl is there.'
17. Bu kütʃük kɨzɨn hoʤasɨ buradadɨr.	'The teacher of this little girl is here.'
18. O kɨzlarɨn güzel kedileri buradadɨr.	'Those girls' pretty cats are here.'
19. Hoʤasɨnɨn büyük köpekleri oradadɨr.	'His teacher's big dogs are there.'
20. Arkadaʃɨmɨn ütʃ büyük kedisi oradadɨr.	'My friends' three big cats are there.'
21. Kütʃük köpeklerimin iki arkadaʃɨ buradadɨr.	'My little dogs' two friends are here.'
22. Ütʃ güzel kɨzɨmɨn arkadaʃlarɨ buradaydɨ.	'My three pretty daughters' friends were here.'
23. Iki kütʃük kɨzɨmɨn ütʃ arkadaʃɨ oradaydɨ.	'My two little daughters' three friends were there.'
24. Bu iki güzel arkadaʃɨn hoʤalarɨ buradaydɨ.	'These two pretty friends' teachers were here.'
25. Iki kütʃük arkadaʃɨnɨn güzel hoʤasɨ oradadɨr.	'His two little friends' pretty teacher is there.'

Dataset 162. Pocomchí (Guatemala)

1. Iril.
   'S/he sees him/her.'

2. Kireht'al.
   'S/he knows them.'

3. Inkoxq'or.
   'They urge him/her.'

4. Kikil.
   'They see them.'

5. Kiroxq'or   re   iʃok   take.
   3s.urge.3p   the   woman   PL
   'She urges the women.'

6. Inkeht'al   re   halak'un   take.
   3p.know.3s   the   child   PL
   'The children know him/her.'

7. Iroxq'or   re   winak.
   3s.urge.3s   the   man
   'The man urges him/her' or 'S/he urges the man.'

8. Kikeht'al   re   halak'un   take.
   3p.know.3p   the   child   PL
   'The children know them, or They know the children.'

9. Ireht'al   re   iʃok   re   halak'un.
   3s.know.3s   the   woman   the   child
   'The child knows the woman.'

10. Kiril   re   halak'un take   re   winak.
    3s.see.3p the   child   PL   the   man
    'The man sees the children.'

11. Inkil   re   winak re   iʃok   take.
    3p.see.3s the   man   the   woman PL
    'The women see the man.'

12. Kikoxq'or   re   iʃok   take   re   winak take.
    3p.urge.3p the   woman   PL   the   man   PL
    'The men urge the women.'

Dataset 163. San Miguel Mixtec (Mexico)

Phonemic tone is not indicated.

1.	Ʒeei.	'A child will eat.'
2.	Kiʃiɲa.	'She will sleep.'
3.	Kĩʔĩde.	'He will go.'
4.	Ʒeeɲa ʒata haku.	'She will eat behind the corral.'
5.	Kiʃii ʔini beʔe.	'A child will sleep in the house.'
6.	Kiʃide ʃini ʒuku.	'He will sleep on the top of the mountain.'
7.	Kĩʔĩɲa ʒata beʔe.	'She will go behind the house.'
8.	Ʒeede ʔini bekaa.	'He will eat in the jail.'
9.	Kĩʔĩi ʃini ʒuku.	'A child will go to the top of the mountain.'

Dataset 164. English

1. Speak.
2. Watch.
3. Speak carefully.
4. Speak casually.
5. Watch carefully.
6. Watch casually.
7. Speak very carefully.
8. Speak less carefully.
9. Speak very casually.
10. Speak less casually.
11. Watch very carefully.
12. Watch less carefully.
13. Watch very casually.
14. Watch less casually.

Dataset 165.   English

1. Run.
2. Walk.
3. Run here.
4. Run there.
5. Walk here.
6. Walk there.
7. Run to town.
8. Walk to town
9. Run to school.
10. Walk to school.
11. Run from town.
12. Walk from town.
13. Run from school.
14. Walk from school.

Laboratory Manual for Morphology and Syntax

Dataset 166. Pocomchí (Guatemala)

1. Inelik.   'He is leaving.'

2. Nel kinʔox ruːkʼ.   'I will go with him.'

3. Yuʔnak nel kinokik wibil.   'I will enter alone now.'

4. Nel inelik ribil.   'He will leave by himself.'

5. Tiʔox pan pat.   'You are going to the house.'

6. Iqal nel telik wuːm.   'Tomorrow I will make you leave.'

7. Inokik ruːm.   'He is making him enter.'

8. Iqal nel inʔox pan kʼaybal awuːkʼ.   'Tomorrow he will go with you to market.'

9. Yuʔnak telik pan kʼaybal awibil.   'Now you are leaving the market by yourself.'

10. Tokik wuːkʼ.   'You are entering with me.'

11. Yuʔnak kinʔox awuːm.   'Now you are making me go.'

12. Nel tokik pan kʼaybal.   'You will enter the market.'

13. Kinʔox.   'I am going.'

14. Telik.   'You are leaving.'

15. Tiʔox ruːm.   'He is making you go.'

16. Nel inokik awuːm.   'You will make him enter.'

17. Kinelik ruːm.   'He is making me leave.'

18. Nel inʔox ribil.   'He will go by himself.'

19. Telik pan pat wuːm.   'I am making you leave the house.'

20. Kinokik pan pat awuːkʼ.   'I am entering the house with you.'

21. Inʔox pan tinamit.   'He is going to town.'

Laboratory Manual for Morphology and Syntax

Dataset 167. Guajajára (Brazil)

1. Oho kuzə ko pe.
   go woman field to
   'The woman went to the field.'

2. Oho kwez kuzə taw pe.
   go that woman town to
   'That woman went to town.'

3. Ur kuzə kwez taw wi.
   come woman that town from
   'The woman came from that town.'

4. Ur mokoz awa ko wi.
   come two man field from
   'Two men came from the field.'

5. Uata kwez awa taw rupi.
   walk that man town Assoc
   'That man walked around town.'

6. Uata mane pehu rupi.
   walk Manuel road Assoc
   'Manuel walked along the road.'

7. Uata mane raʔɨr ko rupi.
   walk Manuel son field Assoc
   'Manuel's son walked around the field.'

8. Ur mane reimaw pehu wi.
   come Manuel dog road from
   'Manuel's dog came from the road.'

9. Oho mokoz mane reimaw ko pe.
   go two Manuel dog field to
   'Two of Manuel's dogs went to the field.'

10. Oho kuzə mane rupi.
    go woman Manuel Assoc
    'The woman went along with Manuel.'

11. Ur mokoz awa wi.
    come two man from
    'He came from the two men.'

12. Uata mane.
    walk Manuel
    'Manuel walked around.'

13. Oho mokoz mane raʔɨr rupi.
    go two Manuel son Assoc
    'He went with Manuel's two sons.'

Laboratory Manual for Morphology and Syntax

Dataset 168. Mezquital Otomí (Mexico)
Phonemic tone is not indicated.

1. Bi-ma.
   ?-go
   'He went.'

2. Bi-bëts'e.
   ?-climb.up
   'He climbed up.'

3. Bi-ma   ra   tsïnt'ï.
   ?-go   the   boy
   'The boy went.'

4. Bi-yït'i mbo   ra   dehe.
   ?-enter   into the   water
   'He entered the water.'

5. Bi-dagi ra   dehe.
   ?-fall   the   water
   'The water fell.'

6. Da-bëts'e ri tsïnt'ï mãɲã ri fani.
   ?-climb   2s boy   onto 2s horse
   'Your boy will climb onto your horse.'

7. Da-ma ma t'aʃa fani   xa   ra   dehe.
   ?-go   1s white horse to   the water
   'My white horse will go to the water.'

8. Da-ma ri dãta tsïnt'ï mbo   ra   t'aʃa ngu.
   ?-go   2s big   boy   into the white house
   'Your big boy will go into the white house.'

9. Da-dagi ra   dehe   xa   ra   hai.
   ?-fall   the   water to   the ground
   'The water will fall to the ground.'

10. Bi-bëts'e mãɲã ma dãta ngu.
    ?-climb   onto 1s big   house
    'He climbed onto my large house.'

11. Da-dagi ma fani   xa   ra   hai.
    ?-fall   1s horse to   the ground
    'My horse will fall to the ground.'

12. Da-yït'i ra   dehe   mbo   ra   hai.
    ?-seep   the water into the ground
    'The water will seep into the ground.'

Dataset 169. Tabasco Chontal (Mexico)

1.	Ahnon.	'I was there.'
2.	Puts²i.	'He fled.'
3.	Puts²on.	'I fled.'
4.	Ahnet tʌ k'ʌnkan.	'You were on an errand.'
5.	Wʌyi tʃitam yaba ump²e ts²eŋ.	'The pig slept under a bed.'
6.	Wʌyi tuyak²o ump²e kah.	'He slept in a town.'
7.	Otʃi a pap tan tʃoh.	'Your father entered the cornfield.'
8.	Otʃon tan tʃoh.	'I entered the cornfield.'
9.	Otʃet tan u tʃoh.	'You entered his cornfield.'
10.	Wʌyon yaba ump²e kʌ ts²eŋ.	'I slept under one of my beds.'
11.	Otʃet tan tʃap²e tʃoh.	'You entered two cornfields.'
12.	Ahni untu kʌ tʃitam tʌ tʃoh.	'One of my pigs was in the cornfield.'
13.	tʃʌmi untu u tʃitam.	'One of his pigs died.'
14.	Puts²i tʃa²tu kʌ tʃitam.	'Two of my pigs fled.'
15.	Wʌyi kʌ pap.	'My father slept.'
16.	tʃʌmi a tʃitam.	'Your pig died.'
17.	tʃʌmi a pap.	'Your father died.'
18.	Ahni untu muluʔ.	'There was a turkey.'
19.	tʃʌmi tʃa²tu muluʔ.	'Two turkeys died.'
20.	Yʌlet tʌ kab.	'You fell to the ground.'
21.	Yʌli winik tʌ kab.	'The man fell to the ground.'
22.	T²ʌbon tʌ ump²e a ts²eŋ.	'I climbed up in one of your beds.'
23.	Ahni ump²e ts²eŋ.	'There was a bed.'

Laboratory Manual for Morphology and Syntax

Dataset 170. English

1. He departed today.
2. She departed yesterday.
3. He called early.
4. She called late.
5. She departs tomorrow.
6. He departs early.
7. She calls today.
8. He calls late.
9. He'll depart today.
10. She'll depart late.
11. He'll call tomorrow.
12. She'll call early.

Dataset 171. English

1. My mother came.
2. Your brother swam.
3. His wife went.
4. My son spoke.
5. Your mother's father came.
6. His brother's daughter went.
7. Her sister's husband swam.
8. My wife's sister's husband spoke.
9. Her husband's brother's son came.
10. Your father's wife's mother's husband went.
11. His daughter's husband's father's mother's brother came.
12. My son's son's wife's father's sister's ... daughter swam.

Dataset 172. Wolaytta (Ethiopia)

1. Ta naʔai ne maʧʧiyo beʔiis.
   'My son saw your wife.'

2. Ne aawai ta aayiyo beʔiis.
   'Your father saw my mother.'

3. Ta maʧʧiya ne aayiyo maddaasu.
   'My wife helped your mother.'

4. Ta iʃai ne iʃaa maʧʧiyo maddiis.
   'My brother helped your brother's wife.'

5. Ne aawaa aawai ne naʔaa beʔiis.
   'Your father's father saw your son.'

6. Ne naʔaa maʧʧiya ta maʧʧiyo aawaa beʔaasu.
   'Your son's wife saw my wife's father.'

7. Ta iʃaa naʔaa maʧʧiyo aayiyo iʃaa ... naʔai ne iʃaa maddiis.
   'My brother's son's wife's mother's brother's ... son helped your brother.'

8. Ne naʔai ne iʃaa naʔaa maʧʧiyo aayiyo iʃaa ... naʔaa maddiis.
   'Your son helped your brother's son's wife's mother's brother's ... son.'

9. Ta aayiyo iʃaa...maʧʧiya ne aawaa iʃaa ... iʃaa beʔaasu.
   'My mother's brother's...wife saw your father's brother's ... brother.'

Dataset 173. Palantla Chinantec (Mexico)

1. Dság^{1}dsa.   'He'll go.'

2. Jií^{1}tsih.   'The child will come.'

3. Júh^2 ti^{3}jmii^{2}tsih.   'The child's father will cough.'

4. Dság^1 mi^{3}chiég^{3}dsa.   'His mother will go.'

5. Jií^1 ti^{3}jmii^2 mi^{3}chiég^{3}tsih.
   'The child's maternal grandfather will come.'

6. Júh^2 mi^{3}chiég^3 ti^{3}jmii^{2}dsa.
   'His paternal grandmother will cough.'

7. Dság^1 ti^{3}jmii^2 ti^{3}jmii^2 mi^{3}chiég^{3}tsih.
   'The child's mother's father's father will go.'

8. Jií^1 ti^{3}jmii^2 mi^{3}chiég^3 mi^{3}chiég^3 ti^{3}jmii^2 ti^{3}jmii^2...tsih.
   'The child's ...'s father's father's mother's maternal grandfather will come.'

Laboratory Manual for Morphology and Syntax

Dataset 174. Tok Pisin (Papua New Guinea)

1.	Mi kam.	'I come.'
2.	Nau yu go.	'You go now.'
3.	Yu kam wantaim mi.	'You come with me.'
4.	Mi go wantaim yu.	'I go with you.'
5.	Mi stap long bus.	'I am in the jungle.'
6.	Yu stap long haus.	'You are in the house.'
7.	Mi go long taun.	'I go to town.'
8.	Bai yu go wantaim mi.	'You'll go with me later.'
9.	Nau mi stap long haus.	'I am in the house now.'
10.	Bai mi stap wantaim yu.	'I'll be with you later.'
11.	Yu go wantaim mi long bus.	'You go with me to the jungle.'
12.	Mi kam wantaim yu long haus.	'I come with you to the house.'
13.	Bai yu kam long bus.	'You'll come to the jungle later.'
14.	Nau yu stap wantaim mi long taun.	'You are with me in the town now.'
15.	Bai mi kam wantaim yu long taun.	'I'll come with you to town later.'

Dataset 175. Rotokas (Papua New Guinea)

1.	Kareuviro.	'He returns all the way.'
2.	Uriopa.	'He is coming.'
3.	Hosi avaera.	'The horse went.'
4.	Avaera kepa iava.	'He went from the house.'
5.	Kakaeto kareuviro.	'The boy returns all the way.'
6.	Uriopa urui iare.	'He is coming to the village.'
7.	Hosi kareuviro evaova iava.	'The horse returns all the way from the tree.'
8.	Kakaeto uriopa kepa iava.	'The boy is coming from the house.'
9.	Kareuviro kepa iare.	'He returns all the way to the house.'
10.	Kakaeto avaera urui iava.	'The boy went from the village.'
11.	Kakaeto avaera evaova iare.	'The boy went to the tree.'
12.	Hosi uriopa evaova iava.	'The horse is coming from the tree.'

Dataset 176. Southern Barasano (Colombia)

Phonemic stress is not indicated.

1. Abĩbĩ.   'He carried (it).'

2. Koebõ kedẽ.   'She washed (it) also.'

3. Wetsikahɨ tsudi abĩbĩ.   'He carried the garment upstream.'

4. To wetsikahɨ abĩbĩ.   'He carried (it) there upstream.'

5. To tsudi koebõ.   'She washed that garment.'

6. Tohɨ koebõ.   'She washed (it) there.'

7. Ti wetsikahɨ koebĩ.   'He washed (it) here upstream.'

8. Tihɨ koebĩ kedẽ.   'He washed (it) here also.'

9. Ti burohɨ abĩbĩ.   'He carried (it) to this hill.'

10. To koaro abĩbĩ kedẽ.   'He carried that gourd also.'

11. To burohɨ ti koaro abĩbõ.   'She carried this gourd to that hill.'

12. Burohɨ abĩbõ.   'She carried (it) to the hill.'

13. tsudi koebõ kedẽ.   'She washed the garment also.'

14. Wetsikahɨ ti tsudi abĩbĩ.   'He carried this garment upstream.'

15. Tohɨ tsudi abĩbĩ.   'He carried the garment there.'

16. Tohɨ ti koebõ kedẽ.   'She washed this one there again.'

17. Burohɨ to abibõ.   'She carried that one to the hill.'

18. Ti wetsikahɨ to koebĩ.   'He washed that one here upstream.'

Laboratory Manual for Morphology and Syntax

Dataset 177. Southern Barasano (Colombia)
Phonemic stress is not indicated.

1. Kũhɨ bɨ̃ɨ̃.   'You stored (it).'

2. Kũbõ tso.   'She will store (it); or She stored (it).'

3. Otebõ tso.   'She will plant (it); or She planted (it).'

4. Otekahɨ yɨ.   'I planted (it).'

5. Otekahɨ bɨ̃.   'You planted (it).'

6. Kĩ kũkahɨ yɨ.   'I stored the cassava.'

7. Yukɨ kũha bɨ.   'You will store (it) now/today.'

8. Kĩ otegoha bɨ.   'You (fem) intend to plant the cassava.'

9. Yukɨ oteha yɨ.   'I will plant (it) now/today.'

10. Yukɨ oteaha bɨ̃.   'You plant (it) now/today.'

11. Yãbõ oteabõ tso.   'She plants the yams.'

12. Yãbõ kũgoha yɨ.   'I (fem) intend to store the yams.'

13. Yãbĩka kũbĩ ĩ.   'He stored (it) yesterday.'

14. Butsiyi kũha yɨ.   'I will store (it) tomorrow.'

15. Yukɨ otegɨbĩ ĩ.   'He intends to plant (it) now/today.'

16. Butsiyi kũgɨha bɨ̃.   'You (masc) intend to store (it) tomorrow.'

17. Ohorika kũaha bɨ̃.   'You store the corn.'

18. Yukɨ kĩ kũgobõ tso.   'She intends to store the cassava now/today.'

19. Ohorika oteaha yɨ.   'I plant the corn.'

20. Butsiyi otegɨha yɨ.   'I (masc) intend to plant (it) tomorrow.'

21. Butsiyi kĩ otebĩ ĩ.   'He will plant the cassava tomorrow.'

22. Yukɨ yãbõ kũabĩ ĩ.   'He stores the yams now/today.'

23. Yukɨ yãbõ otehɨ bɨ̃.   'You planted the yams today.'

24. Tirɨbĩhɨ kũkabõ tso.   'She stored (it) long ago.'

25. Yãbĩka ohorika kũhɨ yɨ.   'I stored the corn yesterday.'

26. Tirɨbĩhɨ ohorika otekabĩ ĩ.   'He planted the corn long ago.'

Dataset 178. Southern Barasano (Colombia)
Phonemic stress is not indicated.

1. Babɨ bĩ.   'You ate (it here).'

2. Babõ tso.   'She ate (it).'

3. Koehɨ yɨ.   'I washed (it there).'

4. Bakabĩ ĩ.   'He ate (it long ago).'

5. Koebõ tso.   'She washed (it).'

6. Koekabõ tso.   'She washed (it long ago).'

7. Yukɨ babĩ ĩ.   'He ate (it) today.'

8. Yãbĭka babĩ ĩ.   'He ate (it) yesterday.'

9. Yukɨ koehɨ bĩ.   'You washed (it there) today.'

10. Tihɨ bakahɨ bĩ.   'You ate (it) here (long ago).'

11. Tohɨ koekahɨ yɨ.   'I washed (it) there (long ago).'

12. Tihɨ kĩ koebĩ ĩ.   'He washed cassava here.'

13. Tohɨ kĩ bahɨ bĩ.   'You ate cassava there.'

14. Tihɨ yãbã babɨ yɨ.   'I ate yams here.'

15. Yukɨ yãbã koebɨ yɨ.   'I washed yams today.'

16. Tohɨ yãbã koebõ tso. 'She washed yams there.'

17. Tihɨ babõ tso, yukɨ. 'She ate (it) here today.'

18. Tirɨbĭhĭ koekahɨ bĩ. 'You washed (it) long ago.'

19. Tohɨ koebĩ ĩ, yãbĭka. 'He washed (it) there yesterday.'

20. Tohɨ bahɨ yɨ, yãbĭka. 'I ate (it) there yesterday.'

21. Tirɨbĭhĭ kĩ bakahɨ yɨ. 'I ate cassava long ago.'

22. Tihɨ koebɨ bĩ, yãbĭka. 'You washed (it) here yesterday.'

23. Tohɨ bakabõ tso, tirɨbĭhĭ. 'She ate (it) there long ago.'

24. Tihɨ koekabĩ ĩ, tirɨbĭhĭ. 'He washed (it) here long ago.'

Laboratory Manual for Morphology and Syntax

Dataset 179. Huave (Mexico)
Phonemic tone is not indicated.

1. Tandok tiʃem. 'He netted shrimp.'
2. Tahond kïet nop naʃey. 'A man dried fish.'
3. Tehants. 'He washed (something).'
4. Apmahants kïet. 'He will wash fish.'
5. Aaga nentʃ apmehants. 'That boy will wash (something).'
6. Apmandok tiʃem aaga nentʃ. 'That boy will net shrimp.'
7. Nop nentʃ tendok. 'A boy netted (something).'
8. Aaga naʃey tehond. 'That man dried (something).'
9. Nop nentʃ apmahond kïet. 'A boy will dry fish.'
10. Nop naʃey apmehond. 'A man will dry (something).'
11. Aaga naʃey tahants tiʃem. 'That man washed shrimp.'
12. Apmendok. 'He will net (something).'
13. Nop naʃey apmandok kïet. 'A man will net fish.'
14. Tahond tiʃem. 'He dried shrimp.'
15. Nop naʃey tahond kïet. 'A man dried fish.'
16. Aaga nentʃ apmehond. 'That boy will dry (something).'
17. Nop nentʃ apmehants. 'A boy will wash (something).'
18. Aaga nentʃ apmandok tiʃem. 'That boy will net shrimp.'

Dataset 180. Highland Mazatec (Mexico)

1. Ki³   tso²ti³.
   went   girl
   'The girl went.'

2. Hi³tʃo¹   ʃʔĩ⁴.
   arrived.there   man
   'The man arrived there.'

3. Hi³tʃo¹   tʃʰõ⁴².
   arrived.there   woman
   'The woman arrived there.'

4. Ki³   tʃʰõ⁴²   ʔnti¹.
   went   woman   little
   'The little woman went.'

5. Ki³sko²ya³   tʃʰõ⁴²   tso²ti³.
   awaited   woman   girl
   'The girl waited for the woman.'

6. Ki³tʰo³nta¹   ʃʔĩ⁴   htʃi¹nka³.
   perspired   man   old
   'The old man perspired.'

7. tsa³ve³   tso²ti³   tʃʰõ⁴²   ʔnti¹.
   saw   girl   woman   small
   'The little woman saw the girl.'

8. Ki³tʰo³nta¹   co²ti³   ntʔe¹.
   perspired   girl   industrious
   'The hard-working girl perspired.'

9. tsa³ve³   ʃʔĩ⁴   tʃʰõ⁴²   htʃi¹nka³.
   saw   man   woman   old
   'The old woman saw the man.'

10. tsa³kʔe¹le⁴   tʃʰõ⁴²   ntʔe¹   ʃʔĩ⁴.
    struck   woman   industrious   man
    'The man hit the hard-working woman.'

11. tsa³kʔe¹le⁴   ʃʔĩ⁴   htʃi¹nka³   tso²ti³.
    struck   man   old   girl
    'The girl hit the old man.'

12. Ki³sko²ya³   tso²ti³   ʔnti¹   ʃʔĩ⁴   ntʔe¹.
    awaited   girl   small   man   industrious
    'The hard-working man waited for the little girl.'

Laboratory Manual for Morphology and Syntax

Dataset 181. Palantla Chinantec (Mexico)

1. Gǿaʔ¹ Be¹³.   'Bob will eat it.'

2. Gǿaʔ¹ Mi²gue³ tang³.   'Mike will eat the avocado.'

3. Hniu¹ Be¹³.   'Bob wants it.'

4. Hniu¹ Mi²gue³ huuh¹².   'Mike wants the orange.'

5. Hniu¹ Sǿa¹³ huuh¹².   'Joe will want the orange.'

6. Ho¹ Mi²gue³.   'Mike will cry.'

7. Ho¹ Sǿa¹³.   'Joe will cry.'

8. Jlíh¹ huuh¹².   'The orange will spoil.'

9. Jlíh¹ tang³.   'The avocado will spoil.'

10. Juǿi¹ huuh¹².   'The orange will ripen.'

11. Juǿi¹ tøg².   'The banana will ripen.'

12. Lóh¹ Be¹³.   'Bob will bathe.'

13. Lóh¹ Sǿa¹³.   'Joe will bathe.'

14. Ŋǿi² Be¹³.   'Bob will laugh.'

15. Ŋǿi² Mi²gue³.   'Mike will laugh.'

16. Téng² Be¹³ tøg².   'Bob will discard the banana.'

17. Téng² Mi²gue³ tang³.   'Mike will discard the avocado.'

18. Téng² Sǿa¹³.   'Joe will discard it.'

19. Tiíh¹ tang³.   'The avocado will fall.'

20. Tiíh¹ tøg².   'The banana will fall.'

Dataset 182. Mandarin Chinese

1. Nǐ   qù.   'You are going.'
   2s   go

2. Nǐ   bù   qù.   'You are not going.'
   2s   not go

3. Nǐ   hǎo.   'You are well.'
   2s   well

4. Tā   hǎo.   'He is well.'
   3s   well

5. Nǐ   hǎo ma.   'Are you well?'
   2s   well ?

6. Tā   lái.   'He is coming.'
   3s   come

7. Tā   lái   ma.   'Is he coming?'
   3s   come ?

8. Tā   lái   le.   'He came.'
   3s   come PST

9. Tā   lái   le   ma.   'Did he come?'
   3s   come PST ?

10. Tā   mǎi shū.   'He buys books.'
    3s   buy book

11. Tā   bù   mǎi shū.   'He doesn't buy books.'
    3s   not buy book

12. Tā   mǎi shū le   ma.   'Did he buy books?'
    he   buy book PST ?

13. Nǐ   bù   kàn shū.   'You do not read books.'
    2s   not read book

14. Tā   kàn shū ma.   'Does he read books?'
    3s   read book ?

15. Tā   kàn shū le   ma.   'Did he read the book?'
    3s   read book PST ?

Dataset 183. Northern Paiute (USA)

1. I   piawabi   tɨkaba   tɨmɨkwɨ.
   1s   old.woman   bread   will.buy
   'My old woman will buy bread.'

2. Tɨkaba   dzagwɨ.
   bread   carry
   'She carries bread.'

3. Tɨkaba   i   geaʔakwɨ.
   bread   1s   will.give
   'She will give me bread.'

4. I   piawabi   tɨkaba   i   makakwɨ.
   1s   old.woman   bread   1s   will.feed
   'My old woman will feed me bread.'

5. Nɨ   tsipisa   dzagwɨkwɨ.
   2s   squirrel   will.carry
   'I will carry ground squirrels.'

6. Tsipisa   yapa   tɨka.
   squirrel carrot   eat
   'The ground squirrel eats wild carrots.'

7. Nɨ   tsipisa   u   geaʔa.
   1s   squirrel   3s   give
   'I give ground squirrels to her.'

8. Nɨ   tsipisa   i   piawabi   maka.
   1s   squirrel   1s   old.woman   feed
   'I feed my old woman ground squirrel.'

9. Nɨ   tsipisa   puni.
   1s   squirrel   see
   'I see the ground squirrel.'

10. I   punikwɨ.
    1s   will.see
    'It will see me.'

Laboratory Manual for Morphology and Syntax

Dataset 184. Pocomchí (Guatemala)

1. ʃniloqˀ iʃim ar. 'I bought corn there.'
2. Kinkˀul ar. 'I arrive there.'
3. ʃkˀul ar. 'He arrived there.'
4. Wilik. 'He is here.'
5. Amol kape ayuʔ. 'You pick coffee here.'
6. Risikˀ kape wuluʔ. 'He looks for coffee over there.'
7. ʃqˀehb. 'He fell down.'
8. Katʃalkin. 'I am alive.'
9. tʃuhnulkat. 'You are seated.'
10. Kinbirxik ayuʔ. 'I hear here.'
11. Tibirxik wuluʔ. 'You hear over there.'
12. Inqˀehb. 'He falls down.'
13. ʃatkˀul wuluʔ. 'You arrived over there.'
14. ʃbirxik ar. 'He heard there.'
15. ʃikˀay kinaqˀ ar. 'He sold beans there.'
16. ʃimol iʃim. 'He picked corn.'
17. Riloqˀ tulul. 'He buys bananas.'
18. Nimol kinaqˀ. 'I pick beans.'
19. Inkˀul. 'He arrives.'
20. Wilkat. 'You are here.'
21. ʃasikˀ iʃim ar. 'You looked for corn there.'
22. Aloqˀ kinaqˀ wuluʔ. 'You buy beans over there.'
23. ʃakˀay tulul. 'You sold bananas.'
24. Katʃalkat. 'You are alive.'
25. ʃatqˀehb ar. 'You fell down there.'
26. Wilkin. 'I am here.'
27. ʃinbirxik ayuʔ. 'I heard here.'
28. Nikˀay kape ayuʔ. 'I sell coffee here.'
29. ʃinqˀehb wuluʔ. 'I fell down over there.'
30. tʃuhnulkin. 'I am seated.'

Dataset 185. Sierra Popoluca (Mexico)

1. Hesʌk heʔm ʃiʃ wiʔkpa ko:pho:m.
   then that cow 3s.will.eat in.meadow
   'Then that cow will eat in the meadow.'

2. Heʔm ʃiʃ ikuʔtpa soʔk ko:pho:m hoymʌ.
   that cow 3s.will.eat grass in.meadow tomorrow
   'That cow will eat grass in the meadow tomorrow.'

3. Apoyum ʌtʃ ka:mho:m.
   ran 1s in.cornfield
   'I ran in the cornfield.'

4. Okmʌ ipetum heʔm ʃiwan tʌk matʌk.
   later 3s.swept that John house yesterday
   'Later yesterday that John swept the house.'

5. Wiʔkum tʃimpa.
   3s.ate dog
   'The dog ate.'

6. Ikuʔtum.
   3s.ate
   'He ate it.'

7. Anuʔkpa.
   1s.will.arrive
   'I will arrive.'

8. Hesʌk tu:m tʃimpa annuusum ʌtʃ tʌkho:m.
   then one dog 1s.held 1s in.house
   'Then I held a dog in the house.'

9. ʃiwan ihuyum tu:m ko:pa.
   John 3s.bought one meadow
   'John bought a meadow.'

10. Miwiʔkpa mitʃ ka:mkʌʌm hoymʌ.
    2s.will.eat 2s at.cornfield tomorrow
    'Tomorrow you will eat at the cornfield.'

11. Mitʃ iŋkuʔtpa sʌk.
    2s 2s.will.eat bean
    'You will eat beans.'

12. Okmʌ heʔm tʃimpa ikuʔtum ʃiʃ.
    later that dog 3s.ate cow
    'Later that dog ate beef.'

13. Mitʃ iɲɲuuspa ʃiwan tʌkkʌʌm.
    2s 2s.will.hold John at.house
    'You will hold John at the house.'

14. Hesʌk anhuypa tu:m ʃiʃ ʌtʃ.
    then 1s.will.buy one cow 1s
    'Then I will buy a cow.'

(Continued)

Dataset 185 continued:

15. Heʔm tʃimpa iwasum heʔm ʃiʃ mawʌʃki.
    that dog 3s.bit that cow yesterday
    'That dog bit that cow day before yesterday.'

16. Poyum ʃiwan.
    3s.ran John
    'John ran.'

17. Mitʃ iɲhuyum tuːm kaːma.
    2s 2s.bought one cornfield
    'You bought a cornfield.'

18. ʌtʃ aŋkuʔtum sʌk.
    1s 1s.ate bean
    'I ate beans.'

19. Okmʌ mipoypa mitʃ koːpkʌʌm.
    later 2s.will.run 2s at.meadow
    'Later you will run at the meadow.'

20. Tuːm ʃiʃ nuʔkpa saːbʌy.
    one cow 3s.will.arrive later
    'A cow will arrive later.'

21. Miɲuʔkpa.
    2s.will.arrive
    'You will arrive.'

22. Ihuyum huumʌ mawʌʃki.
    3s.bought far dat.before.yesterday
    'He bought it far away day before yesterday.'

23. Hesʌk nuʔkpa tʌkhoːm hoymʌ.
    then 3s.will.arrive in.house tomorrow
    'Then he will arrive in the house tomorrow.'

24. Hesʌk ʌtʃ aŋkuʔtpa.
    then 1s 1s.will.eat
    'Then I will eat it.'

25. Aŋwaspa ʌtʃ.
    1s.will.bite 1s
    'I will bite it.'

26. ʃiwan iɲuuspa tsʌːʃi.
    John 3s.will.hold child
    'John will hold the child.'

27. Tsʌːʃi iɲuusum tʃimpa.
    child 3s.held dog
    'The child held the dog.'

28. Sʌk iŋwaspa mitʃ.
    bean 2s.will.bite 2s
    'You will bite beans.'

Laboratory Manual for Morphology and Syntax

Dataset 186. Huichol (Mexico)
Length, juncture, and tone are not indicated.

1. Mepʌyehu.
   'They are going.'

2. Mepʌtekuzatakai.
   'They chatted.'

3. Mepeutuaziyu.
   'They are going hunting.'

4. Tepeutuaziyu.
   'We are going hunting.'

5. Mepʌyehu ʔakitsie.
   'They are going to the canyon.'

6. Tepʌyehu ʔakitsie.
   'We are going to the canyon.'

7. Mepʌtekuzatakai hʌritsie.
   'They chatted in the mountains.'

8. Mepʌtekuzatakai zariukʌ.
   'They chatted by radio.'

9. Mepʌtekuzatakai ʔaki ʔamʌpatsie.
   'They chatted in the big canyon.'

10. Mepʌtekuzatakai zariu ʔamʌpakʌ.
    'They chatted on the big radio.'

11. Mepeutuaziyu ʔʌrʌkʌ.
    'They are going hunting with arrows.'

12. Mepeutuaziyu ʔʌrʌ manuyemʌmʌtsʌkʌ ʔaki ʔamʌpatsie.
    'They are going hunting in the big canyon with sharp arrows.'

13. Tepʌyehu hʌri ʔamʌpatsie.
    'We are going to the big mountains.'

14. Mepʌtekuzatakai zariukʌ ʔaki ʔamʌpatsie.
    'They chatted by radio in the big canyon.'

15. Tepeutuaziyu ʔʌrʌ manuyemʌmʌtsʌkʌ.
    'We are going hunting with sharp arrows.'

16. Mepʌtekuzatakai zariutsie.
    'They chatted on the radio (i.e., they were sitting on top of it).'

Dataset 187. Isthmus Zapotec (Mexico)
Phonemic tone and stress are not indicated

1. Ritʃesa tibigu. — 'A turtle jumps.'
2. Ruʒidʒi tʃupa bigu roʔ. — 'Two big turtles laugh.'
3. Bitʃee biguka. — 'That turtle erred.'
4. Ruyaadu. — 'We dance.'
5. Guza bigu wiinika. — 'That little turtle walked.'
6. Ruyaa tʃupa waga. — 'Two rats dance.'
7. Biʒidʒi tiwaga wiini. — 'A little rat laughed.'
8. Biʒidʒime. — 'It laughed.'
9. Biyaa wagaka. — 'That rat danced.'
10. Rutʃee tʃonna waga roʔ. — 'Three big rats err.'
11. Ritʃesame. — 'It jumps.'
12. Riza bere wiinika. — 'That little chicken walks.'
13. Gutʃesa tʃonna bere. — 'Three chickens jumped.'
14. Bitʃee bereka. — 'That chicken erred.'
15. Riza bere roʔka. — 'That big chicken walks.'
16. Rutʃeebe. — 'He errs.'
17. Ruʒidʒi tileʒu roʔ. — 'A big rabbit laughs.'
18. Biyaa tʃupa leʒu wiini. — 'Two little rabbits danced.'
19. Gutʃesa leʒuka. — 'That rabbit jumped.'
20. Guzadu. — 'We walked.'
21. Ritʃesa kaleʒuka. — 'Those rabbits jump.'
22. Ruyaa kawaga wiinika. — 'Those little rats dance.'
23. Biʒidʒi kabere. — 'The chickens laughed.'
24. Riza tʃupa biguka. — 'Those two turtles walk.'
25. Riza kabigu. — 'The turtles walk.'

Dataset 188. Rotokas (Papua New Guinea)

1. Uriopa.   'He is coming.'

2. Avaera.   'He went.'

3. Araoko uriopa.   'Brother is coming.'

4. Kaakauva avaera.   'He went with the dog.'

5. Popote aite avaera.   'White father went.'

6. Vearo aiteva uriopa.   'He is coming with good father.'

7. Popote voropato avaera.   'White hunter went.'

8. Riro voropatova uriopa.   'He is coming with big hunter.'

9. Aite voropatova uriopa.   'Father is coming with the hunter.'

10. Voropato aiteva uriopa.   'The hunter is coming with father.'

11. Kaakau riro araokova avaera.   'The dog went with big brother.'

12. Popote araoko aiteva uriopa.   'White brother is coming with father.'

13. Voropato vearo araokova uriopa.   'The hunter is coming with good brother.'

14. Riro aite vearo kaakauva avaera.   'Big father went with the good dog.'

15. Riro kaakau popote kaakauva avaera.   'The big dog went with the white dog.'

Dataset 189. Isthmus Zapotec (Mexico)
Phonemic tone and stress are not indicated.

1. Biʒooɲe   leʒu
   ran   rabbit
   'Rabbit ran.'

2. Ruʒooɲe   ngiiu-ka
   runs   man-that
   'The man runs.'

3. Bitʃesa   tʃupa   mistu
   jumped   two   cat
   'The two cats jumped.'

4. Bitʃesa   ti-geuʔ   roʔ
   jumped   one-coyote   big
   'A big coyote jumped.'

5. Bitʃesa   tʃonna   ngiiu   roʔ-ka
   jumped   three   man   big-that
   'Those three big men jumped.'

6. Rukwaagu   ngiiu-ka   leʒu
   hunts   man-that   rabbit
   'The man hunts rabbits.'

7. Bikwaagu tʃupa ngiiu wiini   tʃonna geuʔ
   hunted   two   man   little three   coyote
   'Two little men hunted three coyotes.'

8. Biiya   leʒu   ngiiu-ka
   saw   rabbit   man-that
   'Rabbit saw the man.'

9. Biiya   ngiiu-ka   ti-mistu   wiini
   saw   man-that   one-cat   little
   'The man saw a little cat.'

10. Biiya   ngiiu-ka   tʃonna   geuʔ   roʔ
    saw   man-that   three   coyote   big
    'The man saw three big coyotes.'

11. Rukwaagu   geuʔ   leʒu
    hunts   coyote   rabbit
    'Coyote hunts rabbit.'

12. Rukwaagu   ngiiu-ka   leʒu   wiini-ka
    hunts   man-that   rabbit   little-that
    'The man hunts the little rabbit.'

Dataset 190. Peñoles Mixtec (Mexico)

1. Ní-ʃinu   tée-a͗.
   COMPL-run   man-that
   'That man ran.'

2. Ní-ndua-ʃi.
   COMPL-fall-she
   'She fell.'

3. Ní-ʃiní   tée-a͗   n̄̃   iná.
   COMPL-see   man-that   one   dog
   'That man saw a dog.'

4. Ní-tuʃi-dě   bítú.
   COMPL-hew-he   beam
   'He hewed the beam.'

5. Ní-sáʔa   tée-a͗   déʔe-dé   n̄̃   iná.
   COMPL-give   man-that   child-he   one   dog
   'That man gave his child a dog.'

6. Ní-ʃii-ʃi   ditó-ʃi   n̄̃   kwèndú.
   COMPL-say-she   uncle-she   one   story
   'She told her uncle something.'

Note that the following sentences are ungrammatical (as indicated by *):

7. *Ní-ʃinu   tée-a͗   n̄̃   iná.
   COMPL-run   man-that   one   dog
   'That man ran a dog.'

8. *Ní-ʃiní   tée-a͗.
   COMPL-see   man-that
   'That man saw.'

9. *Ní-sáʔa   tée-a͗   déʔe-dé.
   COMPL-give   man-that   child-he
   'That man gave to his child.'

10. *Ní-sáʔa   tée-a͗   n̄̃   iná.
    COMPL-give   man-that   one   dog
    'That man gave a dog.'

Dataset 191. Choapan Zapotec (Mexico)

The basic order of Zapotec clause constituents is presented in (1).

1. Uyo   benʔ   naʔ   taria   uga   niogue.
   went   man   that   rapidly   there   yesterday
   'That man went there quickly yesterday.'

The arrangements of constituents in (2) through (4) represent focussed constituents, as indicated by underlining in the free translation of each clause.

2. Taria   uyo   benʔ   naʔ   uga   niogue.
   rapidly   went   man   that   there   yesterday
   'That man went there <u>quickly</u> yesterday.'

3. Uga   uyo   benʔ   naʔ   taria   niogue.
   there   went   man   that   rapidly   yesterday
   'That man went <u>there</u> quickly yesterday.'

4. Niogue   uyo   benʔ   naʔ   taria   uga.
   yesterday   went   man   that   rapidly   there
   'That man went there quickly <u>yesterday</u>.'

(5) represents the neutral ordering of additional clause constituents.

5. Bëʔ   benʔ   naʔ   nigula   naʔ   dumi.
   gave   man   that   woman   that   money
   'That man gave money to that woman.'

(6) through (8) show focussed constituents. Ignore the special form of the verb in (6) since you would need more information to handle it properly.

6. Benʔ   naʔ   bëʔneʔ   nigula   naʔ   dumi.
   man   that   gave   woman   that   money
   '<u>That man</u> gave money to that woman.'

7. Nigula   naʔ   bëʔ   benʔ   naʔ   dumi.
   woman   that   gave   man   that   money
   '<u>To that woman</u> that man gave money.'

8. Dumi   bëʔ   benʔ   naʔ   nigula   naʔ.
   money   gave   man   that   woman   that
   '(It was) <u>money</u> (that) that man gave to that woman.'

There are also clauses like (9) for which one (but only one) element can be placed in focus at a time in the same manner as shown above.

9. Bëʔ   benʔ   naʔ   nigula   dumi   tzadicaʔdaoʔ   zan   yuʔu   niogue.
   gave   man   that   woman   money   quickly   in   house   yesterday
   'That man quickly gave money to the woman yesterday in his house.'

Laboratory Manual for Morphology and Syntax

Dataset 192. Palantla Chinantec (Mexico)

1. Ca¹nií¹ hio¹³ gog¹² juøh¹².
   opened woman trunk large
   'The woman opened the large trunk.'

2. Ca¹nií¹ hio¹³ guiugh² gog¹².
   opened woman old trunk
   'The old woman opened the trunk.'

3. Ca¹nií¹ jan² hio¹³ guiugh² gog¹².
   opened one woman old trunk
   'One old woman opened the trunk.'

4. Ca¹nií¹ hio¹³ guiugh² ton¹ gog¹².
   opened woman old two trunks'
   The old woman opened two trunks.'

5. Ca¹nií¹ báh³ hio¹³ gog¹².
   opened AFFIRM woman trunk'
   'The woman opened the trunk.'

6. Hio¹³ báh³ ca¹nií¹ gog¹².
   woman AFFIRM opened trunk
   'It was the woman who opened the trunk.'

7. Gog¹² báh³ ca¹nií¹ hio¹³.
   trunk AFFIRM opened woman
   'It was the trunk the woman opened.'

8. Ton¹ gog¹² báh³ ca¹nií¹ hio¹³.
   two trunk AFFIRM opened woman
   'It was two trunks the woman opened.'

9. Ton¹ báh³ gog¹² ca¹nií¹ hio¹³.
   two AFFIRM trunk opened woman
   'It was two trunks the woman opened.'

10. Gog¹² juøh¹² báh³ ca¹nií¹ hio¹³ guiugh².
    trunk large AFFIRM opened woman old
    'It was the large trunk the old woman opened.'

11. Jan² hio¹³ guiugh² báh³ ca¹nií¹ gog¹².
    one woman old AFFIRM opened trunk
    'It was one old woman who opened the trunk.'

12. Jan² báh³ hio¹³ guiugh² ca¹nií¹ gog¹².
    one AFFIRM woman old opened trunk'
    'It was one old woman who opened the trunk.'

13. *Jan² hio¹³ báh³ guiugh² ca¹nií¹ gog¹².

14. *Ton¹ gog¹² báh³ juøh¹² ca¹nií¹ hio¹³.

Dataset 193. Sierra Popoluca (Mexico)

1. Nʌkpa peːtoh.
   'Peter is going.'

2. Nʌkpa ʃiwan aːtebet.
   'John is going to Soteapan.'

3. Luːʃ miɲpa hoymʌ kawahyukmʌ.
   'Louis is coming tomorrow on horseback.'

4. Matʌk nʌkum labrada puymʌ.
   'He went to Piedra Labrada yesterday on foot.'

5. Miɲum matʌk kamyonyukmʌ peːtoh.
   'Peter came yesterday on a truck.'

6. Kamyonyukmʌ nʌkpa mina luːʃ.
   'Louis is going to Minatitlan on a truck.'

7. Kawahyukmʌ nʌkum ʃiwan aːtebet.
   'John went to Soteapan on horseback.'

8. Hoymʌ nʌkpa labrada peːtoh puymʌ.
   'Peter is going to Piedra Labrada tomorrow on foot.'

9. Wʌstʌkmʌ miɲpa ʃiwan.
   'John is coming day after tomorrow.'

10. Puymʌ miɲpa luːʃ wʌstʌkmʌ.
    'Louis is coming day after tomorrow on foot.'

11. Nʌkpa luːʃ aːtebet hoymʌ.
    'Louis is going to Soteapan tomorrow.'

12. Nʌkum ʃiwan matʌk aːtebet.
    'John went to Soteapan yesterday.'

13. Mina nʌkpa hoymʌ luːʃ.
    'Louis is going to Minatitlan tomorrow.'

14. Nʌkum puymʌ mina matʌk.
    'He went to Minatitlan yesterday on foot.'

Laboratory Manual for Morphology and Syntax

Dataset 194. Tabasco Chontal (Mexico)
Phonemic stress is not indicated.

1. Anume.   'You pass by'
2. AyʌIo.   'You fall.'
3. Kʌkʔuʃnan.   'I eat.'
4. Kʌyʌlo nanti.   'I fall way over there.'
5. Ubon ʧʔoye.   'He gets up frequently.'
6. Nanti kʌʧʔoye.   'I get up way over there.'
7. Aʧʔoye wida.   'You get up here.'
8. Akʔalin kʔuʃnan.   'You eat well.'
9. Unume nanti.   'He passes by way over there.'
10. Yaʔi kʌnume.   'I pass by there.'
11. Wida ukʔuʃnan.   'He eats here.'
12. Upʌpʌʔ yʌlo.   'He falls without cause.'
13. Akʔuʃnan yaʔi.   'You eat there.'
14. Ukʔuʃnan wida.   'He eats here.'
15. Wida kʌkʔalin yʌlo.   'I fall here well.'
16. Kʌbon nume wida.   'I pass by here frequently.'
17. Yaʔi abon ʧʔoye.   'You get up there frequently.'
18. Kʌpʌpʌʔ ʧʔoye nanti.   'I get up way over there without cause.'
19. Nanti upʌpʌʔ nume.   'He passes by aimlessly way over there.'
20. Ubon yʌlo yaʔi.   'He falls there frequently.'

Laboratory Manual for Morphology and Syntax

Dataset 195. Tabasco Chontal (Mexico)

Phonemic stress is not indicated.

1. Umʌneʔ buʔu.   'He buys beans.'
2. Ukʼuʃi iʃim.   'He ate corn.'
3. Kʌtʼʌbo.   'I climb up.'
4. Akʼʌb yʌlet.   'You fell at night.'
5. Akʼʌb ukʼuʃeʔ weʔe.   'He eats meat at night.'
6. Kʌmʌni buʔu akʼʌb.   'I bought beans at night.'
7. Yʌli isʼapan.   'He fell early in the morning.'
8. Akʼuʃi weʔe akʼʌb.   'You ate meat at night.'
9. Ayʌlo.   'You fall.'
10. Isʼapan kʌmʌneʔ iʃim.   'I buy corn early in the morning.'
11. Utʃʌpi buʔu.   'He cooked beans.'
12. Pʼiʃon.   'I woke up.'
13. Isʼapan kʌyʌlo.   'I fall early in the morning.'
14. Upʼiʃo isʼapan.   'He wakes up early in the morning.'
15. Tʼʌbon akʼʌb.   'I climbed up at night.'
16. Atʃʌpeʔ weʔe isʼapan.   'You cook meat early in the morning.'
17. Tʼʌbet.   'You climbed up.'
18. Isʼapan amʌni weʔe.   'You bought meat early in the morning.'
19. Utʼʌbo isʼapan.   'He climbs up early in the morning.'
20. Kʌkʼuʃeʔ buʔu.   'I eat beans.'
21. Pʼiʃi akʼʌb.   'He woke up at night.'
22. Akʼʌb kʌtʃʌpi iʃim.   'I cooked corn at night.'
23. Utʃʌpeʔ iʃim.   'He cooks corn.'
24. Akʼʌb apʼiʃo.   'You wake up at night.

Dataset 196. Southern Barasano (Colombia)

Phonemic stress is not indicated.

1. Wadibĩ ĩ.   'He came.'

2. Wadibɨ bĩ, yukɨ.   'You came today.'

3. Yãbĩka wadibɨ yɨ.   'I came yesterday.'

4. Bãhabɨ yɨ.   'I ascended.'

5. Yukɨ bãhabĩ ĩ.   'He ascended today.'

6. Bãhabõ tso, yãbĩka.   'She ascended yesterday.'

7. Yukɨ tsena ĩabõ tso.   'She saw the pineapple today.'

8. Wai ĩabɨ bĩ.   'You saw the fish.'

9. Yetse ĩabĩ ĩ, yãbĩka.   'He saw the pig yesterday.'

10. Yãbĩka wai babĩ ĩ.   'He ate fish yesterday.'

11. Yetse babõ tso.   'She ate the pig(-meat).'

12. Tsena babɨ yɨ, yukɨ.   'I ate the pineapple today.'

13. Ĩre ekabõ tso, tsena, yãbĩka.   'She fed the pineapple to him yesterday.'

14. Ĩre ekabɨ yɨ.   'I fed (it) to him.'

15. Yukɨ bĩre ekabɨ yɨ, wai.   'I fed the fish to you today.'

16. Tsore ekabĩ ĩ, yukɨ.   'He fed (it) to her today.'

17. Tsore ekabɨ bĩ, yetse.   'You fed the pig(-meat) to her.'

18. Yãbĩka yɨre ekabɨ bĩ.   'You fed (it) to me yesterday.'

19. Yɨre ĩtsibĩ ĩ, yetse, yukɨ.   'He gave the pig to me today.'

20. Yukɨ bĩre ĩtsibĩ ĩ.   'He gave (it) to you today.'

21. Yãbĩka tsore ĩtsibɨ yɨ, tsena.   'I gave the pineapple to her yesterday.'

22. Ĩre ĩtsibɨ bĩ, yãbĩka.   'You gave (it) to him yesterday.'

23. Bĩre ĩtsibõ tso, wai.   'She gave fish to you.'

24. Yɨre ĩtsibõ tso.   'She gave (it) to me.'

Dataset 197. Waorani (Ecuador)

FYI: One of the verb roots in the following sentences is **a** 'see, look'.

1. Tepæ̃ kĩŋæ̃ põ bei ɲõwõ.   'Come quickly now and drink cassava drink!'

2. Kĩŋæ̃ põ beida æ̃mæ̃mã.   'You two come across (river) fast and drink!'

3. Ɲõwõ yowẽ iyikii põ beidãni.   'You all come close by now and eat tree grapes!'

4. Ɲõwõ ao go beboi iyikii.   'Now I'll go right here nearby and eat Inga fruit!' or 'Now let me go ... !'

5. Iyikii tepæ̃ põ bekãi wãtæpiyæ̃.   'He'll come near and drink cassava drink in awhile!' or 'Let him ... !'

6. Kĩŋæ̃ põ aida.   'You two come look, fast!'

7. Ɲõwõ æ̃mæ̃mã kĩŋæ̃ go bekãi.   'He'll hurry across now and drink!' or 'Let him ... !'

8. Kiŋæ̃ iyikii go ai.   'Go right here nearby quickly and see!'

9. Yowẽ go aida æ̃mæ̃mã.   'You two go look at the tree grapes on the other side!'

10. Wãtæpiyæ̃ yowẽ põ ai.   'Come see the tree grapes afterwhile!'

11. Põ aidãni ɲõwõ.   'You all come look now!'

12. Ɲõwõ kĩŋæ̃ ao põ akãi.   'He'll come quickly now and see the Inga fruit!' or 'Let him ... !'

13. Ɲõwõ go beboida.   'I'll go drink now, you two!' or 'Let me ... !'

14. æ̃mæ̃mã go aboi.   'I'll go across and see!' or 'Let me ... !'

15. Wãtæpiyæ̃ põ beboidãni.   'I'll come and drink afterwhile, you all!' or 'Let me ... !'

16. Põ akãida.   'He'll come and look, you two!' or 'Let him ... !'

17. Tepæ̃ põ bekãidãni.   'He'll come and drink cassava drink, you all!' or 'Let him ... !'

18. Kĩŋæ̃ ao go ai.   'Go quickly and see the Inga fruit!'

19. Go aboida æ̃mæ̃mã.   'I'll go across and see, you two!' or 'Let me ... !'

Laboratory Manual for Morphology and Syntax

Dataset 198. Tlingit (USA)
Phonemic tone is not indicated.

Note: treat **awʌ-** as a 3s perfective prefix.

1. Hɪt t'ex² awʌdʒʌk we kʌʁak.
   house behind he.killed that mouse
   'He killed the mouse behind the house.'

2. As ganx² awʌhun.
   tree outside he.sold
   He sold the timber outside.'

3. Quk t'et awʌχɪtʃ we x²ʋx².
   box behind he.threw that book
   He threw the book behind the box.'

4. Awʌt'e we x²ʋx².
   he.found that book
   He found the book.'

5. Quk tʌyix² awʌdʒʌq.
   box under he.killed
   He killed it under the box.'

6. Gant awʌχɪtʃ we yiʔʌt.
   outside he.threw that bed
   He threw the bed outside.'

7. As χʌndʌχ awʌt'e.
   tree near he.found
   He found it near the tree.'

8. Quk hɪt tʌyit awʌχɪtʃ.
   box house under he.threw
   He threw the box under the house.'

9. Gandʌχ awʌt'e.
   outside he.found
   He found it outside.'

10. Awʌχɪtʃ.
    he.threw
    He threw it.'

(continued)

Dataset 198 continued:

11. Hɪt   yix²   awʌhun.
    house in   he.sold
    He sold it in the house.'

12. Quk   yɪkdʌχ   awʌt²e.
    box   in   he.found
    He found it in the box.'

13. Awʌhun   we   hɪt.
    he.sold   that   house
    He sold the house.'

14. Hɪt   χʌnx²   awʌʤʌq   we   xuts.
    house near   he.killed that   brown.bear
    He killed the brown bear near the house.'

15. Hɪt   yix²   awʌʤʌq.
    house in   he.killed
    He killed it in the house.'

16. X²ʊx²   χʌnt   awʌχɪʧ.
    book   near   he.threw
    He threw it near the book.'

17. Yiʔʌt   t²edʌχ   awʌt²e   we   quk.
    bed   behind   he.found   that   box
    He found the box behind the bed.'

18. Xuts   as   χʌnx²   awʌʤʌq.
    brown.bear   tree   near   he.killed
    He killed the brown bear near the tree.'

19. Kʌʁak   yiʔʌt   tʌyidʌχ   awʌt²e.
    mouse   bed   under   he.found
    He found the mouse under the bed.'

20. X²ʊx²   xuts   t²et   awʌχɪʧ.
    book   brown.bear   behind   he.threw
    'He threw the book behind the brown bear.'

Laboratory Manual for Morphology and Syntax

Dataset 199. Northern Puebla Totonac (Mexico)

Note: Do not attempt morphology.

1. Wal.
   'He spoke.'

2. Aːkalistaːn wal Pedro.
   then
   'After that Peter spoke.'

3. Kiːwal Pedro.
   'Peter went to speak.'

4. Kiːwal Pedro aʔntsa.
   there
   'Peter went to speak there.'

5. Qoːtan   wal Pedro.
   yesterday
   'Yesterday Peter spoke.'

6. Pedro wal laqaːtʃu.
   everywhere
   'Peter spoke everywhere.'

7. Aːkalistaːn Pedro wal pahtsu qoːtan.
   then   nearby yesterday
   'After that Peter spoke nearby yesterday.'

8. Nawan aʔntsa   laqali.
   there   tomorrow
   'He will speak there tomorrow.'

9. Nawan maqluwa   laqali   tuʃumaʔn.
   many.times tomorrow day.after.tomorrow
   'He will speak many times in the future.'

10. Stuʔnkwa nawan laqaːtʃu   kaːtsisaːt.
    certainly   everywhere early
    'He will certainly speak early everywhere.'

11. tʃuʔntsa nawan.
    thus
    'Thus he will speak.'

12. Aːkalistaːn nawan Pedro lakapal.
    then   quickly
    'Then Peter will speak quickly.'

13. tʃoʔla   wal pahtsu lakapal.
    probably   nearby quickly
    'He probably spoke quickly nearby.'

(Continued)

Dataset 199 continued:

14. ʧoʔla   Pedro laqali   nawan.
    probably   tomorrow
    'Peter will probably speak tomorrow.'

15. Wal aʔtsa qoːtan   tuʃumaʔntsa.
       here   yesterday day.before.yesterday
    'He spoke here in the past.'

16. Stuʔnkwa wal tuʃumaʔntsa.
    certainly   day.before.yesterday
    'He certainly spoke day before yesterday.'

17. Wal ʃiwaːn laqaːʧu   wampala ʧoʔh.
            everywhere again   today
    'John spoke everywhere again today.'

18. ʧuʔnca Pedro qoːtan   wal pahtsu.
    thus   yesterday   nearby
    'Peter thus spoke nearby yesterday.'

19. Stuʔnkwa ʃiwaːn ʧoʔh kiːwal maqluwa.
    certainly   today   many.times
    'John certainly went to speak many times today.'

20. Kaːtsisaːt Pedro kiːwal wampala.
    early   again
    'Peter went early to speak again.'

21. Laqali   ʃiwaːn nakiːwan pahtsu ʃaʔnka.
    tomorrow   nearby well
    'Tomorrow John will go to speak well nearby.'

22. Tuʃumaʔn   Pedro nawan.
    day.after.tomorrow
    'Peter will speak day after tomorrow.'

23. ʧoʔh ʃiwaːn nakiːwan aʔntsa.
    today   there
    'John will go to speak there today.'

24. Wal ʃaʔnka qoːtan.
       well   yesterday
    'He spoke well yesterday.'

25. Nawan lakapal tuʃumaʔn.
           quickly day.after.tomorrow
    'He will speak quickly day after tomorrow.'

26. Kiːwal ʃiwaːn pahtsu.
           nearby
    'John went nearby to speak.'

(Continued)

Dataset 199 continued:

27. Nawan Pedro aʔtsa ʃaʔnka.
                 here well
    'Peter will speak well here.'

28. tʃuʔntsa kaːtsisaːt tʃoʔh nawan wampala.
    thus   early   today   again
    'He will thus speak again this morning.'

29. Qoːtan   tuʃumaʔntsa   wal aʔtsa maqluwa.
    yesterday day.before.yesterday   here many.times
    'He spoke here many times in the past.'

30. tʃoʔla   Pedro kiːwal aʔntsa maqluwa   kaːtsisaːt tʃoʔh.
    probably   there many.times early   today
    'Peter probably went to speak there many times this morning.'

Dataset 200. Palantla Chinantec (Mexico)

Note: underlining indicates emphasis.

1. Ca¹dsiég¹ dsa².   'Someone arrived.'

2. Jní² ca¹lóh¹ ja³ná³.   'I bathed there.'

3. Dsa² ca¹dsiég¹ ja³ió¹ dsiég².   'Someone arrived way over there yesterday.'

4. Ja³la² ca¹ŋøa¹ dsa² jo¹.   'Someone walked here day before yesterday.'

5. Jní² ca¹ŋøa¹ ja³la².   'I walked here.'

6. Ja³ió¹ ca¹ŋøa¹ jní².   'I walked way over there.'

7. Dsiég² ca¹lóh¹ jní².   'Yesterday I bathed.'

8. Jo¹ ca¹dsiég¹ dsa² ja³ná³.   'Day before yesterday someone arrived there.'

9. Dsa² ca¹lóh¹.   'Someone bathed.'

10. Ca¹dsiég¹ jní² ja³ió¹ jo¹.   'I arrived way over there day before yesterday.'

Dataset 201. Northern Tepehuán (Mexico)
Phonemic tone is not indicated.

Note: underlining indicates emphasis.

1. Koi.	'Slept.'	9. Maikoipʌʃi api.	'You didn't sleep?'
2. Tʌʌ.	'Saw.'	10. Maitʌʌpʌʃi.	'You didn't see?'
3. Koiɲʃi anʌ.	'I slept?'	11. Apipʌʃi koi.	'You slept?'
4. Tʌʌɲʃi.	'I saw?'	12. Apipʌʃi tʌʌ.	'You saw?'
5. Koipʌʃi.	'You slept?'	13. Apipʌʃi maikoi.	'You didn't sleep?'
6. Tʌʌpʌʃi api.	'You saw?'	14. Apipʌʃi maitʌʌ.	'You didn't see?'
7. Maikoiɲʃi.	'I didn't sleep?'	15. Maitapʌʃi koi api.	'You didn't sleep?'
8. Maitʌʌɲʃi anʌ.	'I didn't see?'	16. Maitapʌʃi tʌʌ.	'You didn't see?'

Dataset 202. Carib (Guatemala)

1. Lariha wã María.	'John saw Mary.'
2. Lariha wã ãũli le.	'John saw the dog.'
3. Tariha María ãũli le.	'Mary saw the dog.'
4. Tariha María wã.	'Mary saw John.'
5. Wã lariha María.	'It was John who saw Mary.'
6. María tariha wã.	'It was Mary who saw John.'
7. María lariha wã.	'It was Mary whom John saw.'
8. Wã tariha María.	'It was John whom Mary saw.'
9. Ãũli le tariha María	'It was the dog that Mary saw.'

Laboratory Manual for Morphology and Syntax

Dataset 203. Vietnamese
Phonemic tone is not indicated.

1.	Ʌwŋ hawk.	'You study.'
2.	Toy hawk.	'I study.'
3.	Toy ŋu.	'I sleep.'
4.	Ʌwŋ ŋu hay zë.	'You slept two hours.'
5.	Ʌwŋ hawk baw zë.	'How many hours did you study?'
6.	Toy hawk baw lʌw.	'How long did I study?'
7.	Hay zë toy ŋu.	'I will sleep two hours.'
8.	Baw lʌw Ʌwŋ ŋu.	'How long will you sleep?'
9.	Baw lʌw toy hawk.	'How long will I study?'
10.	Baw zë toy ŋu.	'How many hours will I sleep?'

Dataset 204. Finnish

1.	Etsin karitsaa.	'I look for the lamb.'
2.	Koira etsii lehmää.	'The dog looks for the cow.'
3.	Sisko etsii enoa.	'Sister looks for mother's brother.'
4.	Naapuri etsii üstävää.	'The neighbor looks for a friend.'
5.	Katson koiraa.	'I look at the dog.'
6.	Katsot isää.	'You look at father.'
7.	üstävä katsoo karitsaa.	'A friend looks at the lamb.'
8.	Isä katsoo naapuria.	'Father looks at the neighbor.'
9.	Kuuntelet naapuria.	'You listen to a neighbor.'
10.	Lehmä kuuntelee siskoa.	'The cow listens to sister.'
11.	Eno kuuntelee isää.	'Mother's brother listens to father.'
12.	Karitsa kuuntelee koiraa.	'The lamb listens to the dog.'

Dataset 205. Japanese

1. Kodomo ga aruku.
   'The child walks.'

2. Josei ga aruku.
   'The woman walks.'

3. Kodomo ga kuru.
   'The child comes.'

4. Dansei no kodomo ga kuru.
   'The man's child comes.'

5. Kodomo ga hon o miru.
   'The child sees the book.'

6. Kodomo ga josei no okashi o miru.
   'The child sees the woman's cake.'

7. Josei no kodomo ga hon o mitsukeru.
   'The woman's child finds the book.'

8. Josei ga hon o kodomo ni ageru.
   'The woman gives the child the book.'

9. Josei ga okashi o dansei ni ageru.
   'The woman gives the man the cake.'

10. Dansei ga okashi o josei no kodomo ni motteiku.
    'The man takes the woman's child the cake.'

Dataset 206. Russian

1. Dʲévatʃka   ísɨt   sabáku.
   little.girl   look.for   dog
   'The little girl is looking for the dog.'

2. Sabáka   ísɨt   bʲélku.
   dog   look.for   squirrel
   'The dog is looking for the squirrel.'

3. Bʲélku   ganʲáɨt   sabáka.
   squirrel   chase   dog
   'The dog is chasing the squirrel.'

4. Ganʲáɨt   sabáku   dʲévatʃka.
   chase   dog   little.girl
   'The little girl is chasing the dog.'

5. Ísɨt   sabáka   dʲévatʃku.
   look.for   dog   little.girl
   'The dog is looking for the little girl.'

Dataset 207. German

1. Der Küster zeigt dem Sohn den Schuh.
   The sexton shows the son the shoe.'

2. Der Onkel zeigt dem Küster den Hund.
   The uncle shows the sexton the dog.'

3. Der Sohn verkauft dem Onkel den Hund.
   The son sells the uncle the dog.'

4. Der Küster verkauft dem Onkel den Schuh.
   The sexton sells the uncle the shoe.'

5. Der Hund beisst den Küster.
   The dog bites the sexton.'

6. Der Sohn beisst den Onkel.
   The son bites the uncle.'

7. Der Hund jagt den Onkel.
   The dog chases the uncle.'

8. Der Onkel jagt den Sohn.
   The uncle chases the son.'

Dataset 208. Pitjantjatjara—Ooldea (Australia)

1. Kuḻpirpa ŋaʎapiṭaŋu.
   kangaroo came
   'The kangaroo came.'

2. Yuṇṯalpa pakanu.
   daughter got.up
   '[My] daughter got up.'

3. Ŋali ŋaʎapiṭaŋu.
   1d came
   'We (two) came.'

4. Ɲura pakanu.
   2s got.up
   'You got up.'

5. Ampintu kuḻpirpa ɲaŋu.
   Ampin kangaroo saw
   'Ampin saw the kangaroo.'

6. Ɲura yuṇṯalpa kulinu.
   2s daughter heard
   'You heard [my] daughter.'

7. Kuḻpirtu ɲuraɲa ɲaŋu.
   kangaroo 2s saw
   'The kangaroo saw you.'

8. Yuṇṯaltu ŋaliɲa kulinu.
   daughter 1d heard
   '[My] daughter heard us (two).'

9. Ŋali kuḻpirpa ɲaŋu.
   1d kangaroo saw
   'We (two) saw the kangaroo.'

Laboratory Manual for Morphology and Syntax

Dataset 209. Pitjantjatjara—Ooldea (Australia)

1. Watiŋku kuʎpirpa ŋaʎakatiŋu.   'The man brought the kangaroo.'

2. Ṭiṭi ŋuraŋka ɲinaŋu.   'The child sat in camp.'

3. Papa paṇaŋka ɲinaŋu.   'The dog sat on the ground.'

4. Papaŋku ṭiṭi paṭaŋu.   'The dog bit the child.'

5. Ṭiṭi yulaŋu.   'The child cried.'

6. Ŋayulu ṭiṭi kulinu.   'I heard the child.'

7. Watiŋku ŋura wantiŋu.   'The man left the camp.'

8. Watiŋku kuʎpirpa kuʎṭuŋu.   'The man speared the kangaroo.'

9. Kuʎpirtu wati pirinu.   'The kangaroo scratched the man.'

10. Yuṇṭaltu ṭiṭi manṭinu.   'The daughter picked up the child.'

11. Miɲma ŋaʎakulpaŋu.   'The woman returned.'

12. Miɲmaŋku ŋayuɲa ɲaŋu.   'The woman saw me.'

13. Ŋayulu miɲma waṭaŋu.   'I told the woman.'

14. Ŋayulu mirpaɲariŋu.   'I became angry.'

15. Ɲura ŋayuɲa ɲaŋu.   'You saw me.'

16. Miɲmaŋku ɲuraɲa ɲaŋu.   'The woman saw you.'

17. Yuṇṭalpa ŋaʎapiṭaŋu.   'The daughter came.'

18. Kuʎpirpa iluriŋu.   'The kangaroo died.'

19. Miɲma mapiṭaŋu.   'The woman went away.'

20. Ŋayulu ṭiṭi makatiŋu.   'I carried the child away.'

Continued

Dataset 209 continued:

21.	Ṇuṇulu ŋayuɲa ɲaŋu.	'Nunu saw me.'
22.	Paluúu wati waṭaṇu.	'He told the man.'
23.	Watiŋku paluɲa kulinu.	'The man heard him.'
24.	Watiŋku ampinɲa yaʎʈiŋu.	'The man called Ampin.'
25.	Ampinɲa pakaṇu.	'Ampin got up.'
26.	Paluúu mapiṭaŋu.	'He went away.'
27.	Ɲura ŋaʎapiṭaŋu.	'You came.'
28.	Ampintu ɲuraɲa ɲaŋu.	'Ampin saw you.'
29.	Ŋanaɲa ɲinakatiŋu.	'We (pl) sat down.'
30.	Ŋanaɲa yunʈalpa yaʎʈiŋu.	'We called the daughter.'
31.	Ŋali yunʈalpa ṭapinu.	'We (2) asked the daughter.'
32.	Watiŋku ŋanaɲaɲa wanaṇu.	'The man followed us (pl).'
33.	Ampintu ŋaliɲa yaʎʈiŋu.	'Ampin called us (2).'
34.	Ɲuramuka ṭiṭi kulinu.	'You (pl) heard the child.'
35.	Pililu ɲuramukaɲa ɲaŋu.	'Pili saw you (pl).'
36.	Ṭana ṭiṭi makatiŋu.	'They (pl) took the child away.'
37.	Ṭiṭiŋku ṭanaɲa pirinu.	'The child scratched them (pl).'
38.	Ṭana ṭiṭiŋka ɲinaŋu.	'They (pl) sat on the child.'
39.	Ṭana pakaṇu.	'They (pl) got up (arose).'
40.	Piliɲa mirpaɲariŋu.	'Pili was angry.'
41.	Watiŋku piliɲa puŋu.	'The man hit Pili.'

Dataset 210. Jungle Quichua (Ecuador)

1. Wawa ʃamun.
   child come
   'The child comes.'

2. Kay wawa ʃayahurka.
   this child was.standing
   'This child was standing.'

3. ʃayahun   atun kari.
   is.standing big man
   'The big man is standing.'

4. tʃi itʃiʎa mama ʃamurka.
   that small mother came
   'That small mother came.'

5. Mama kay atun wawata kayan.
   mother this big child   call
   'Mother calls this big child.'

6. Kay itʃiʎa karita kayahun ali   wawa.
   this small man   is.calling good child
   'The good child is calling this small man.'

7. Itʃiʎa wawata kari rikun.
   small child   man watch
   'The man watches the small child.'

8. Kay karita mama   kayarka.
   this man   mother called
   'Mother called this man.'

9. tʃi atun mama kay itʃiʎa wawata maskahun.
   that big   mother this small child   is.seeking
   'That big mother is seeking this small child.'

10. Kay wawa kayahurka tʃi ali   karita.
    this child was.calling that good   man
    'This child was calling that good man.'

11. tʃi atun mamata ali   wawa maskahurka.
    that big   mother good child was.seeking
    'The good child was seeking that big mother.'

12. Itʃiʎa kari atun karita rikuhurka.
    small man big man   was.watching
    'The small man was watching the big man.'

Dataset 211. Latin

1. Filia columbam liberat.
   'The daughter frees the dove.'

2. Femina filiam amat.
   'The woman loves the daughter.'

3. Filiae columbas amant.
   'The daughters love the doves.'

4. Aquila feminam salvat.
   'The eagle saves the woman.'

5. Aquilae columbas portant.
   'The eagles carry the doves.'

6. Feminae aquilam liberant.
   'The women free the eagle.'

7. Femina latas longas columbas amat.
   'The woman loves the long, wide doves.'

8. Magna aquila parvam columbam pugnat.
   'The big eagle fights the small dove.'

9. Magna alba aquila alas duas portat.
   'The big white eagle carries two wings.'

10. Mea filia gratas tuas picturas duas amat.
    'My daughter loves your two fine paintings.'

11. Magnae meae aquilae duae parvam columbam pugnant.
    'My two big eagles fight the small dove.'

12. Albae magnae meae columbae duae bellicosas tuas aquilas pugnant.
    'My two big white doves fight your warlike eagles.'

13. Longae latae meae aquilae duae puellas amant.
    'My two long, wide eagles love girls.'

14. Magnae aquilae parvas columbas duas pugnant.
    'The big eagles fight two small doves.'

15. Mea filia albas magnas tuas columbas duas liberat.
    'My daughter frees your two big white doves.'

Dataset 212. Rotokas (Papua New Guinea)

1.	Ikauuepa.	'You hurried.'
2.	Avaraepa.	'I went.'
3.	Avarovere.	'He'll go.'
4.	Avauvere evoa.	'You'll go over there.'
5.	Urua paurivere.	'You'll build a bed.'
6.	Kepa kipuava.	'I painted a house.'
7.	Ikauravere evoa.	'I'll hurry over there.'
8.	Ikauroepa ragaiva.	'He hurried with me.'
9.	Avauepa ragaiva.	'You went with me.'
10.	Avaravere rerava.	'I'll go with him.'
11.	Kepa pauavere evoa.	'I'll build a house over there.'
12.	Rerapa urua paureva.	'He built a bed for him.'
13.	Ikaurovere varavira.	'He'll hurry down to the coast.'
14.	Opuruva pauava viiva.	'I built a canoe with you.'
15.	Ikauraepa viiva varavira.	'I hurried with you down to the coast.'
16.	Ikauuvere rerava evoa.	'You'll hurry with him over there.'
17.	Rerapa opuruva kipuriva.	'You painted a canoe for him.'
18.	Kepa kipurevere varavira.	'He'll paint a house down on the coast.'
19.	Avaroepa viiva varavira.	'He went with you down to the coast.'
20.	Opuruva kipurivere ragaiva.	'You'll paint a canoe with me.'
21.	Viipa urua kipuavere rerava.	'I'll paint a bed with him for you.'
22.	Kepa pauriva rerava varavira.	'You built a house with him down on the coast.'
23.	Viipa opuruva paurevere ragaiva.	'He'll build a canoe with me for you.'
24.	Ragaipa urua kipureva viiva evoa.	'He painted a bed with you for me over there.'

Laboratory Manual for Morphology and Syntax

Dataset 213. Rotokas (Papua New Guinea)

1. Opuruvaepa voa. — 'The canoe was here.'
2. Opuruvapere ipavira. — 'The canoe will be up in the mountains.'
3. Papapakepaepa ipavira. — 'The airplane was up in the mountains.'
4. Papapakepapere voa. — 'The airplane will be here.'
5. Viiepa rerava voa. — 'You were with him here.'
6. Viivere rerava ipavira. — 'You will be with him up in the untains.'
7. Reraepa viiva ipavira. — 'He was with you up in the mountains.'
8. Reravere rerava voa. — 'He will be with him here.'
9. Vii uriouepa rerava voa. — 'You came with him here.'
10. Rera uriorovere viiva ipavira. — 'He will come with you up to the mountains.'
11. Opuruva urioepa ipavira. — 'The canoe came up to the mountains.'
12. Papapakepa uriopere voa. — 'The airplane will come here.'
13. Opuruva virupere ipavira. — 'The canoe will move up to the mountains.'
14. Papapakepa viruepa voa. — 'The airplane moved here.'
15. Vii viruuvere rerava ipavira. — 'You will move with him up to the mountains.'
16. Rera viruroepa rerava voa. — 'He moved with him here.'
17. Rera papapakepa purarevere viiva voa. — 'He will make the airplane with you here.'
18. Vii papapakepa voririva ipavira. — 'You bought the airplane in the mountains.'
19. Rera papapakepa purareva voa. — 'He made the airplane here.'
20. Vii opuruva voririvere rerava voa. — 'You will buy the canoe with him here.'
21. Vii epao rerava ipavira. — 'You are/were with him up in the mountains.'
22. Rera epao viiva voa. — 'He is/was with you here.'
23. Opuruva epao voa. — 'The canoe is/was here.'
24. Papapakepa epao ipavira. — 'The airplane is/was up in the mountains.'
25. Vii opuruva purariva rerava ipavira. — 'You made the canoe with him up in the mountains.'
26. Rera opuruva vorireva rerava ipavira. — 'He bought the canoe with him up in the mountains.'

Dataset 214. Walmaṭari (Australia)

1. Kuɲaȓpa lapaṇi.
   dog   ran
   'The dog ran.'

2. Kuɲaȓpa lapaṇi mana ʤaṭi.
   dog   ran   stick
   'The dog ran with a stick.'

3. Kakaʤipa lapaṇi.
   goanna   ran
   'The goanna ran.'

4. Ŋanpayipa lapaṇi yawaṭa ʤaṭi.
   man   ran   horse
   'The man rode a horse.'

5. Manapa ɲaɲa ŋanpayiḷu.
   stick   saw man
   'The man saw the stick.'

6. Yawaṭapa ɲaɲa ŋanpayiḷu.
   horse   saw man
   'The man saw the horse.'

7. Kuɲaȓpa ɲaɲa ŋanpayiḷu yawaṭa ʤaṭiḷu.
   dog   saw man   horse
   'The man on the horse saw the dog.'

8. Ŋanpayipa kuȓapapa ʤani kakaʤiḷu.
   man   hand   bit goanna
   'The goanna bit the man on the hand.'

9. Kuɲaȓpa piɲa ŋanpayiḷu kuȓapaḷu.
   dog   hit man   hand
   'The man hit the dog with his hand.'

10. Kuɲaȓpa piɲa ŋanpayiḷu mana ʤaṭiḷu.
    dog   hit man   stick
    'The man hit the dog with a stick.'

11. ʤiŋalpa kaɲʤiṇi ŋanpayiḷu ʤinaḷu.
    spear   trod   man   foot
    'The man trod on the spear with his foot.'

12. ʤiŋalpa kaɲʤiṇi ŋanpayiḷu puut ʤaṭiḷu.
    spear   trod   man   boot
    'The man trod on the spear with his boot.'

Dataset 215. Cashinahua (Peru)

1. ɨ bɨtsã tsakakɨ̃.   'My brother shoots it.'
2. ɨ bɨtsã isu haida tsakakɨ̃.   'My brother shoots many spider monkeys.'
3. ɨ bɨtsã piawɨ̃ isu tsakakɨ̃.   'My brother shoots spider monkey with arrows.'
4. ɨ isu tsakai kaʂũ.   'I hunted (went shooting) spider monkey.'
5. Miaɾã ɨ ũĩʂũ.   'I saw you.'
6. Habu butukɨ̃.   'He goes down.'
7. Mɨ̃ kaʂũ.   'You went.'
8. ɨ bɨtsã hasɨ̃ ũĩkɨ̃.   'My brother sees wild turkey.'
9. Haaɾã haʃiwɨ̃ ɨ̃nã imawawaʂũ.   'Mine killed him with a spear.'
10. Hasɨ̃ ɨ bɨtsa ũĩkɨ̃.   'A wild turkey sees my brother.'
11. Hasɨ̃ kuʃi kakɨ̃.   'A wild turkey goes fast (runs).'
12. ɨ bɨtsã tsakabãĩkɨ̃.   'My brother shoots it, going along.'
13. Kumã isu ɨwopa ũĩʂũ.   'The partridge saw a big spider monkey.'
14. Hunɨ̃ isu ɨwopa haida ũĩʂũ.   'The man saw a very big spider monkey.'
15. Kuma haidã huni ũĩnũ.   'Many partridges will see the man.'
16. ɨ kuka yeʃ tsakai kanũ.   'My father-in-law will hunt (go shooting) armadillo.'
17. Yeʃã ɨ kukã ũĩkɨ̃.   'My father-in-law sees armadillo.'
18. ɨ kuka pɨpã isu ũĩʂũ.   'My good father-in-law saw a spider monkey.'
19. ɨ tʃe haidã tsakabubuʂũ.   'My many brothers-in-law shot it from place to place.'
20. ɨ isu pɨʂupiʃta ũĩ kanũ.   'I'll go seeing a little spider monkey.'
21. Hɨ̃sɨ̃sã ɨ ũĩbãĩkɨ̃.   'Going along I see ants.'
22. ɨ isu ʂɨta ũĩnũ.   'I'll see spider monkey teeth.'
23. Habũna tsakabubui kakɨ̃.   'His hunts them from place to place.'
24. Isu kuɾũ mɨ̃na ũĩʂũ.   'The grey spider monkey saw yours.'
25. Habũ bɨtsã ɨ kuma haida ũĩʂũ.   'His brother saw my many partridges.'
26. Mɨ̃ kukã isu ʂɨta ũĩʂũ.   'Your father-in-law saw spider monkey teeth.'
27. Kuma ɨwopa haida kuʃi kanũ.   'The very big partridge will run.'
28. ɨ isu bɨsu ũĩkɨ̃.   'I see a spider monkey face.'
29. Isu ɨwopa haidã pia ũĩnũ.   'A very big spider monkey will see the arrows.'
30. Hunɨɾã pia haidawɨ̃ ɨ tsakakɨ̃.   'I shoot men with many arrows.'
31. Kawɨ.   'Go!
32. ɨ bɨtsaɾã ɨ des pɨpã ũĩnũ.   'My good nephew will see my brother.'
33. ɨaɾã ɨ bɨtsã ũĩkɨ̃.   'My brother sees me.'

Continued

Laboratory Manual for Morphology and Syntax

Dataset 215 Continued:

34.	Mĩnã hasĩ pɨi bɨtʃikĩ.	'Yours wants wild turkey feathers.'
35.	tsakai kawɨ.	'Hunt!
36.	Habũ isuɾã ĩnã ũĩkĩ.	'Mine sees his spider monkey.'
37.	Isu imawawai inawɨ.	'Go up killing monkey!
38.	ĩnaɾã habũ isũ bɨtʃibãĩnũ.	'His spider monkey will want mine going along.'
39.	ĩna tsakawɨ.	'Shoot mine!
40.	Isu mɨkĩnã huni haidã ũĩkĩ.	'Many men see a monkey hand.'
41.	Niwɨ.	'Walk!
42.	Hasĩ batʃiɾã habũ bɨtʃikĩ.	'He wants wild turkey eggs.'
43.	Habũnã mia ũĩbubunũ.	'His will see you from place to place.'
44.	Kuʃi butuwɨ.	'Go down fast!
45.	Huni ɨwopã niʃi bɨtʃikĩ.	'The big man wants a rope.'
46.	Haa imawawawɨ.	'Kill him!
47.	Hĩsĩs haida inakãĩșũ.	'Many ants ascended going along.'
48.	Habũ kukã haʃi ũĩbãĩșũ.	'His father-in-law saw the spear going along.'
49.	Inawɨ.	'Go up!
50.	tʃe pɨpa kakukukĩ.	'Good brothers-in-law go from place to place.'
51.	Mĩ tʃe pɨpa haida kuʃi kakukușũ.	'Your very good brother-in-law ran from place to place.'
52.	Yeʃ bɨtʃiwɨ.	'Want armadillo!
53.	ĩ hasĩ batʃi bɨtʃinũ.	'I'll want wild turkey eggs.'
54.	Mĩna tsakai kașũ.	'Yours hunted it.'
55.	Uĩĩ butuwɨ.	'Seeing go down!
56.	Habũ kuka pɨpa kuʃi butunũ.	'His good father-in-law will descend fast.'
57.	ĩ kukã kuma pɨi bɨtʃișũ.	'My father-in-law wanted partridge feathers.'
58.	Binuɾã ĩ bɨtʃișũ.	'I wanted a club.'
59.	ĩ Imawawai kașũ.	'I went killing it.'
60.	Habu kuʃi nikukușũ.	'He walked fast from place to place.'
61.	Hașĩ inu imawawașũ.	'The spear killed the jaguar.'
62.	Hasĩnã ĩ bɨtsa pɨpa haidã ũĩkĩ.	'My very good brother sees a wild turkey.'
63.	ĩ bɨtsa ĩ isu pɨșupiʃta ũĩĩ inașũ.	'My brother, seeing my little spider monkey, went up.'
64.	Habũ dẽs pia haidawɨ isu tsakașũ.	'His nephew shot spider monkeys with many arrows.'
65.	Mĩ kuma ɨwopa haidã haa ũĩkĩ.	'Your very big partridge sees him.'
66.	Habũ binuwɨ imawawabãĩkĩ.	'He going along kills with a club.'

Continued

Dataset 215 Continued:

67. Kumarã habũ binuwĩ ĩ imawawanũ.
    'I'll kill partridge with his club.'

68. Huni ɨwopa haidarã kuma ɨwopã ũĩs̡ũ.
    'The big partridge saw the very big man.'

69. Habũ habũ isu pɨs̡upiʃta haida tsakas̡ũ.
    'He shot his very small spider monkey.'

70. Mĩ bɨtsa isu kũĩ bɨtʃibãĩni butukĩ.
    'Your brother, going along wanting real monkeys, descends.'

71. Habũ isu pɨs̡upiʃtarã ĩ pia haidã imawawakĩ.
    'My many arrows kill his little spider monkey.'

72. Hasĩ haidarã hĩsĩs bɨtʃii butukukus̡ũ.
    'The ants wanting many wild turkeys went down from place to place.'

73. Mĩnarã piawĩ habu imawawabãĩni kakĩ.
    'He, going along killing yours with arrows, goes.'

74. Isurã ĩ pia haidawĩ ĩ tsakai inakĩ.
    'I, shooting a spider monkey with my many arrows, go up.'

75. ĩ bɨtsã pia ɨwopa haidawĩ kuma tsakabãĩkĩ.
    'My brother going along shoots a partridge with a very big arrow.'

76. Mĩ isu haidarã ĩ pia ɨwopawĩ ĩ tsakabubui kanũ.
    'I'll hunt your many spider monkeys from place to place with my big arrows.'

77. Mĩ isu kũĩ ĩ niʃi kũĩwĩ habũna imawawanũ.
    'Your real monkey will kill his with my real rope.'

78. Yeʃã haʃi ɨwopawĩ habu imawawai inakukunũ.
    'He, killing armadillo with a big spear, will go up from place to place.'

79. Isu kũĩnã habũ s̡itawĩ inu ɨwopa haidã imawawabubukĩ.
    'The very big jaguar kills real monkeys with his teeth from place to place.'

80. ĩ ĩ binu haidawĩ mĩ yeʃ imawawai nikĩ.
    'I walk killing your armadillo with my many clubs.'

81. ĩ tʃe haidã haʃi ɨwopawĩ inu imawawabãĩs̡ũ.
    'My many brothers-in-law going along killed a jaguar with a big spear.'

82. ĩ isu pɨs̡upiʃta haidarã binu pɨs̡upiʃta haidawĩ mĩ imawawakĩ.
    'You kill my very small spider monkey with a very little club.'

83. Habũnarã mĩ binu ɨwopa haidawĩ mĩ imawawas̡ũ.
    'You killed his with your very big club.'

84. Inũ habũ s̡itawĩ huni pɨs̡upiʃta imawawakĩ.
    'The jaguar kills the little man with his teeth.'

85. Huni habũ binu ɨwopa haidawĩ yeʃ imawawai nikãĩnũ.
    'The man will walk going along, killing armadillo with his very big club.'

Laboratory Manual for Morphology and Syntax

Dataset 216. Sayula Popoluca (Mexico)
Phonemic stress is not indicated.

1. Minʌʃp huypay.   'You go buying.'

2. Nʌʃp toʔkpay.   'He goes selling.'

3. Tʌnʌʃkap huypay.   'We (not you) go buying.'

4. Nanʌʃkap huypay.   'We all go buying.'

5. Miganʌʃkawu toʔkpay.   'You all didn't go selling.'

6. Tʌnʌʃp ʃiʃhuypay.   'I go meat-buying.'

7. Tʌʃiʃhuyp.   'I meat-buy.'

8. Nʌʃp huypay ʔinaʔw.   'Her husband goes buying.'

9. Nʌʃp toʔkpay tʌnyaʔw.   'My husband goes selling.'

10. Tʌʃiʃhuykap.   'We (not you) meat-buy.'

11. Miʃiʃtoʔkw.   'You meat-sold.'

12. ʃiʃtoʔkah.   'He will meat-sell.'

13. Migaʃiʃtoʔkah.   'You will not meat-sell.'

14. Kanʌʃu ʃiʃtoʔkpay.   'He did not go meat-selling.'

15. Tʌgaʃiʃtoʔkp.   'I do not meat-sell.'

16. Naganʌʃkawu ʃiʃhuypay.   'We all did not go meat-buying.'

17. Tʌganʌʃkaah ʃiʃtoʔkpay.   'We (not you) will not go meat-selling.'

18. Nʌʃah ʃiʃhuypay ʔinaʔw.   'Her husband will go meat-buying.'

19. Kanʌʃu ʃiʃtoʔkpay ʔinyaʔw.   'Your husband did not go meat-selling.'

Laboratory Manual for Morphology and Syntax

Dataset 217. Sierra Popoluca (Mexico)

1. Hěm ʃiwan nʌkum hoːyi kaːmhoːm.   'John went for a walk in the cornfield.'

2. Peːtoh miɲpa wiˀːki tʌkkʌ́ːm.   'Peter will come to eat at the house.'

3. Ʌtʃ nʌkpa atʃiːɲi nʌʌkʌ́ːm.   'I will go to bathe at the river.'

4. Mitʃ oyum miwiˀːki peːtohkʌ́ːm.   'You went to eat at Peter's house and returned.'

5. Hěm tʃimpa miɲum wiˀːki.   'The dog came to eat.'

6. Hěm peːtoh mohum mʌːtʃi ʃiwankʌ́ːm.   'Peter began to play at John's place.'

7. Ʌtʃ ahoːypa.   'I will go for a walk.'

8. Mitʃ miwiˀkpa.   'You will eat.'

9. tʃimpa tʃiŋpa.   'A dog will bathe.'

10. Heˀm tʃimpa mʌːtʃpa tʌkhoːm.   'The dog will play inside the house.'

11. Peːtoh wiˀkum.   'Peter ate.'

12. Anʌkpa.   'I will go.'

13. Mitʃ mioyum kaːmkʌ́ːm.   'You went to the cornfield and returned.'

14. Nʌkpa tʃiːŋi.   'He will go to bathe.'

15. Ʌtʃ mohpa awiˀːki tʌkhoːm.   'I will begin to eat inside the house.'

16. Mitʃ miɲum mimʌːtʃi nʌ́ːhoːm.   'You came to play in the water.'

Laboratory Manual for Morphology and Syntax

Dataset 218. English

1. I study.
   I can study.
   I may study.
   I shall study.

2. I am studying.
   I can be studying.
   I may be studying.
   I shall be studying.

3. I have studied.
   I can have studied.
   I may have studied.
   I shall have studied.

4. I have been studying.
   I can have been studying.
   I may have been studying.
   I shall have been studying.

5. I studied.
   I could study.
   I might study.
   I should study.

6. I was studying.
   I could be studying.
   I might be studying.
   I should be studying.

7. I had studied.
   I could have studied.
   I might have studied.
   I should have studied.

8. I had been studying.
   I could have been studying.
   I might have been studying.
   I should have been studying.

9. I do not study.
   I cannot study.
   I may not study.
   I shall not study.

10. I am not studying.
    I cannot be studying.
    I may not be studying.
    I shall not be studying.

11. I have not studied.
    I cannot have studied.
    I may not have studied.
    I shall not have studied.

12. I have not been studying.
    I cannot have been studying.
    I may not have been studying.
    I shall not have been studying.

13. I did not study.
    I could not study.
    I might not study.
    I should not study.

14. I was not studying.
    I could not be studying.
    I might not be studying.
    I should not be studying.

15. I had not studied.
    I could not have studied.
    I might not have studied.
    I should not have studied.

16. I had not been studying.
    I could not have been studying.
    I might not have been studying.
    I should not have been studying.

Dataset 219. Huixtec Tzotzil (Mexico)

1. Mólun.   'I am old.'
2. Mólat.   'You are old.'
3. Lékun.   'I am fine.'
4. Lékat.   'You are fine.'
5. Tʃikóm.   'I will stay.'
6. Tʃakóm.   'You will stay.'
7. Tʃibát.   'I will go.'
8. Nibát.   'I went.'
9. Natál.   'You came.'
10. Tʃalík.   'You will begin.'
11. Tʃiláx.   'I will finish.'
12. Niʔátin.   'I bathed.'
13. Tʃaʔábtex.   'You will work.'
14. Nikóm ʔátinukun.   'I stayed and bathed.'
15. Tʃakóm ʔátinukat.   'You will stay and bathe.'
16. Tʃibát ʔátinukun.   'I will go and bathe.'
17. Nabát ʔátinukat.   'You went and bathed.'
18. Nitál ʔábtexukun.   'I came and worked.'
19. Nalík ʔábtexukat.   'You began to work.'
20. Tʃaláx ʔábtexukat.   'You will finish working.'

Dataset 220. Siona (Colombia)

1. Wekɨbi ũihi.
   tapir   be.lying.down

   'The tapir is lying down.'

2. Wɨʔebi tãibi.
   house   fell.down

   'The house fell down.'

3. Kuyabi wɨibi.
   stranger got.up

   'The stranger got up.'

4. Wɨbi mɨihi.
   agouti go.up

   'The agouti goes up.'

5. ɫhagɨbi ãihi.
   chief   eat

   'The chief eats.'

6. Kudabi saihi.
   chicken go

   'The chicken goes.'

7. Yaibi daihi.
   jaguar come

   'The jaguar comes.'

8. ɫhagɨbi wɨde ũabi.
   chief   agouti laid.down

   'The chief laid the agouti down.'

9. Yaibi kudade tãhi.
   jaguar chicken drop

   'The jaguar drops the chicken.'

10. Kuyabi wekɨde wɨabi.
    stranger tapir   lifted

    'The stranger lifted the tapir.'

11. Yaibi wɨde mɨahi.
    jaguar agouti take.up

    'The jaguar takes the agouti up.'

12. Kuyabi yaide sahi.
    stranger jaguar take

    'The stranger takes the jaguar.'

13. ɫhagɨbi kudade dabi.
    chief   chicken brought

    'The chief brought the chicken.'

14. Kuyabi wekɨde wɨohi.
    stranger tapir   make.get.up

    'The stranger makes the tapir get up.'

15. Wekɨbi kuyade mɨobi.
    tapir   stranger made.go.up

    'The tapir made the stranger go up.'

16. Kuyabi yaide ãobi.
    stranger jaguar fed

    'The stranger fed the jaguar.'

17. ɫhagɨbi kuyade saobi.
    chief   stranger sent

    'The chief sent the stranger.'

Continued

Dataset 220 Continued:

18. Kuyabi łhagɨde daohi.   'The stranger sends the chief here.'
    stranger chief   send.here

19. Wɨbi   sai mɨihi.   'The agouti going ascends.'
    agouti go go.up

20. Yaibi wɨde   da   mɨahi.   'The jaguar bringing the agouti raises it.'
    jaguar agouti bring take.up

21. Wekɨbi kuyade dao   mɨobi.   'The tapir made the stranger come ascending.'
    tapir   stranger send.here made.go.up

    *Wekɨbi kuyade dai mɨobi.
    *Wekɨbi kuyade dai mɨabi.
    *Wekɨbi kuyade da mɨobi.
    *Wekɨbi kuyade da mɨibi.
    *Wekɨbi kuyade dao mɨabi.
    *Wekɨbi kuyade dao mɨibi.

Dataset 221. Palantla Chinantec (Mexico)

1. Uen^{12} dsǿa^{12} Juøn^{13} quianh^{13} ti^{3}jmii^{2}dsa.
   hard   heart John   with   father.3
   'John and his father are mean.'

2. Uen^{12} dsǿa^{12} Juøn^{13} ja^3 cog^2 ti^{3}jmii^{2}dsa.
   hard   heart John   toward   father.3
   'John is mean to his father.'

3. Ca^{1}ŋó^1 Juøn^{13} quianh^{13} ti^{3}jmii^{2}dsa.'
   went(sg) John   with   father.3
   'John went with his father.'

4. Ca^{1}ŋi^{1}lén^2 Juøn^{13} quianh^{13} ti^{3}jmii^{2}dsa.
   went(pl) John   with   father.3.
   'John and his father went.'

5. Ca^{1}bú^2 Juøn^{13} quianh^{13} hma^2.
   struck John   with   wood
   'John struck (someone) with a stick.'

6. Quianh^{13} Juøn^{13} ti^{3}jmii^{2}dsa.
   with   John   father.3
   (a) 'John's father is with him.'
   (b) 'John is with his father.'

   *Ja^3 cog^2 Juøn^{13} ti^{3}jmii^{2}dsa.

   *Quianh^{13} Juøn^{13} hma^2.

Dataset 222. Colorado (Ecuador)

1. Na   ano   fi-e.   'The child ate plantains.'
   child plantain eat-DECL

2. Unila kucu   ka-e.   'The man got cassava.'
   man   cassava get-DECL

3. tsatsika ka-n.   'Did he get meat?'
   meat   get-INTERR

4. Ka-e.   'He got it.'
   get-DECL

5. Susu fi-e.   'The dog ate it.'
   dog   eat-DECL

6. Na   tsatsika fari-e.   'The child asked for meat.'
   child meat   ask-DECL

7. Na   ho-n.   'Is he a child?'
   child BE-INTERR

8. Ano   fari-no ho-e.   'He should ask for plantain.'
   plantain ask-INF BE-DECL

9. Fi-no   ho-n.   'Should he eat?'
   eat-INF BE-INTERR

10. Unila ka-no   ho-e.   'The man should get it.'
    man   get-INF BE-DECL

11. Kutsu   fi-ka   ho-e.   'He has eaten cassava.'
    cassava eat-PTCPL BE-DECL

12. Ano   fari-ka   ho-n.   'Has he asked for plantain?'
    plantain ask-PTCPL   BE-INTERR

13. Unila tsatsika munara-e.   'The man needs meat.'
    man   meat   need-DECL

14. Fi-no   munara-e.   'He needs to eat.'
    eat-INF need-DECL

15. Na   susu fari-no munara-n.   'Need the child ask for the dog?'
    child dog ask-INF need-INTERR

Dataset 223. Kalagan (Philippines)

Regularized.

1. Magdala   ya kuda? sa eseg.
   will.carry the horse the man
   'The horse will carry the man.'

2. Magkamang ya   bubay sa umay adti be?en.
   will.get   the   woman the rice   at   basket
   'The woman will get the rice from the basket.'

3. Maglugpat ya idu? sa kauy.
   will.jump the dog the wood
   'The dog will jump the wood.'

4. Miglabet ya eseg sa kuda? na   kauy.
   beat   the man the horse with stick
   'The man beat the horse with a stick.'

5. Kamangen na idu? ya kauy adti umay.
   will.get   the dog the stick at   rice.field
   'The dog will get the stick at the rice field.'

6. Dala?an   na eseg ya be?en sa umay.
   will.carry the man at basket the rice
   'The man will carry the rice to the basket.'

7. Lugpatan na kuda?ya umay   sa kauy.
   will.jump the horse at rice.field the wood
   'The horse will jump over the wood at the rice field.'

8. Labetan   na eseg ya umay   sa idu?.
   will.beat the man at rice.field the dog
   'The man will beat the dog at the rice field.'

9. Pigdala na kuda? ya   be?en sa umay adti eseg.
   carried the horse with basket the rice   at   man
   'The horse used the basket to carry the rice to the man.'

10. Paglugpat na bubay ya   kauy sa be?en.
    will.jump the woman with stick the basket
    'The lady will use a stick to jump over the basket.'

(continued)

Laboratory Manual for Morphology and Syntax

Dataset 223 continued:

11. Piglugpat na eseg ya kauy sa iduʔ.
    jumped the man with stick the dog
    'The man used the stick to jump over the dog.'

12. Piglabet na bubay ya kauy sa iduʔ adti umay.
    beat the woman with stick the dog at rice.field
    'The woman used the stick to beat the dog at the rice field.'

13. Magdala ya eseg.
    will.carry the man
    The man will carry.'

14. Pagkamang na eseg ya beʔen sa umay adti iduʔ.
    will.get the man with basket the rice at dog
    'The man will get the rice from the dog in the basket.'

15. Lugpaten na iduʔ ya kudaʔ.
    will.jump the dog the horse
    'The dog will jump over the horse.'

16. Pagdala na bubay ya beʔen sa umay adti eseg.
    will.carry the woman with basket the rice at man
    'The woman will use the basket to carry the rice to the man.'

17. Piglugpatan na kudaʔ ya beʔen.
    jumped the horse at basket
    'The horse jumped at the place of the basket.'

18. Pigdalaʔan na beʔen ya iduʔ sa umay.
    carried the basket at dog the rice
    'The basket carried the rice to the dog.'

19. Migkamang ya umay sa beʔen adti eseg.
    got the rice the basket at man
    'The rice got the basket from the man.'

20. Migdala ya eseg sa umay na beʔen adti bubay.
    carried the man the rice with basket at woman
    'The man carried the rice in a basket to the woman.'

(continued)

Dataset 223 continued:

21. Pigkamang na bubay ya beʔen sa umay adti eseg.
    got   the woman with basket the rice   at   man
    'The woman used a basket to get the rice from the man.'

22. Miglugpat ya beʔen adti umay.
    jumped   the basket at   rice
    'The basket jumped into the rice.'

23. Kamangan na iduʔ ya beʔen sa umay.
    will.get   the dog at basket the rice
    'The dog will get the rice from the basket.'

24. Pigkamangan na iduʔ ya eseg sa umay na beʔen.
    got   the dog at man the rice   with basket
    'The dog got the rice in a basket from the man.'

25. Dalaʔen   na bubay ya iduʔ na beʔen adti eseg.
    will.carry the woman the dog with basket at   man
    'The woman will carry the dog to the man in a basket.'

26. Maglabet ya eseg.
    will.hit   the man
    'The man will hit.'

27. Labeten na bubay ya kudaʔ na kauy.
    will.beat the woman the horse with stick
    'The woman will beat the horse with a stick.'

28. Paglabet na eseg ya kauy sa kudaʔ adti umay.
    will.beat the man with stick the horse at   rice.field
    'The man will beat the horse with a stick at the rice field.'

29. Piglabetan na eseg ya umay   sa kudaʔ.
    beat   the man at rice.field the horse
    'The man beat the horse at the rice field.'

Laboratory Manual for Morphology and Syntax

Dataset 224. Kalagan (Philippines)
Regularized.

1. Magkita? ya utaw sa balay.   'The man sees the house.'
2. Kita?en na utaw ya balay.   'The man sees the house.'
3. Magdet ya bata? sa usa.   'The boy hunts the pig.'
4. Deten na bata? ya usa.   'The boy hunts the pig.'
5. Magtawag ya bata? sa utaw.   'The boy calls the man.'
6. Tawagen na bata? ya utaw.   'The boy calls the man.'
7. Magdala ya utaw sa usa.   'The man carries the pig.'
8. Dala?en na utaw ya usa.   'The man carries the pig.'
9. Magtuway ya utaw sa bata?.   'The man guides the boy.'
10. Tuwayen na utaw ya bata?.   'The man guides the boy.'

11. Migdet ya bata? sa usa adti pawa?.
    'The boy hunted the pig at the farm.'

12. Deten na utaw ya suwagan adti magalet.
    'The man hunts the deer in the jungle.'

13. Pigtawag na utaw ya usa.
    'The man called the pig.'

14. Magdali? ya utaw sa umay adti be?en.
    'The man mixes the rice in a basket.'

15. Dali?an na bata? ya be?en sa umay.
    'The boy mixes the rice in a basket.'

16. Lutu?en na utaw ya umay adti kulun.
    'The man cooks the rice in a pot.'

17. Miglutu? ya bata? sa suwagan adti kulun.
    'The boy cooked the deer in a pot.'

18. Piglutu?an na bata? ya kulun sa umay
    'The boy cooked the rice in a pot.'

19. Tawagan na utaw ya pawa? sa bata?
    'The man calls the boy at the farm.'

20. Pigdetan na utaw ya magalet sa usa
    'The man hunted the pig in the jungle.'

Continued

Dataset 224 continued:

21. Tawagen na utaw ya bataʔ adti magalet
    'The man calls the boy in the jungle.'

22. Pigdaliʔ na bataʔ ya umay adti beʔen
    'The boy mixed the rice in a basket.'

23. Miglutuʔ ya maglutuʔ sa usa
    'The one who cooks cooked the pig.'

24. Magtawag ya utaw sa maglutuʔ adti balay
    'The man calls the cook to the house.'

25. Lutuʔen na bataʔ ya usa adti kulun
    'The boy cooks the pig in the pot.'

26. Pigtuwayan na maglutuʔ ya magalet sa magdet
    'The cook guided the hunter in the jungle.'

27. Migdet ya magdet na sinapang adti pawaʔ
    'The hunter hunted at the farm with a gun.'

28. Magtimbak ya maglutuʔ sa usa adti magalet
    'The cook shoots the pig in the jungle.'

29. Pagdaliʔ na bataʔ ya beʔen sa umay adti balay
    'The boy mixes the rice in a basket at the house.'

30. Daliʔen na maglutuʔ ya umay adti beʔen
    'The cook mixes the rice in a basket.'

31. Magdaliʔ ya magtuway sa umay
    'The guide mixes the rice.'

32. Pagtimbak na utaw ya sinapang adti balay
    'The man shoots the gun in the house.'

33. Timbakan na magdet ya pawaʔ sa usa na sinapang
    'The hunter shoots the pig at the farm with a gun.'

34. Pigdaliʔ na magtimbak ya kulun sa sitaw adti abu
    'The shooter mixed the beans in a pot in the kitchen.'

35. Pigdet na magtuway ya usa na sinapang adti pawaʔ
    'The guide hunted the pig with a gun at the farm.'

36. Pigtimbak na maglutuʔ ya magtimbak sa usa adti pawaʔ
    'The cook shot a pig with a gun (with a shooter) at the farm.'

37. Pigtimbak na bataʔ ya usa na sinapang
    'The boy shot the pig with a gun.'

Dataset 225. Western Bukidnon Manobo (Philippines)

1. Midtibas a kenikew.   'I slashed you.'

2. Midtibas ku sikew.   'I slashed you.'

3. Edtibas a kenikew.   'I slash you.'

4. Edtibasen ku sikew.   'I slash you.'

5. Neketibas a kenikew.   'I was able to slash you.'

6. Netibas ku sikew.   'I was able to slash you.'

7. Ebpeketibas a kenikew.   'I am able to slash you.'

8. Egketibas ku sikew.   'I am able to slash you.'

9. Intibas ku heʔini kenikew.   'I slashed you with this.'

10. Idtibas ku heʔini kenikew.   'I slash you with this.'

11. Iŋketibas ku heʔini kenikew.   'I was able to slash you with this.'

12. Igketibas ku heʔini kenikew.   'I am able to slash you with this.'

13. Mibpetibas a kenikew te sundaru.   'I had the soldier slash you.'

14. Mibpetibas ku sikew te sundaru.   'I had the soldier slash you.'

15. Ebpetibas a kenikew te sundaru.   'I have the soldier slash you.'

16. Ebpetibasen ku sikew te sundaru.   'I have the soldier slash you.'

17. Nekepetibas a kenikew te sundaru.   'I was able to have the soldier slash you.'

18. Nepetibas ku sikew te sundaru.   'I was able to have the soldier slash you.'

19. Ebpekepetibas a kenikew te sundaru.   'I am able to have the soldier slash you.'

20. Egkepetibas ku sikew te sundaru.   'I am able to have the soldier slash you.'

21. Impetibas ku heʔeyan te sundaru.   'I had the soldier slashed with that.'

22. Ibpetibas ku heʔeyan te sundaru.   'I have the soldier slashed with that.'

23. Iŋkepetibas ku heʔeyan te sundaru.   'I was able to have the soldier slashed with that.'

Continued

Dataset 225 continued:

24. Igkepetibas ku he?eyan te sundaru.   'I am able to have the soldier slashed with <u>that</u>.'

25. Waza? a medtibas kenikew.   '<u>I</u> did not slash you.'

26. Waza? ku sikew tibasa.   'I did not slash <u>you</u>.'

27. Waza? ku he?ini itibas kinikew .   'I did not slash you with <u>this</u>.'

28. Waza? a meketibas kenikew.   '<u>I</u> was not able to slash you.'

29. Waza? ku sikew metibas .   'I was not able to slash <u>you</u>.'

30. Waza? ku he?ini iketibas kinikew .   'I was not able to slash you with <u>this</u>.'

31. Mibpenibas a kinikew .   '<u>I</u> slashed you all up.'

32. Mibpenibas ku sikew .   'I slashed <u>you</u> all up.'

33. Impenibas ku he?ini kinikew .   'I slashed you all up with <u>this</u>.'

34. Nekepenibas a kinikew .   '<u>I</u> was able to slash you all up.'

35. Nepenibas ku sikew .   'I was able to slash <u>you</u> all up.'

36. Iŋkepenibas ku he?ini kinikew .   'I was able to slash you all up with <u>this</u>.'

37. Mibegayan a kinikew te vegas.   'You gave <u>me</u> rice.'

38. Ebegayan a kinikew te vegas.   'You (will) give <u>me</u> rice.'

39. Nebegayan a kinikew te vegas.   'You were able to give <u>me</u> rice.'

40. Egkebegayan a kinikew te vegas.   'You are able to give <u>me</u> rice.'

41. Mibpebegayan a kinikew te vegas.   'You had someone give <u>me</u> rice.'

42. Ebpebegayan a kinikew te vegas.   'You (will) have someone give <u>me</u> rice.'

43. Nepebegayan a kinikew te vegas.   'You were able to have someone give <u>me</u> rice.'

44. Egkepebegayan a kinikew te vegas.   'You are able to have someone give <u>me</u> rice.'

45. Waza? a begayi kinikew te vegas.   'You did not give <u>me</u> rice.'

46. Waza? a kenikew mebegayi te vegas.   'You were not able to give <u>me</u> rice.'

Dataset 226. English

1. I washed myself.
2. I washed you.
3. I washed him.
4. You washed me.
5. You washed yourself.
6. You washed him.
7. He washed me.
8. He washed you.
9. He washed him.
10. He washed himself.
11. Wash me!
12. Wash yourself!
13. Wash him!

Dataset 227. Palantla Chinantec (Mexico)

1. Jŋie^{12} dsa^2.   'He rests.'
2. Tsa^{1}jŋie^{12} dsa^2.   'He does not rest.'
3. Ca^{1}jŋie^1 dsa^2.   'He rested.'
4. Janh^3 hning^2.   'You rest.'
5. Tsa^{1}janh^3 hning^2.   'You do not rest.'
6. Ca^{1}jŋieh^3 hning^2.   'You rested.'
7. Jŋie^3!   'Rest!'
8. Tsa^{1}jan^3!   'Don't rest!'
9. Ho^{12} dsa^2.   'He cries.'
10. Høgh^2 hning^2.   'You cry.'
11. Tsa^{1}høg^2!   'Don't cry!
12. Ca^{1}hagh^3 hning^2.   'You cried.'
13. Hag^3!   'Cry!
14. Ca^{1}lóh^2 dsa^2.   'He bathed.'
15. Lóh^2 hning^2.   'You bathe.'
16. Tsa^{1}lóh^2!   'Don't bathe!
17. Ca^{1}lioh^{12} hning^2.   'You bathed.'
18. Lioh^{12}!   'Bathe!

Dataset 228. Huixtec Tzotzil (Mexico)

The following examples illustrate the formation of a negative injunctive clause:

1.	ʃabát.	'You go.'
2.	ʃabátme.	'You go (emphatic).'
3.	Mú ʃabát.	'You do not go.'
4.	Múme ʃabát.	'Don't go!'

The following examples illustrate the formation of injunctive stative clauses:

5.	Kólun.	'I am free.'
6.	Kólot.	'You are free.'
7.	Kólukun.	'May I become free!'
8.	Kólukot.	'May you become free!'

The following examples illustrate the formation of an injunctive second-person active intransitive clause:

9.	ʃibát.	'I go.'
10.	ʃabát.	'You go.'
11.	ʃbát.	'He goes.'
12.	Bátan.	'Go!

The remaining examples illustrate the formation of an injunctive second-person active transitive clause:

13.	Xpás.	'I do it.'
14.	ʃapás.	'You do it.'
15.	ʃpás.	'He does it.'
16.	Páso.	'Do it!'

Laboratory Manual for Morphology and Syntax

Dataset 229. Urim Commands (Papua New Guinea)

1. Kupm antam namu.
   1s   boil   plantain
   'I am boiling plantains.'

2. Wet kupm antam namu.
   just 1s   boil   plantain
   'I just boiled plantains.'

3. Mpa kupm intam namu.
   will 1s   boil   plantain
   'I will boil plantains.'

4. Kitn antam.
   2s   boil
   'You are boiling it/them.'

5. Kitn kaki wayu.
   2s   peel taro
   'You are peeling taro.'

6. Wet kitn kaki wayu.
   just 2s   peel taro
   'You just peeled taro.'

7. Mpa kitn kiki wayu.
   will 2s   peel taro
   'You will peel taro.'

8. Intam wayu o.
   boil taro IMPV
   'Boil the taro!'

9. Kiki wayu o.
   peel taro IMPV
   'Peel the taro!'

10. Kiki o.
    peel IMPV
    'Peel it/them!'

11. Kitn intam o.
    2s   boil IMPV
    'You, boil it/them!'

12. Kitn intam namu   o.
    2s   boil plantain IMPV
    'You, boil the plantains!'

Laboratory Manual for Morphology and Syntax

Dataset 230. Luganda (Uganda)

1. Omulenzi mulangira.   'The boy is a prince.'
2. Omulenzi muwanvu.   'The boy is tall.'
3. Emmere nnungi.   'The food is good.'
4. Emmere eyokya.   'The food is hot.'
5. Emmere matooke.   'The food is bananas.'
6. Omulenzi yalya emmere.   'The boy ate the food.'
7. Omulenzi yalya matooke.   'The boy ate bananas.'
8. Omulenzi yafuuka mulangira.   'The boy became a prince.'
9. Omulenzi yasigala nga mulangira.   'The boy remained a prince.'
10. Emmere yasigala nga eyokya.   'The food remained hot.

Dataset 231. Engenni (Nigeria)

1. Aδiδä nä wu.
rich.man the died   'The rich man died.'

2. Edei δemu nä du eseni.
man fat the bought fish   'The fat man bought fish.'

3. Ade do eseni.
Ade stole fish   'Ade stole fish.'

4. Edei nä aδiδä.
man the rich.man   'The man is a rich man.'

5. Edei dori nä ade.
man tall the Ade   'The tall man is Ade.'

6. Ade doriya.
Ade tall   'Ade is tall.'

7. Aδiδä nä δemuya.
rich.man the big   'The rich man is fat.'

Dataset 232. Michoacán Nahuatl (Mexico)

1. Nitʃoka.   'I cry.'
2. Maltik in ʃolul.   'The child bathed.'
3. Nisiwal.   'I am a woman.'.
4. Timaltia.   'You bathe.'
5. Temuk se ʃolul.   'A child descended.'
6. Niʃolul.   'I am a child.'
7. Tilakal.   'You are a man.'
8. Kotʃi in siwal.   'The woman sleeps.'
9. Temua.   'He descends.'

10. Tiʃolul.   'You are a child.'
11. tʃokak se siwal.   'A woman cried.'
12. Wala in lakal.   'The man comes.'
13. Lakal.   'He is a man.'
14. Tikotʃik.   'You slept.'
15. Siwal.   'She is a woman.'
16. Nimolaluk.   'I ran.'
17. Timolalua.   'You run.'
18. Niwalak.   'I came.'

Dataset 233. Lalana Chinantec (Mexico)
Phonemic tone is not indicated.

1. ʥa hmi: ʃi:ʔ ʥuhn.
   3 chinantec boy good
   'The good boy is a Chinantec.'

2. ʥa ʥuhn ʃ:ʔ kye:n ʥa ha:n.
   3 good boy of   3 old
   'The old people's boy is good.'

3. ʥa ʥuhn ʥa hmi:.
   3 good 3 chinantec
   'The Chinantec people are good.'

4. ʥa ʔwe:ʔn ʃi:ʔ.
   3 strong boy
   'The boy is strong.'

5. ʃi:ʔ ʔwe:ʔn ʃi:ʔ ʥuhn kye:n mih.
   boy strong boy good of   woman
   'The woman's good boy is strong.'

6. ʥa ʔwe:ʔn ʃi:ʔ kye:n ʥa hmi:.
   3 strong boy of   3 chinantec
   'The Chinantec people's boy is strong.'

7. ʃi:ʔ ʥuhn ʃi:ʔ ʔwe:ʔn kye:n ʥa ha:n.
   boy good boy strong of   3 old
   'The old people's strong boy is good.'

Dataset 234. Trique of Copala (Mexico)

1. Ananh ȝana.
   weave woman
   'The woman weaves.'

2. Unanh ȝana.
   run.away woman
   'The woman runs away.'

3. Neh waa ȝana.
   ugly BE woman
   'The woman is ugly.'

4. Ananh ȝana zaʔ.
   weave woman pretty
   'The pretty woman weaves.'

5. Yaan ȝinii.
   sit boy
   'The boy is sitting.'

6. Neh waa ȝinii.
   ugly BE boy
   'The boy is ugly.'

7. Ranʔ ȝinii.
   sick boy
   'The boy is sick.'

8. ʔyah ȝana.
   make woman
   'The woman makes it.'

9. ʔyah ȝinii weʔ.
   make boy house
   'The boy builds a house.'

10. ʔyah ȝinii weʔ ʃih.
    make boy house big
    'The boy builds a large house.'

11. Zaʔ waa ȝana ʃih.
    pretty BE woman big
    'The large woman is pretty.'

12. Weʔe waa ȝana.
    good.looking BE woman
    'The woman is good-looking.'

    *ranʔ waa ȝinii
    sick BE boy

Dataset 235. Urim (Papua New Guinea)

1. kil kul.
   3 come
   'S/he comes.'

2. Yantwilm ɨrpma.
   Yantwilm sit
   'Yantwilm is here/alive.'

3. Yantwilm ɨrpma ti.
   Yantwilm sit   here
   'Yantwilm is here.'

4. Yantam kul ti   ɨse.
   Yantam come here already
   'Yantam has come here.'

5. Mayen   kil kul   ti.
   old.woman 3   come here
   'The old woman comes here.'

6. Kiɲ   wor kul.
   woman good come
   'The good/pretty woman comes.'

7. Melnum wailwail kul   ɨse.
   person important come already
   'The important person has come.'

8. Mamik mayen a Yantam kul.
   grandmother of Yantam come
   'Yantam's grandmother comes.'

9. Kil wor.
   3   good
   'S/he is good/pretty.'

10. Yantam kil watin.
    Yantam 3   long
    'Yantam is tall.'

11. Kil melnum wailwail.
    3   person important
    'S/he is an important person.'

12. Yantwilm kil mayen.
    Yantwilm 3   old.woman
    'Yantwilm is an old woman.'

13. Kil yar.
    3   sorcerer
    'He is a sorcerer.'

14. Yantam kil ɨpma   waket.
    Yantam 3   stomach hot
    'Yantam is angry.'

15. Yikal pa a Yantam.
    bow   it of Yantam
    'The bow is Yantam's.'

Dataset 236. Northern Paiute (USA)

1. Nɨ taunawai tɨkaba tɨmɨ.
   1s town.in bread buy
   'I bought bread in town.'

2. I hamaʔa idziʔi taunawai tɨkaba tɨmɨ.
   my sister yesterday town.in bread buy
   'My sister bought bread in town yesterday.'

3. I piawabi tɨkaba tɨmɨkwɨ.
   1s wife bread buy.FUT
   'My wife will buy bread.'

4. Nɨ idziʔi taunawai.
   1s yesterday town.in
   'I was in town yesterday.'

5. I hamaʔa kuiyuiwai.
   1s sister Nixon.in
   'My sister is in Nixon.'

6. I paba piawabi taunawai.
   1s big wife town.in
   'My big wife is in town.'

7. Kuiyui pabahiu.
   Nixon big
   'Nixon is big.'

8. I piawabi pabahiu.
   1s wife big
   'My wife is big.'

Laboratory Manual for Morphology and Syntax

Dataset 237. Mezquital Otomí (Mexico)
Phonemic tone is not indicated.

1. Da-ma ra ʔɲëhë.
FUT-go the man
'The man will go.'

2. Da-zëhë ma tʼï.
FUT-arrive 1s son
'My son will arrive.'

3. Nu ra bãtsi go ma tʼï.
that the child BE 1s son
'That child is my son.'

4. Bi-ma.
PST-go
'He went.'

5. Stin-tsʼo ra dãnga ndã.
FUT-bad the big chief
'The big chief will be bad.'

6. Nu ma dãnga tʼï go ri ndã.
that 1s big son BE 2s chief
'That big son of mine is your boss.'

7. Da-ma ma tʼïka tʼï.
FUT-go 1s little son
'My little son will go.'

8. ʃman-tsæ ma bãtsi.
PST-cold 1s child
'My child was cold.'

9. Nu ri tʼï go ra tʼïka ʔɲëhë.
that 2s son BE the little man
'That son of yours is the little man.'

10. Bi-ma ri dãnga bãtsi.
PST-go 2s big child
'Your big child went.'

11. ʃman-tsʼo ra tsæ dehe.
PST-bad the cold water
'The cold water was bad.'

12. Nu ra tsʼo ʔɲëhë go ra dãnga ndã.
that the bad man BE the big chief
'That bad man is the big chief.'

13. Da-ma ri tsʼo bãtsi.
FUT-go 2s bad child
'Your bad child will go.'

Continued

Dataset 237 Continued:

14. Stin-tsæ ra tsˀo dehe.
    FUT-cold the bad water
    'The bad water will be cold.'

15. Bi-zëhë ra dehe.
    PST-arrive the water
    'The water arrived.'

16. ʃman-tsˀæ ra dãnga ndã.
    PST-bad the big chief
    'The big chief was bad.'

17. Nu ra tsæ bãtsi go ri tˀï.
    that the cold child BE 2s son
    'That cold child is your son.'

18. ʃman-tsæ.
    PST-cold
    'It was cold.'

Dataset 238. Nepali

1. Yo kukur ho.	'This is a dog.'
2. Yo kitaab ho.	'This is a book.'
3. Yo gher ho.	'This is a house.'
4. Yo nani ho.	'This is a child.'
5. Yo Thulo kitaab ho.	'This is a big book.'
6. Yo saano kitaab ho.	'This is a small book.'
7. Yo raato kukur ho.	'This is a red dog.'
8. Kitaab saano ho.	'The book is small.'
9. Gher Thulo ho.	'The house is big.'
10. Yo kitaab raato ho.	'This book is red.'
11. Yo gher Thulo ho.	'This house is big.'
12. Raato kitaab Thulo ho.	'The red book is big.'
13. Yo saano kukur kaalo ho.	'This small dog is black.'
14. Nani gher dekhche.	'The child sees the house.'
15. Yo nani Thulo kitaab dekhche.	'This child sees the big book.'
16. Nani yo saano gher dekhche.	'The child sees this small house.'
17. Yo nani kukurlai dekhche.	'This child sees the dog.'
18. Nani saano kukurlai dekhche.	'The child sees the small dog.'
19. Saano kukur Thulo nanilai dekhche.	'The small dog sees the big child.'
20. Yo raato kukur nanilai dekhche.	'This red dog sees the child.

Laboratory Manual for Morphology and Syntax

Dataset 239. English

1. bad — badness
   good — goodness
   big — bigness
   sick — sickness
   thick — thickness

2. bright — brighten
   cheap — cheapen
   dark — darken
   deep — deepen
   thick — thicken

3. glad — gladly
   open — openly
   normal — normally
   sad — sadly
   rhythmical — rhythmically

4. arrive — arrival
   refuse — refusal
   deny — denial
   approve — approval
   reverse — reversal

5. joy — enjoy
   rage — enrage
   trance — entrance
   power — empower
   train — entrain

6. wood — wooden
   earth — earthen
   gold — golden
   wool — woolen
   silk — silken

7. instruct — instructive
   select — selective
   create — creative
   possess — possessive
   prevent — preventive

8. brown — brownish
   small — smallish
   red — reddish
   young — youngish
   big — biggish

9. despot — despotism
   heathen — heathenism
   Mohammedan — Mohammedanism
   Calvin — Calvinism
   McCarthy — McCarthyism

10. day — daily
    hour — hourly
    week — weekly
    month — monthly
    year — yearly

Dataset 240. Turkish

1. ʧaliʃan adam ʧoʤuktan kaʧtɨ.   'The working man ran from the boy.'
2. Kuʃ evde ötüyor.   'The bird is singing in the house.'
3. Büyüyen ʧoʤuk uyuyor.   'The growing boy is sleeping.'
4. Uyuyan kedi agaʧtan düʃtü.   'The sleeping cat fell from the tree.'
5. Düʃen agaʧ kumda büyümüʃtü.   'The falling tree had grown in the sand.'
6. Adam gülüyor.   'The man is laughing.'
7. Ölen kuʃ agaʧta uyudu.   'The singing bird slept in the tree.'
8. Ölen adam ʧaliʃiyordu.   'The dying man was working.'
9. Gülen ʧoʤuk evde ölmüʃtü.   'The laughing boy had died in the house.'
10. Büyüyordu.   'He was growing.'
11. Evden kaʧmiʃti.   'He had fled from the house.'
12. Katʃan adam düʃtü.   'The fleeing man fell.'

Dataset 241. Huave (Mexico)

1. Aaga naʃey taʃip.   'That man got fat.'
2. Aaga nakats nenʧ tahants tiʃem.   'That wet boy washed shrimp.'
3. Tiʃem apmahaw aaga nenʧ.   'The shrimp will see that boy.'
4. Aaga nenʧ apmakats.   'That boy will get wet.'
5. Aaga naʃey tandok nadam kïet.   'That man netted the big fish.'
6. Tahaw nop naʃip nenʧ.   'He saw a fat boy.'
7. Tadam.   'It got big.'
8. Apmahond tiʃem.   'He will dry shrimp.'
9. Aaga naʃey apmaʃip.   'That man will get fat.'
10. Nop naʃip naʃey apmandok kïet.   'A fat man will net fish.'
11. Apmahants nadam tiʃem.   'He will wash the big shrimp.'
12. Apmadam.   'It will get big.'
13. Nop nenʧ tahond kïet.   'A boy dried the fish.'
14. Nop nenʧ takats.   'A boy got wet.'

Laboratory Manual for Morphology and Syntax

Dataset 242. Palantla Chinantec (Mexico)

1. Juen^{12} bøa^3 quiing^2.   'The dry stick will break.'
2. Quián^1 hma^2 jliu^{12}.   'The crooked board will fall.'
3. Táih^1 hma^2 dsøg^{12}.   'The straight board will reach.'
4. Tsa^{1}juen^1 ta^{12}.   'The ladder will not break.'
5. Tsa^{1}quián^1 bøa^3.   'The stick will not fall.'
6. Tsa^{1}táih^1 ta^{12} jliu^{12}.   'The crooked ladder will not reach.'
7. Li^{1}hli^2 hma^2.   'The board will get wet.'
8. Li^{1}quiing^2 hma^2 hli^2.   'The wet board will dry.'
9. Tsa^{1}li^{1}dsøg^{12} ta^{12}.   'The ladder will not straighten.'
10. Tsa^{1}li^{1}jliu^{12} bøa^3 dsøg^{12}.   'The straight stick will not become crooked.'

Dataset 243. Lalana Chinantec (Mexico)
Phonemic tone is not indicated.

1. Kalakwaː kwɨː liːʔ.   'The beautiful corn grew.'
2. Liːʔ kalakwaː kwɨː.   'The corn grew beautifully.'
3. Kalaroːh kwɨː ne.   'The yellow corn ripened.'
4. Dʒö kalane kwɨː kya.   'My corn yellowed well.'
5. Kaladʒö kwɨː.   'The corn turned out well.'
6. Kalaliːʔ kwɨː dʒö.   'The good corn became beautiful.'
7. Dʒö kalaroːh moːh ne kya.   'My yellow pineapples ripened well.'
8. Kaladʒö moːh kya.   'My pineapples turned out well.'
9. Kalane moːh.   'The pineapples became yellow.'
10. Kalaroːh kwɨː kwaː.   'The tall corn became ripe.'
11. Liːʔ kalane kwɨː kwaː kya.   'My tall corn yellowed beautifully.'
12. Mɨlakwaː kwɨː.   'The corn has grown.'
13. Mɨladʒö moːh kya.   'My pineapples have turned out well.'
14. Liːʔ kaʔya kwɨː.   'The corn germinated beautifully.'
15. Kakɨʔn kwɨː roːh.   'The ripe corn fell over.'
16. Mɨʔya kwɨː.   'The corn has germinated.'

Laboratory Manual for Morphology and Syntax

Dataset 244. Rotokas (Papua New Guinea)

1. Vii ikauuei.   'You hurry.'

2. Vii rovouvere.   'You will begin.'

3. Rera iparoepa.   'He ascended.'

4. Rera vararoei.   'He descends.'

5. Ragai iraravere.   'I will precede.'

6. Rera siraorovere.   'He will sorrow.'

7. Vii irauei kepaia.   'You precede to the house.'

8. Ragai vararavere.   'I will descend.'

9. Vii ipauvere voari.   'You will ascend over there.'

10. Rera rovoroei iravira.   'He begins ahead.'

11. Vii siraovira varauepa.   'You descended sorrowfully.'

12. Rera vararoepa iravira.   'He descended ahead.'

13. Ragai rovovira iparaei.   'I ascend at first.'

14. Rera siraovira iraroepa.   'He preceded sorrowfully.'

15. Ragai ikauraepa ipavira.   'I hurried up above.'

16. Ragai siraoraei varavira.   'I sorrow down below.'

17. Vii rovovira siraouepa voari.   'You sorrowed at first over there.'

18. Rera ikauvira ikaurovere kepaia.   'He will hurry quickly to the house.'

19. Ragai rovovira iraravere ipavira.   'I will precede at first up above.'

20. Ragai ikauvira rovoraepa varavira.   'I began quickly down below.'

Dataset 245. Rotokas (Papua New Guinea)

1. Vii opuruva taparivere.   'You will hit a canoe.'
2. Vii papapakepa purariva.   'You made an airplane.'
3. Ragai opuruva kekeavere.   'I will see a canoe.'
4. Vii opuruva kaekaepieriva.   'You lengthened a canoe.'
5. Vii vearo wiliwili kekeriva.   'You saw a good bicycle.'
6. Vii papapakepa riropierivere. 'You will enlarge an airplane.'
7. Ragai papapakepa vuripieava.   'I ruined an airplane.'
8. Ragai opuruva vearopieavere.   'I will improve a canoe.'
9. Ragai riro papapakepa tapaava. 'I hit a big airplane.'
10. Ragai vuri wiliwili puraavere. 'I will make a bad bicycle.'
11. Vii vuri papapakepa vearopieriva. 'You improved a bad airplane.'
12. Vii vearo wiliwili vuripierivere. 'You will ruin a good bicycle.'
13. Ragai kaekae opuruva riropieava. 'I enlarged a long canoe.'
14. Ragai riro wiliwili kaekaepieavere. 'I will lengthen a big bicycle.'

Dataset 246. Sierra Popoluca (Mexico)

1. Ipetpa tʌk.   'He will sweep the house.'
2. Ampetpa tʌk.   'I will sweep the house.'
3. Ihuypa tʌk.   'He will buy the house.'
4. Anhuypa petkuy.   'I will buy the broom.'
5. Anhuyum maʔykuy.   'I bought things to sell.'
6. Ammaʔypa mok.   'I will sell corn.'
7. Imaʔyum haykuy.   'He sold the pen.'
8. Anhaypa to:to.   'I will write a book.'
9. Aŋwatum tʌk.   'I built the house.'
10. Aŋwatpa ɲipkuy.   'I will make a planting stick.'
11. Iɲippa mok.   'He will plant corn.'
12. Aɲɲippa sʌk.   'I will plant beans.'

Dataset 247. Palantla Chinantec (Mexico)

1. Jmé^2 móa^{12}.   'The medicine dissolves.'
2. Nih^{12} mói^2.   'The ball bursts.'
3. Rø^2 jóg^3.   'The argument is settled [smooth].'
4. Léi^{13} jóg^3.   'The word is manifest.'
5. Mi^{2}jmé^2 Dsie^3 móa^{12}.   'Bill dissolves the medicine.'
6. Mi^{2}nih^{12} Ca^{31} mói^2.   'Dick bursts the ball.'
7. Mi^{2}rø^2 Dsie^3 jóg^3.   'Bill settles the argument.'
8. Mi^{2}léi^{13} Ca^{31} jóg^3.   'Dick reveals the word.'

Dataset 248. Rotokas (Papua New Guinea)

1. Rera rovo-ro-ei.
   3s   start-3s-PRES
   'He starts.'

2. Vii vore-u-ei.
   2s return-2s-PRES
   'You return.'

3. Vii kovo-u-epa.
   2s work-2s-PST
   'You work.'

4. Rera wiliwili keke-re-va.
   3s   bicycle see-3s-PST
   'He saw the bicycle.'

5. Vii papapakepa pura-ri-voi.
   2s airplane   make-2s-PRES
   'You make the airplane.'

6. Rera opuruva kae-re-voi.
   3s   canoe   carry-3s-PRES
   'He carries the canoe.'

7. Rera wiliwili rovo-pie-re-va.
   3s   bicycle start-CAUS-3s-PST
   'He started the bicycle.'

8. Vii papapakepa vore-pie-ri-va.
   2s airplane   return-CAUS-2s-PST
   'You made the airplane come back.'

9. Rera opuruva kovo-pie-re-voi.
   3s   canoe   work-CAUS-3s-PRES
   'He uses the canoe.'

Laboratory Manual for Morphology and Syntax

Dataset 249. Tlingit (USA)

1. ʌχ gʌni   χwaxaʃ.
   1s   firewood 1s.sawed.off

   'I sawed off my firewood.'

2. Una χwatʔe.
   gun 1s.found

   'I found a gun.'

3. Qa tʔutʃʔ xʌʃa awʌtʔe.
   man black saw 3s.found

   'A man found a black saw.'

4. Qa gʌn   awʌxaʃ.
   man firewood 3s.sawed.off

   'A man sawed off firewood.'

5. We qa   ʃawʌt awʌgwʌl.
   that man woman 3s.stabbed

   'That man stabbed a woman.

6. We ʃawʌt sʔisa awʌusʔ.
   that woman cloth 3s.washed

   'That woman washed a cloth.'

7. Du dlet   usʔayi awʌtʔe.
   3s white soap   3s.found

   'S/he found his/her white soap.'

8. ʃawʌt we dlet   sʔisa awʌhun.
   woman that white cloth 3s.sold

   'A woman sold that white cloth.'

9. We tʔutʃʔ qa   usʔa awʌhun.
   that black man soap 3s.sold

   'That black man sold soap.'

10. ʌχ xʌʃayi awʌhun.
    1s saw   3s.sold

    'S/he sold my saw.'

11. Tʔutʃʔ gwʌla awʌtʔe.
    black dagger 3s.found

    'S/he found a black dagger.'

12. Du gwʌlayi we qa   awʌdʒʌq.
    3s dagger that man 3s.killed

    'His/her dagger killed that man.'

13. We qa   wacix awʌun.
    that man caribou 3s.shot

    'That man shot a caribou.'

14. ʌχ dlet wacixi ʃawʌt awʌdʒʌq.
    1s white caribou woman 3s.killed

    'My white caribou killed a woman.'

Laboratory Manual for Morphology and Syntax

Dataset 250. Michoacán Nahuatl (Mexico)

1. Ni-kotʃi-k.
   1sSu-sleep-PST
   'I slept'

2. Kotʃi-k   i-ʃolul.
   sleep-PST 3sPo-child
   'His child slept.'

3. Ti-yuli.
   2sSu-live
   'You live.'

4. Yuli mo-siwal.
   live 2sPo-wife
   'Your wife lives.'

5. Netʃ-lamatʃilti-a.
   3sDO-inform-PRES
   'He informs me.'

6. Ki-lamatʃilti-k   no-siwal.
   3sDO-inform-PST 1sPo-wife
   'He informed my wife.'

7. Ti-wehkawa.
   2sSu-endure
   'You endure.'

8. Wehkawa no-tʃikawalisli.
   endure   1sPo-strength
   'My strength holds out.'

9. Ni-lami-k.
   1sSu-end-PST
   'I finished.'

10. Lami mo-lamatʃiltilisli.
    end   2sPo-news
    'Your news ends.'

11. Lami-k i-tʃikawalisli.
    end-PST 3sPO-strength
    'His strength gave out.'

12. Mih-tʃikawa-k.
    2sDO-strengthen-PST
    'He strengthened you.'

13. Ki-tʃikawa.
    3sDO-strengthen
    'He strengthens him.'

14. Ki-tʃikawa   no-ʃolul.
    3sDO-strengthen 1sPo-child
    'He strengthens my child.'

15. Ki-polu-a.
    3sDO-lose-PRES
    'He loses it.'

16. Ki-polu-a   kotʃilisli.
    3sDO-lose-PRES sleep
    'He loses sleep.'

17. Ki-polu-k   i-tʃikawalisli.
    3sDO-lose-PST 3sPo-strength
    'He lost his strength.'

18. Netʃ-wililti-a.
    1sDO-empower-PRES
    'He empowers me.'

19. Mits-wililti-k.
    2sDO-empower-PST
    'He empowered you.'

20. Ki-wililti-a   mo-ʃolul.
    3sDO-empower-PRES 2sPo-child
    'He empowers your child.'

21. Netʃ-neki.
    1sDO-desire
    'He loves me.'

22. Ki-neki   yulilisli.
    3sDO-desire life
    'He wants life.'

23. Ki-neki   i-siwal.
    3sDO-desire 3sPo-wife
    'He loves his wife.'

24. Ki-neki-k   no-wililtilisli.
    3sDO-desire-PST 1sPo-power
    'He wanted my power.'

Dataset 251. Turkish

1. Demir taʃɨdɨ.
   'He carried the iron.'

2. ʃekerdʒiler ʃeker taʃidɨ.
   'The confectioners carried sugar.'

3. tʃifttʃiler tʃiftler taʃidɨ.
   'The farmers carried ploughs.'

4. tʃitʃektʃiden tʃitʃekler taʃidɨ.
   'He carried flowers from the florist.'

5. Demirdʒiler tʃifttʃilerden tʃift taʃidɨ.
   'The smiths carried the plough from the farmers.'

6. tʃitʃektʃi demirdʒilerden tʃitʃek taʃidɨ.
   'The florist carried the flower from the smiths.'

7. Demirdʒi ʃekerdʒiden ʃeker taʃidɨ.
   'The smith carried sugar from the confectioner.'

8. ʃekerdʒi tʃifttʃiden tʃift taʃidɨ.
   'The confectioner carried the plough from the farmer.'

9. tʃitʃektʃiler ʃekerdʒilerden tʃitʃekler taʃidɨ.
   'The florists carried flowers from the confectioners.'

10. tʃifttʃi demirdʒiden demir taʃidɨ.
    'The farmer carried iron from the smith.

Dataset 252. Turkish

1. On adam beʃinʤi günde beʃ elma verdiler.
   'Ten men gave five apples on the fifth day.'

2. Beʃ adam sekiz gün itʃin onunʤu adama elma verdiler.
   'Five men gave apples to the tenth man for eight days.'

3. Dokuz adam beʃimize on elma verdiler.
   'Nine men gave ten apples to five of us.'

4. Adam onumuza beʃer elma verdi.
   'The man gave ten of us five apples apiece.'

5. Sekizinʤi ayda on elma verdi.
   'He gave ten apples in the eighth month.'

6. Dokuzumuza sekizer elma aldɨ.
   'He took nine of us eight apples apiece.'

7. Onunʤu adam dokuz ay itʃin beʃ adama elma verdi.
   'The tenth man gave five men apples for nine months.'

8. Beʃinʤi adam sekizimize elma aldɨ.
   'The fifth man took eight of us apples.'

9. Sekizinʤi adam beʃ elma verdi.
   'The eighth man gave five apples.'

10. Onumuz dokuzunʤu günde adama sekiz elma aldɨk.
    'Ten of us took the man eight apples on the ninth day.'

11. Sekizimiz on ay itʃin onlara dokuzar elma verdik.
    'Eight of us gave them nine apples apiece for ten months.'

12. Dokuzumuz sekiz adama onar elma verdik.
    'Nine of us gave eight men ten apples apiece.'

Dataset 253. English

1. I like to eat ice cream at bedtime.
2. Do you like to eat ice cream at bedtime?
3. When do you like to eat ice cream?
4. What do you like to eat for breakfast?
5. I like to eat banana cream pie for breakfast.
6. I would like some right now.
7. Would you like some now?
8. Who likes chocolate mousse?
9. Which mousse do you like best?
10. Where does a chocolate mousse live during the hunting season?
11. How does he keep out of the sun?
12. How many pounds of mousse can you eat in one sitting?
13. Can you eat two pounds

Dataset 254. Northern Paiute

The Paiute verb is here unmarked for tense and can be translated as either 'see' or 'saw'.

1. Nɨ tɨkabɨ poni.	'I saw the bread.'
2. Nɨ puku poni.	'I saw a horse.'
3. Puku poni.	'Saw a horse (subj unspecified).'
4. Nɨ tauna-wai puku poni.	'I saw a horse in town.'
5. Nɨ idziʔi puku poni.	'I saw a horse yesterday.'
6. Nɨ idziʔi tauna-wai puku poni.	'I saw a horse in town yesterday.'
7. Pukuha poni.	'Did see the horse (subj unspecified)?'
8. Ɨha puku poni.	'Did you see the horse?'
9. Idziʔiha puku poni.	'Yesterday saw the horse (subj unspec.)?'

Dataset 255. Mandarin Chinese

1. Tā lái.	'He is coming.'
2. Tā lái ma.	'Is he coming?'
3. Nǐ lái ma.	'Are you coming?'
4. Tā bù lái.	'He is not coming.'
5. Nǐ lái bù lái.	'Are you coming or not?'
6. Nǐ lái háishi bù lái.	'Are you coming or not?'
7. Tā lái bù lái.	'Is he coming or not?'
8. Tā mǎi shū.	'He buys books.'
9. Nǐ bù kàn shū.	'You do not read books.'
10. Tā mǎi shū bù mǎi shū.	'Does he buy books or not?'
11. Tā mǎi shū bù mǎi.	'Does he buy books or not?'
12. Tā mǎi bù mǎi shū.	'Does he buy books or not?

Dataset 256. Roglai (Vietnam)

1. Kəu nau.	'I go.'
2. Ɲu nau.	'He goes.'
3. Ɲu nau ata.	'He goes far.'
4. Kəu ʔduaːiʔ.	'I run.'
5. Hã ʔduaːiʔ ata.	'You run far.'
6. Hã ʔduaːiʔ suka.	'You run fast.'
7. Ɲu nau luʔ.	'Does he go?'
8. Ɲu ʔduaːiʔ ata luʔ.	'Does he run far?'
9. Hã nau suka luʔ.	'Do you go fast?'
10. ʔduaːiʔ.	'Run!
11. ʔduaːiʔ hã.	'You! Run!
12. Nau suka ɲu.	'He goes fast!
13. Nau.	'Go!
14. Nau ata kəu.	'I go far!

Dataset 257. Huixtec Tzotzil (Mexico)

1. ʧibát té.   'I will go there.'
2. Nibát té.   'I went there.'
3. ʧbát yóʔ.   'He will go to the same place.'
4. ʧkóm yóʔ.   'He will stay in the same place.'
5. Navéʔ yóʔ.   'You ate in the same place.'
6. Bú nabát.   'Where did you go?'
7. Bú ʧikóm.   'Where will I stay?'
8. Bú ʧavéʔ.   'Where will you eat?'

9. Láx yíl ʔíʃim tidóktor té.
PST see corn the.doctor there
'The doctor saw corn there.'

10. Bú láx yíl ʔíʃim tidóktor.
where? PST see corn the.doctor
'Where did the doctor see corn?'

11. Kʼusi láx yíl tidóktor té.
what? PST see the.doctor there
'What did the doctor see there?'

12. Láx yál mántal tiprésidentee.
PST say command the.president
'The president gave a command.'

13. Bú láx yál mántal tiprésidentee.
where? PST say command the.president
'Where did the president give a command?'

14. Kʼusi láx yál tiprésidentee.
what? PST say the.president
'What did the president say?'

Dataset 258. Palantla Chinantec (Mexico)

1. Dság¹ Juøn¹³ jø³juøi² hiá¹.
   go.3s John town tomorrow
   'John will go to town tomorrow.'

2. Dság¹ Juøn¹³ jø³juøi² jmai³ Sa³¹.
   go.3s John town day Saturday
   'John will go to town on Saturday.'

3. Dság⁴¹ Juøn¹³ jø³juøi² hiá¹.
   go.3s? John town tomorrow
   'Will John go to town tomorrow?'

4. Ha²tøah¹ dság¹ Juøn¹³ hiá¹.
   where? go.3s John tomorrow
   'Where will John go tomorrow?'

5. Ha²løih² dság¹ Juøn¹³ jø³juøi².
   When? go.3s John town
   'When will John go to town?'

6. He² jmai³ dság¹ Juøn¹³ jø³juøi².
   what? day go.3s John town
   'What day will John go to town?'

7. He²løa¹ dság¹ Juøn¹³ jø³juøi² hiá¹.
   Why? go.3s John town tomorrow
   'Why will John go to town tomorrow?'

8. Dság¹ Juøn¹³ jø³juøi² hiá¹ dih³ hniu¹ dsa láh¹jøng².
   go.3s John town tomorrow because want 3 thus
   'John will go to town tomorrow because he wants to.'

9. Hein² dság¹ jø³juøi² hiá¹.
   who? go.3s town tomorrow
   'Who will go to town tomorrow?'

10. Hein² quianh¹³ dság¹ Juøn¹³ jø³juøi² hiá¹.
    who? with go.3s John town tomorrow
    'With whom will John go to town tomorrow?'

11. Dság¹ Juøn¹³ jø³juøi² hiá¹ quianh¹³ og¹ hlég².
    go.3s John town tomorrow with two soldiers
    'John will go to town tomorrow with two soldiers.'

12. Ha¹cónh² hlég² dsø¹lén² jø³juøi² hiá¹ quianh¹³ Juøn¹³.
    how.many? soldier go.3p town tomorrow with John
    'How many soldiers will go to town tomorrow with John?'

Laboratory Manual for Morphology and Syntax

Dataset 259. Vietnamese

Data from Ken Gregerson; Orthography from Nguyen Dinh Hoa. 1967.
Vietnamese-English Student Dictionary. Southern Illinois University Press.

1. Toy di cë.
   1s go market
   'I am going to market.'

2. Toy thʌy kɔn gay.
   1s see CLS girl
   'I see the girl.'

3. Toy an sway.
   1s eat mango
   'I am eating a mango.'

4. Kɔn gay xʌwŋ an sway.
   CLS girl NEG eat mango
   'The girl is not eating a mango.'

5. Toy xʌwŋ thʌy ka.
   1s NEG see fish
   'I do not see any fish.'

6. Kɔn gay xʌwŋ di cë.
   CLS girl NEG go market
   'The girl is not going to the market.'

7. Kɔn gay di cë xʌwŋ.
   CLS girl go market NEG
   'Is the girl going to the market?'

8. Kɔn gay thʌy sway xʌwŋ.
   CLS girl see mango NEG
   'Does the girl see the mango?'

9. Kɔn gay an ka xʌwŋ.
   CLS girl eat fish NEG
   'Is the girl eating fish?'

Laboratory Manual for Morphology and Syntax

Dataset 260. Vietnamese

Data from Ken Gregerson; Orthography from Nguyen Dinh Hoa. 1967.
Vietnamese-English Student Dictionary. Southern Illinois University Press.

1. Kɔn gay thʌy kɔn tray.
   CLS girl see CLS boy
   'The girl sees the boy.'

2. Kɔn gay an sway.
   CLS girl eat mango
   'The girl ate the mango.'

3. Kɔn gay thʌy ay.
   CLS girl see who?
   'Who did the girl see?'

4. Ay thʌy kɔn gay.
   who? see CLS girl
   'Who saw the girl?'

5. Ay an sway.
   who? eat mango
   'Who ate the mango?'

6. Kɔn gay an kayzi.
   CLS girl eat what?
   'What did the girl eat?'

7. Kɔn gay di cë ngay hom nay.
   CLS girl go market today
   'The girl went to market today.'

8. Kɔn gay di cë xi naw.
   CLS girl go market when?
   'When did the girl go to market?'

9. Kɔn gay di dʌw.
   CLS girl go where?
   'Where did the girl go?'

Dataset 261. Northern Kankanay (Philippines)

1. Nin?awit nan lalaki is ɨwɨs.
   carried   man   blanket
   'The man carried a blanket.'

2. Ay nin?awit nan lalaki is ɨwɨs.
   ? carried   man   blanket
   Did the man carry a blanket?'

3. Sino nan naŋ?awit is ɨwɨs.
   who?   carried   blanket
   'Who carried a blanket?'

4. Ay sino nan naŋ?awit is ɨwɨs.
   ? who?   carried   blanket
   'Who carried a blanket?'

5. Sino nan baba?i.
   who?   woman
   'Who is that woman?'

6. ?inawit nan lalaki nan ɨwɨs.
   carried   man   blanket
   'The man carried a blanket.'

7. Ŋan nan ?inawit nan lalaki.
   what?   carried   man
   'What did the man carry?'

8. Ay ŋan nan ?inawit nan lalaki.
   ? what?   carried   man
   'What did the man carry?'

9. Binadaŋan nan lalaki id kob?a.
   helped   man   yesterday
   'The man helped yesterday.'

10. Ɨg?an nan binadaŋan nan lalaki.
    when?   helped   man
    'When did the man help?'

11. ?inmayan nan lalaki id ba?ɨy.
    went   man   house
    'The man went into the house.'

12. Into nan ?inmayan nan lalaki.
    where?   went   man
    'Where did the man go?'

13. Into nan ɨwɨs.
    where?   blanket
    'Where is the blanket?'

Dataset 262. Urim (Papua New Guinea)

1. Weti kiɲ   antam wayu kai wri.
   today woman cooked taro   at   garden
   'The woman cooked taro in the garden today.'

2. Weti mla antam wayu kai wri.
   today who? cooked taro   at   garden
   'Who cooked taro in the garden today?'

3. Weti kiɲ   antam   kuɲa   kai wri.
   today woman cooked what? at   garden
   'What did the woman cook in the garden today?'

4. Weti kiɲ   antam wayu kai ahi.
   today woman cooked taro   at where?
   'Where did the woman cook taro today?'

5. Wa karke kiɲ   antam wayu kai wri.
   when?   woman cooked taro   at   garden
   'When did the woman cook taro in the garden?'

6. Kiɲ   wek antam wayu.
   woman two cooked taro
   'Two women cooked taro.'

7. Kiɲ   aripm   antam wayu.
   woman how.many? cooked taro
   'How many women cooked taro?'

8. Kiɲ   ari manto numpet wek.
   woman saw pig   sick   two
   'The woman saw two sick pigs.'

9. Kiɲ   ari manto numpet aripm.
   woman saw pig   sick   how.many?
   'How many sick pigs did the woman see?'

10. Kiɲ   ari manto kuɲa   wek.
    woman saw pig   what? two
    'Which two pigs did the woman see?'

Laboratory Manual for Morphology and Syntax

Dataset 263. English

1. I admire the gal who likes chocolate mousse.
2. I admire the moose which hid throughout the hunting season.
3. I admire the gal (whom) you saw with the chocolate mousse.
4. I admire the food (which) you eat for breakfast.
5. I admire the gal whose chocolate mousse you ate.
6. I admire the gal whom you ate chocolate mousse with.
7. I admire the gal with whom you ate chocolate mousse.
8. I admire the gal whom you gave chocolate mousse (to).
9. I admire the gal to whom you gave chocolate mousse.
10. I admire the gal that likes chocolate mousse.
11. I admire the moose that hid throughout the hunting season.
12. I admire the gal (that) you saw with the chocolate mousse.
13. I admire the food (that) you eat for breakfast.
    *I admire the gal that's chocolate mousse you ate.
14. I admire the gal (that) you ate chocolate mousse with.
    *I admire the gal with that you ate chocolate mousse.
15. I admire the gal (that) you gave chocolate mousse (to).
    *I admire the gal to (that) you gave chocolate mousse.

Dataset 264. English

This is the farmer sowing his corn
that kept the cock that crowed in the morn
that waked the priest all shaven and shorn
that married the man all tattered and torn
that kissed the maiden all forlorn
that milked the cow with the crumpled horn
that tossed the dog
that worried the cat
that killed the rat
that ate the malt
that lay in the house
that Jack built.

Dataset 265. Colorado (Ecuador)

1. Sona   hi-e.
woman went-DECL
'The woman went.'

2. Sona   watsa fari-e.
woman fish requested-DECL
'The woman asked for fish.'

3. Manpi watsa fi-ka ho-e.
uncle fish   eaten BE-DECL
'Uncle has eaten fish.'

4. Manpi sana kutsu   fi-e.
uncle raw cassava ate-DECL
'Uncle ate the raw cassava.'

5. Uwan miya na-ka   neya-e.
tall   chief child-ACC sought-DECL
'The tall chief looked for the child.'

6. Kutsu fi-min   sona   ha-e.
cassava eat-NOM woman came-DECL
'The woman who ate the cassava came.'

7. Tsatsika fi-min   hi-e.
meat   eat-NOM went-DECL
'The one who ate meat departed.'

8. Ha-min   na   kutsu   fari-e.
come-NOM child cassava requested-DECL
'The child who came asked for cassava.'

9. Unila watsa fi-min   na-ka   neya-e.
man fish eat-NOM child-ACC sought-DECL
'The man looked for the child who had eaten the fish.'

10. Na-ka   neya-min unila sona   fi-ka ho-n watsa fari-e.
child-ACC seek-NOM man woman eaten BE   fish requested-DECL
'The man who looked for the child asked for the fish which the woman had eaten.'

11. Unila sona   neya-ka ho-n-ka kira-e.
man   woman sought BE-ACC saw-DECL
'The man saw the one for whom the woman had looked.'

12. Miya sona   neya-ka ho-n unila-ka neya-e.
chief woman sought BE   man-ACC sought-DECL
'The chief looked for the man for whom the woman had looked.'

13. Sona   kira-ka ho-n miya ha-e.
woman seen   BE   chief came-DECL
'The chief whom the woman had seen came.'

Laboratory Manual for Morphology and Syntax

Dataset 266. Vietnamese (Part 1)

1. Tôi mua xoài.
   1s buy mango
   'I bought a mango.'

2. Cô gái ấy đã ăn xoài.
   CLS girl that PST eat mango
   'That girl ate a mango.'

3. Xoài đó là xoài thật lớn.
   mango that BE mango really big.
   'That mango is really big.'

4. Trái xoài lớn đó là xoài thối.
   CLS mango big that BE mango rotten.
   'That big mango is rotten.'

5. Cô gái ấy là cô gái thật xinh-đẹp.
   CLS girl that BE CLS girl really pretty
   'That girl is really pretty.'

6. Cô gái xinh-đẹp ấy đã ăn trái xoài lớn đó
   CLS girl pretty that PST eat CLS mango big that
   'That pretty girl ate that big mango.'

7. Cô gái đã ăn xoài là cô gái thật xinh-đẹp.
   CLS girl PST eat mango BE CLS girl really pretty
   'The girl who ate the mango is a really pretty girl.'

8. Trái xoài cô gái đã ăn là xoài thật lớn.
   CLS mango CLS girl PST eat BE mango really big.
   'The mango that the girl ate is a really big mango.'

9. Trái xoài mà cô gái đã ăn là xoài thật lớn.
   CLS mango REL CLS girl PST eat BE mango really big.
   'The mango that the girl ate is a really big mango.'

10. Trái xoài mà cô gái ấy đã ăn là xoài thối.
    CLS mango REL CLS girl that PST eat BE mango rotten.
    'The mango that that girl ate is a rotten mango.'

11. Tôi ăn xoài cô gái ấy đã mua.
    1s eat mango CLS girl that PST buy
    'I ate the mango that that girl bought.'

12. Tôi đã ăn xoài mà cô gái xinh-đẹp ấy mua.
    1s PST eat mango REL CLS girl pretty that buy
    'I ate the mango that that pretty girl bought.'

    *Cô gái mà đã ăn xoài là cô gái thật xinh-đẹp.
    CLS girl REL PST eat mango BE CLS girl really pretty
    'The girl who ate the mango is a really pretty girl.'

    *Cô gái là cô gái xinh-đẹp đã ăn xoài.
    CLS girl BE CLS girl pretty PST eat mango
    'That girl who is pretty ate the mango.'

Dataset 266. Vietnamese (Part 2)

13. Anh đã tặng tôi món quà.
    2s PST give 1s CLS gift
    'You gave me a gift.'

14. Món quà mà anh đã tặng tôi là quà thật lớn.
    CLS gift REL 2s PST give 1s BE gift really big
    'The gift that you gave me is a really big gift.'

15. Cô gái anh đã tặng quà là cô gái thật xinh-đẹp.
    CLS girl 2s PST give gift BE CLS girl really pretty
    'The girl that you gave a gift to is a very pretty girl.'

16. Cô gái mà anh đã tặng quà là cô gái thật xinh-đẹp.
    CLS girl REL 2s PST give gift BE CLS girl really pretty
    'The girl that you gave a gift to is a very pretty girl.'

17. Cô gái đã tặng anh món quà đó thích anh.
    CLS girl PST give 2s CLS gift that like 2s
    'The girl who gave you that gift likes you.'

18. Tôi thích cô gái đã tặng anh món quà đó.
    1s like CLS girl PST give 2s CLS gift that
    'I like the girl who gave you that gift.'

19. Tôi đã để xoài trong cái hộp mà anh đã tặng tôi.
    1s PST put mango in CLS box that 2s PST give 1s
    'I put the mango in the box that you gave me.'

20. Cái hộp tôi đã để xoài là cái hộp thật lớn.
    CLS box 1s PST put mango BE CLS box really big
    'The box I put the mango in is really large.'

21. Cái hộp nơi tôi đã để xoài là cái hộp thật lớn.
    CLS box place 1s PST put mango BE CLS box really big
    'The box I put the mango in is really large.'

    *Tôi thích cô gái mà đã tặng anh món quà đó.
    1s like CLS girl REL PST give 2s CLS gift that
    'I like the girl who gave you that gift.'

    *Cái hộp mà tôi đã để xoài là cái hộp thật lớn.
    CLS box REL 1s PST put mango BE CLS box really big
    'The box I put the mango in is really large.'

    *Cái hộp mà nơi tôi đã để xoài là cái hộp thật lớn.
    CLS box REL place 1s PST put mango BE CLS box really big
    'The box I put the mango in is really large.'

Laboratory Manual for Morphology and Syntax

Dataset 267. Northern Kankanay (Philippines)

1. Nin?awit nan lalaki.
   carried   man
   'The man carried (it).'

2. Nin?awit nan lalaki is ɨwɨs.
   carried   man   blanket
   'The man carried a blanket.'

3. Nin?awit nan lalaki is ɨwɨs   isnan ba?ɨy.
   carried   man   blanket   house
   'The man carried a blanket into the house.'

4. ?inawit nan lalaki nan ɨwɨs   isnan ba?ɨy.
   carried   man   blanket   house
   'The man carried the blanket into the house.'

5. ?inawit nan lalaki nan ɨwɨs   isnan baba?i.
   carried   man   blanket   woman
   'The man carried the blanket to the woman.'

6. Ninbadang nan lalaki.
   helped   man
   'The man helped.'

7. Nintimpak nan lalaki is onga.
   slapped   man   child
   'The man slapped a child.'

8. Binadang nan lalaki nan onga.
   helped   man   child
   'The man helped the child.'

9. Ninbadang nan lalaki ay nangtimpak isnan baba?i.
   helped   man   slapped   woman
   'The man who slapped the woman helped.'

10. Ninbadang nan lalaki ay nangdayaw isnan baba?i is onga.
    helped   man   praised   woman   child
    'The man who praised the woman helped a child.'

11. Ninbadang nan lalaki ay dinayaw nan baba?i.
    helped   man   praised   woman
    'The man whom the woman praised helped.'

12. Ninbadang nan lalaki ay tinimpak nan baba?i is onga.
    helped   man   slapped   woman   child
    'The man whom the woman slapped helped a child.'

13. Binadang nan lalaki ay nangtimpak isnan baba?i nan onga.
    helped   man   slapped   woman   child
    'The man who slapped the woman helped the child.'

Continued

Dataset 267 continued:

14. Binadang nan lalaki ay tinimpak nan baba?i nan onga.
    helped   man   slapped   woman   child
    'The man whom the woman slapped helped the child.'

15. Dinayaw nan baba?i nan lalaki ay nangbadang isnan onga.
    praised   woman   man   helped   child
    'The woman praised the man who helped the child.'

16. Tinimpak nan baba?i nan onga ay binadang nan lalaki.
    slapped   woman   child   helped   man
    'The woman slapped the child whom the man helped.'

17. Nindayaw nan gawis ay baba?i is onga.
    praised   good   woman   child
    'The good woman praised a child.'

18. Dinayaw nan baba?i nan onga ay gawis ay nangbadang isnan lalaki.
    praised   woman   child   good   helped   man
    'The woman praised the good child who helped the man.'

19. Gawis nan onga.
    good   child
    'The child is good.'

20. Ninbadang nan gawis ay onga.
    helped   good   child
    'The good child helped.'

21. Ninbadang nan onga ay gawis.
    helped   child   good
    'The child who is good helped.'

22. Lalaki nan nangdayaw isnan onga.
    man   praised   child
    'The praiser of the child is a man.'

23. Baba?i nan tinimpak nan lalaki.
    woman   slapped   man
    '[She whom] the man slapped is a woman.'

24. Onga nan nangbadang.
    child   helped
    '[The one who] helped is a child.'

25. Onga nan gawis ay nangbadang.
    child   good   helped
    'The good helper is a child.'

26. Onga nan nangbadang ay gawis.
    child   helped   good
    '[The one who] helped well is a child.'

Dataset 268. Rotokas (Papua New Guinea)

1. Vii ipa-u-vere.
   2s ascend-2s-FUT
   'You will go up.'

2. Voea ava-a-vere.
   3p   go-3p-FUT
   'They will go.'

3. Reitai vore-ro-epa.
   Reitai come.back-3sm-PST
   'Reitai came back.'

4. Ragai kare-ra-epa   voa.
   1s   return-1s-PST here
   'I returned here.'

5. Rera ikau-ro-epa   kepaia.
   3sm hurry-3sm-PST house
   'He hurried to the house.'

6. Ipa-ro-epa   rera ira urio-ro-vere.
   ascend-3sm-PST 3sm 3sm come-3sm-FUT
   'He who will come went up.'

7. Urio-ro-epa   reitai ira ikau-ro-vere   kepaia.
   come-3sm-PST Reitai 3sm hurry-3sm-FUT house
   'Reitai who will hurry to the house came.'

8. Ava-ra-epa kepaia ragai ragoa vara-ra-epa.
   go-1s-PST house 1s   1s   decend-1s-PST
   'I who went down went to the house.'

9. Vore-a-vere   voa voea oea kare-a-vere   kepaia.
   come.back-3p-FUT here 3p   3p return-3p-FUT house
   'They who will return to the house will come back here.'

10. Kare-u-vere   kepaia vii viigoa vore-u-vere   voa.
    return-2s-FUT house 2s 2s   come.back-2s-FUT here
    'You who will come back here will return to the house.'

Dataset 269. Rotokas (Papua New Guinea)

1. Oira rera-ia   sirao-o-epa.
   3sf 3sm-ACC sorrow-3sf-PST
   'She sorrowed for him.'

2. Rera voea-ia tarai-ro-epa.
   3sm 3p-ACC know-3sm-PST
   'He knew them.'

3. Voea oira-ia siposipo-a-vere.
   3p   3sf-ACC teach-3p-FUT
   'They will teach her.'

4. Voea tarai-a-epa   oira-ia iria rera-ia   sirao-o-vere.
   3p   know-3p-PST 3sf-ACC 3sf 3sm-ACC sorrow-3sf-FUT
   'They knew her who will sorrow for him.'

5. Rera uriri-ro-vere rera-ia   ira voea-ia tarai-ro-epa
   3sm fear-3sm-FUT 3sm-ACC 3sm 3p-ACC know-3sm-PST
   'He will fear him who knew them.'

6. Voea sirao-a-vere   rera-ia   ira-ia   sirao-ro-vere   rera.
   3p   sorrow-3p-FUT 3sm-ACC 3sm-ACC sorrow-3sm-FUT 3sm
   'They will sorrow for him for whom he will sorrow.'

7. Oira tarai-o-vere   voea-ia oea-ia uriri-ro-epa rera.
   3sf know-3sf-FUT 3p-ACC 3p-ACC fear-3s-PST 3sm
   'She will know them whom he feared.'

8. Voea uriri-a-epa oira-ia iria-ia siposipo-o-epa oira.
   3p   fear-3p-PST 3sf-ACC 3sf-ACC teach-3sf-PST   3sf
   'They feared her whom she taught.'

9. Rera sirao-ro-vere   voea-ia oea oira-ia siposipo-a-vere.
   3sm sorrow-3sm-FUT 3p-ACC 3p 3sf-ACC teach-3p-FUT
   'He will sorrow for them who will teach her.'

10. Rera siposipo-ro-epa oira-ia iria-ia tarai-a-vere   voea.
    3sm teach-3sm-PST 3sf-ACC 3sf-ACC know-3p-FUT 3p
    'He taught her whom they will know.'

11. Voea-ia siposipo-o-vere oira iria-ia sirao-ro-vere   rera.
    3p-ACC teach-3sf-FUT   3sf 3sf-ACC sorrow-3sm-FUT 3sm
    'She for whom he will sorrow will teach them.'

12. Rera-ia   uriri-a-epa voea oea rera-ia   tarai-a-epa.
    3sm-ACC fear-3p-PST 3p 3p 3sm-ACC know-3p-PST
    'They who knew him feared him.'

Laboratory Manual for Morphology and Syntax

Dataset 270. Japanese

1. Josei   ga kita.
   woman   came
   'The woman came.'

2. Kodomo ga hon o miru.
   child   book   see
   'The child sees the book.'

3. Josei   ga kodomo ni okashi o motteitta.
   woman   child   cake   carried
   'The woman took the child a cake.'

4. Dansei ga yoi   okashi o mitsuketa.
   man   good cake   found
   'The man found the good cake.'

5. Dansei ga kita   ka.
   man   came
   'Did the man come?'

6. Dono kodomo ga kita   ka.
   which child   came
   'Which child came?'

7. Chiisai kodomo ga okashi o totta ka.
   small   child   cake   took
   'Did the small child take the cake?'

8. Josei   ga dono kodomo ga kita   ka o mita.
   woman   which child   came   saw
   'The woman saw which child came.'

9. Kodomo ga josei   ga mitsuketa hon o mita.
   child   woman   found   book saw
   'The child saw the book the woman found.'

10. Dansei ga hon   o mitsuketa josei   o mita.
    man   book found   woman   saw
    'The man saw the woman who found the book.'

11. Kodomo ga josei   ga dono okashi o totta ka o mita.
    child   woman   which cake   took   saw
    'The child saw which cake the woman took.'

12. Dansei ga yoi   kodomo ni okashi o motteitta ka.
    man   good child   cake   carried
    'Did the man take the good child a cake?'

13. Dansei ga hon o totta josei   ni okashi o ageta.
    man   book took woman   cake   gave
    'The man gave the cake to the woman who took the book.'

Continued

Dataset 270 continued:

14. Dare ga kita   ka.
    who   came
    'Who came?'

15. Dare ga kodomo o mita ka.
    who   child   saw
    'Who saw the child?'

16. Kodomo ga nani o mita ka.
    child   what   saw
    'What did the child see?'

17. Josei ga dare ni okashi o ageta ka.
    woman   who   cake   gave
    'To whom did the woman give the cake?'

18. Josei ga dare ga kita   ka o mita.
    woman   who   came   saw
    'The woman saw who came.'

19. Josei ga kodomo ga nani o mitsuketa ka o mita.
    woman   child   what   found   saw
    'The woman saw what the child found.'

20. Josei ga kodomo ga okashi o ageta dansei o mita.
    woman   child   cake   gave   man   saw
    'The woman saw the man to whom the child gave the cake.'

21. Dansei ga dare ga kita   ka o mita ka.
    man   who   came   saw
    'Did the man see who came?'

22. Dansei ga kodomo ga nani o totta ka o mita ka.
    man   child   what   took   saw
    'Did the man see what the child took?'

23. Josei   ga kodomo ga dare ni hon o motteitta ka o mita ka.
    woman   child   who   book   carried   saw
    'Did the woman see to whom the child took the book?'

24. Okashi o mitsuketa dansei ga hon o totta.
    cake   found   man   book   took
    'The man who found the cake took the book.'

25. Dansei ga kodomo ga josei ni motteitta okashi o mita.
    man   child   woman   carried   cake   saw
    'The man saw the cake the boy took to the woman.'

26. Kodomo ga okashi o motteitta dansei ga kita.
    child   cake   carried   man   came
    'The man to whom the boy took the cake came.'

27. Dansei ga kodomo ga dare ni hon o motteitta ka o mita.
    man   child   who   book   carried   saw
    'The man saw to whom the child took the book.'

Laboratory Manual for Morphology and Syntax

Dataset 271. Mandarin Chinese

1. Bǎolì mài shū.
   Baoli sell book
   'Baoli sells books.'

2. Wǒ xǐhuān yifú.
   1s enjoy clothes
   'I enjoy clothes.'

3. Nǐ kàn shū.
   2s read book
   'You read books.'

4. Shū yǒu yìsi.
   book have meaningful
   'Books are meaningful.'

5. Yīfú hěn guì.
   clothes very expensive
   'Clothes are very expensive.'

6. Bǎolì hěn hǎo.
   baoli very good
   'Baoli is very nice.'

7. Bǎolì xǐhuān hěn hǎo de yīfú.
   baoli enjoy very good of clothes
   'Baoli enjoys very good clothes.'

8. Wǒ mài bǎolì de shū.
   1s sell baoli of book
   'I am selling Baoli's books.'

9. Wǒ de shū yǒu yìsi.
   1s of book have meaningful
   'My books are meaningful.'

10. Nǐ de hěn guìde yīfú hěn hǎo.
    1s of very expensive clothes very good
    'Your very expensive clothes are very good.'

11. Bǎolì màide shū hěn hǎo.
    baoli sell book very good
    'The books Baoli sells are very good.'

12. Wǒ xǐhuān nǐ kànde shū.
    1s enjoy 2s read book
    'I enjoy the books you read.'

13. Nǐ kàn yǒu yìsi de shū.
    2s study have meaning of book
    'You study books which are meaningful.'

Dataset 272. Copainalá Zoque (Mexico)

1. Minba.
   'He comes.'

2. Ho?pit minu.
   'He came next day.'

3. Homih nu?kpa yʌy.
   'He will arrive here tomorrow.'

4. Homih tsu?kumyahpa.
   'They will set out tomorrow.'

5. Ki?mu?k nu?kyahu ?ʌmʌ.
   'They arrived there when he went up.'

6. Minyahpa?k tsu?kumba.
   'He will set out when they come.'

7. Minba?k nu?kyahpa yʌy.
   'They will arrive here when he comes.'

8. Nu?kyahu?k ?ʌmʌ minu.
   'He came when they arrived there.'

9. Minyahu nu?kpamʌy.
   'They came to where he will arrive.'

10. Ki?myahpa tsu?kumbamʌy homih.
    'They will go up to where he will set out tomorrow.'

11. Ho?pit nu?ku ki?mumʌy.
    'Next day he arrived where he went up.'

Dataset 273. Southern Barasano (Colombia)
Phonemic stress is not indicated.

1. Ehabɨ yɨ.   'I arrived.'
2. Tɨdibɨ bĩ.   'You returned.'
3. Wabetibõ tso.   'She did not go.'
4. Tsore ĩabɨ bĩ.   'You saw her.'
5. Wadibetibĩ ĩ.   'He did not come.'
6. Ĩre bãtsibɨ yɨ.   'I knew of him.'
7. Bĩre gotibõ tso.   'She told of you.'
8. Yɨre ahibetibĩ ĩ.   'He did not hear of me.'
9. Yɨ wasere gotibɨ bĩ.   'You told that I went.'
10. Tso wadibetire ahibɨ yɨ. 'I heard that she did not come.'
11. Ĩ tɨdisere ĩabetibõ tso. 'She did not see that he returned.'
12. Bĩ ehabetire bãtsibetibĩ ĩ. 'He did not know that you did not arrive.'

Laboratory Manual for Morphology and Syntax

Dataset 274. Palantla Chinantec (Mexico)

1. Ŋó^{12}=dsa.
   go   3
   'He goes.'

2. Ŋó^{12}=dsa máh^2.
   go   3   mountain
   'He goes to the mountain.'

3. Guǿ^{12} guiuh^{13} máh^2.
   sit   Sir   mountain
   'The gentleman lives on the mountain.'

4. Dsiég^{12}=dsa máh^2.
   arrive   3   mountain
   'He arrives at the mountain.'

5. Dsiég^{12}=dsa ja^3 guǿ^{12} guiuh^{13}.
   arrive   3   where sit   Sir
   'He arrives where the gentleman lives.'

6. Guǿ^{12}=dsa.
   sit   3
   'He is at home.'

7. Jŋie^{12}=dsa ja^3 dsiég^{12}=dsa máh^2.
   rest   3   where arrive   3   mountain
   'He rests where he arrives on the mountain.'

8. Guǿ^{12} guiuh^{13} ja^3 jŋie^{12}=dsa.
   sit   Sir   where rest   3
   'The gentleman lives where he rests.'

9. Ŋáh^{12} =dsa.
   go.back   3
   'He returns home.'

Dataset 275. Palantla Chinantec (Mexico)

1. Gǿah¹   =dsa.
   will.eat 3
   'He will eat.'

2. Ca¹-co¹ tsih².
   PST-play child
   'The child played.'

3. Co¹   =dsa na¹.
   will.play 3   today
   'He will play today.'

4. Ca¹-gǿah¹ guiuh¹³ dsiég².
   PST-eat   Sir   yesterday
   'The gentleman ate yesterday.'

5. Ca¹-gǿah¹=dsa mi³   ca¹-co¹   =dsa.
   PST-eat   3   when PST-will.play 3
   'He ate when he had played.'

6. Co¹   tsih² na³ ca¹-gǿah¹ tsih².
   will.play child when PST-eat   child
   'The child will play when he has eaten.'

7. Gǿah¹   guiuh¹³ na³   ca-¹co¹   =dsa na¹.
   will.eat Sir   when PST-play 3   today
   'The gentleman will eat when he has played today.'

8. Ca¹-co¹ =dsa mi³   ca¹-gǿah¹=dsa dsiég².
   PST-play 3   when PST-eat   3   yesterday
   'He played when he had eaten yesterday.'

9. Co¹   =dsa na³ ca¹-gǿah¹ tsih² na¹.
   will.play 3   when PST-eat   child today
   'He will play when the child has eaten today.'

Dataset 276. Pocomchí (Guatemala)

1. A-kʼuʃum.
   2s-eat
   'You eat.'

2. Ri-kʼulik.
   3s-arrive
   'He arrives.'

3. Hat a-loqʼ.
   2s 2s-buy
   'You buy.'

4. Ihin ni-kʼamam.
   1s 1s-work
   'I work.'

5. A-kʼamam tʃi= a-kʼuʃum.
   2s-work that 2s-eat
   'You work to eat.'

6. Reʔ ri-loqʼ tʃi= ri-kʼuʃum.
   3s 3s-buy that 3s-eat
   'He buys to eat.'

7. Ri-loqʼ tʃi= hat a-loqʼ.
   3s-buy that 2s 2s-buy
   'He buys so you buy.'

8. A-kʼulik tʃi= ihin ni-kʼamam.
   2s-arrive that 1s   1s-work
   'You arrive so I work.'

9. Ihin ni-kʼuʃum tʃi= reʔ ri-kʼamam.
   1s 1s-eat   that 3s 3s-work
   'I eat so he works.'

10. Ni-loqʼ tʃi= a-kʼuʃum tʃi= a-kʼamam tʃi= a-kʼulik
    1s-buy that 2s-eat   that 2s-work   that 2s-arrive

       tʃi= ihin ni-kʼulik tʃi=   ...
       that 1s   1s-arrive that
    'I buy so that you eat so that you work so that you arrive so that I arrive so that ...'

Dataset 277. Palantla Chinantec (Mexico)

1. Júh^{2}dsa.   'He coughs.'

2. Ŋǿi^{2}jni.   'I laugh.'

3. Ca^{1}cuú^{2}dsa.   'He sneezed.'

4. Ca^{1}ho^{1}dsa.   'He cried.'

5. Ho^{12}jni huu^{13} júh^{2}jni.   'I cry because I cough.'

6. Cuú^{2}jni huu^{13} cuú^{2}dsa.   'I sneeze because he sneezes.'

7. Ŋǿi^{2}dsa huu^{13} ca^{1}ho^{1}jni.   'He laughs because I cried.'

8. Ca^{1}júh^{2}dsa huu^{13} ca^{1}ŋǿi^{2}dsa. 'He coughed because he laughed.'

9. Cuú^{2}jni huu^{13} ca^{1}ho^{1}jni huu^{13} ca^{1}ŋǿi^{2}jni.

10. Cuú^{2}dsa huu^{13} ŋǿi^{2}jni huu^{13} ho^{12}dsa huu^{13} ho^{12}jni huu^{13} ca^{1}ŋǿi^{2}dsa huu^{13} ca^{1}cuú^{2}jni huu^{13} ca^{1}júh^{2}jni huu^{13} ca^{1}ŋǿi^{2}dsa huu^{13}...

Dataset 278. English

1. I know who likes chocolate mousse.
2. I know what you eat for breakfast.
3. I know which cereal you eat for breakfast.
4. I know how much cereal you eat for breakfast.
5. I know how many pounds of mousse you eat in one sitting.
6. I know how he keeps out of the sun.
7. I know why he hides during hunting season.
8. I remember the time when we used to eat ice cream together.
9. I remember the time we used to eat ice cream together.
10. I remember when we used to eat ice cream together.
11. I know a place where a chocolate mousse lives.
12. I know a place a chocolate mousse lives.
13. I know where a chocolate mousse lives.
14. I know (that) you like to eat ice cream at bedtime.
15. I marvel that you like to eat banana cream pie for breakfast.
16. That you would like some right now amazes me.

Dataset 279. Lalana Chinantec (Mexico)
Phonemic tone is not indicated.

1. Haːn hmiː.
   old   father.3
   'His father is old.'

2. ʤuhn ʃiːʔ.
   good boy
   'The boy is good.'

3. ʣoːʔ mɨh.
   sick woman
   'The woman is sick.'

4. Ɲi hmiː ʃi ʤuhn ʃiːʔ.
   'His father knows whether the boy is good.'

5. Hoː mɨh ʃi ʣoːʔ hmiː.
   'The woman sees whether her father is sick.'

6. Ɲi ʃiːʔ ʃi haːn mɨh.
   'The boy knows whether the woman is old.'

7. Hoː mɨh ʔe ʤuhn ʃiːʔ.
   'The woman sees that the boy is good.'

8. Hoː hmiː ʔe haːn mɨh.
   'His father sees that the woman is old.'

9. Ɲi ʃiːʔ ʔe ʣoːʔ hmiː.
   'The boy knows that his father is sick.'

10. Ɲi mɨh ʔe ʣoːʔ ʃiːʔ.
    'The woman knows that the boy is sick.'

Dataset 280. Lalana Chinantec (Mexico)
Phonemic tone is not indicated.

1. Hoː hi   hmiː.
   see paper father.3
   'His father reads.'

2. Hmeːta   hmiː.
   do   work father.3
   'His father works.'

3. Nuː huːh mɨh.
   hear word woman
   'The woman hears the message.'

4. Hoː ta   ʃiːʔ.
   see work boy
   'The boy sees the work.'

5. ʔeː ta hoː hmiː.
   'What work does his father see?'

6. ʔeː hi hmeː mɨh.
   'What message does the woman write?'

7. ʔeː huːh nuː ʃiːʔ.
   'What message does the boy hear?'

8. ʔeː huːh hmeː mɨh.
   'What does the woman discuss?'

9. Hoː mɨh ʔeː hi hmeː ʃiːʔ.
   'The woman sees what the boy writes.'

10. Nuː ʃiːʔ ʔeː huːh nuː hmiː.
    'The boy hears what message his father hears.'

11. Nuː hmiː ʔeː ta hmeː ʃiːʔ.
    'His father hears what work the boy does.'

12. Hoː ʃiːʔ ʔeː hi hoː mɨh.
    'The boy sees what paper the woman reads.'

Dataset 281. Palantla Chinantec (Mexico)

1. Cuø^{12} Dsie^3 cog^3.
   give Bill money
   'Bill gives money.'

2. Hniu^1 Juøn^{13} cang^3.
   want John rock
   'John wants the rock.'

3. Jái^{12} Be^{13} jǿg^3.
   see Bob word
   'Bob takes care of the problem.'

4. Hioh^{12} Søa^{13} cog^3.
   hate Joe money
   'Joe hates the money.'

5. Cuø^{12} Søa^{13} cang^3 jái^{12} Juøn^{13}.
   give Joe rock see John
   'Joe gives the rock John sees.'

6. Hniu^1 Dsie^3 jǿg^3 hioh^{12} Be^{13}.
   want Bill word hate Bob
   'Bill wants the arrangement that Bob hates.'

7. Jái^{12} Juøn^{13} cog^3 hniu^1 Dsie^3.
   see John money want Bill
   'John provides the money Bill wants.'

8. Hioh^{12} Be^{13} cang^3 cuø^{12} Søa^{13}.
   hate Bob rock give Joe
   'Bob hates the rock Joe gives.'

9. Hniu^1 Søa^{13} cuø^{12} Juøn^{13} jǿg^3.
   want Joe give John word
   'Joe wants John to give permission.'

10. Jái^{12} Dsie^3 jái^{12} Søa^{13} cog^3.
    see Bill see Joe money
    'Bill sees Joe looking at the money.'

11. Hioh^{12} Juøn^{13} hniu^1 Be^{13} cang^3.
    hate John want Bob rock
    'John hates it that Bob wants the rock.'

12. Cuø^{12} Be^{13} jái^{12} Juøn^{13} cang^3 hniu^1 Dsie^3 cuø^{12} Søa^{13} jái^{12} Go^3.
    give Bob see John rock want Bill give Joe see Greg
    'Bob permits John to see the rock Bill wants Joe to let Greg see.'

13. Hioh^{12} Søa^{13} hniu^1 Be^{13} cuø^{12} Dsie^3 jái^{12} Juøn^{13} cang^3 hniu^1 Be^{13}.
    hate Joe want Bob give Bill see John rock want Bob
    'Joe hates it that Bob wants Bill to let John see the rock that Bob wants.'

Dataset **282**. Colorado (Ecuador)

14. Hi-e.
    go-DECL
    '(S/he) went.'

15. Sona   ha-e.
    woman   came-DECL
    'The woman came.'

16. Unila kutsu   munara-e.
    man   cassava want-DECL
    'The man wants cassava.'

17. Miya manpi-ka mira-e.
    chief uncle-ACC know-DECL
    'The chief knows uncle.'

18. Na   hi-n.
    child go-INTERROG
    'Did the child go?'

19. Munara-n.
    want-INTERROG
    'Does (s/he) want (it)?'

20. Mo-ka   neya-n.
    who-ACC seek-INTERROG
    'For whom did (s/he) look?'

21. Manpi watsa fi-n.
    uncle fish eat-INTERROG
    'Did uncle eat fish?'

22. Mo hi-n.
    who went-INTERROG
    'Who went?'

23. Mo sona-ka   neya-n.
    who? woman-ACC seek-INTERROG
    'Who looked for the woman?'

24. Unila mo-ka   mira-n.
    man   who-ACC know-INTERROG
    'Whom does the man know?'

25. Miya ti   fari-n.
    chief what ask.for-INTERROG
    'What did the chief ask for?'

26. Fi-no   munara-e.
    eat-INF want-DECL
    '(S/he) wants to eat.'

Continued

Dataset 282 continued:

27. Fari-no   mira-n.
    ask.for-INF know-INTERROG
    'Does (s/he) know how to ask for (it)?'

28. Sona   ha-no   munara-e.
    woman come-INF want-DECL
    'The woman wants to come.'

29. Na   kutsu   fi-no   munara-e.
    child cassava eat-INF want-DECL
    'The child wants to eat cassava.'

30. Unila manpi-ka neya-no munara-n.
    man   uncle-ACC seek-INF want-INTERROG
    'Does the man want to look for uncle?'

31. Manpi ti   fari-no   munara-n.
    uncle what ask.for-INF   want-INTERROG
    'What does uncle want to ask for?'

32. Mo   miya-ka   mira-no munara-n.
    who chief-ACC know-INF want-INTERROG
    'Who wants to know the chief?'

33. Miya na-ka   neya-no mira-e.
    chief child-ACC seek-INF know-DECL
    'The chief knows how to look for the child.'

34. Na   ti   fi-no   mira-n.
    child what eat-INF know-INTERROG
    'What does the child know how to eat?'

35. Manpi neya-sa   munara-e.
    uncle seek-SUBJN want-DECL
    'Uncle wants (him/her) to look for (it).'

36. Watsa fi-sa   munara-e.
    fish eat-SUBJN want-DECL
    '(S/he) wants (him/her) to eat fish.'

37. Sona   munara-e manpi kutsu   fari-sa.
    woman want-DECL uncle cassava ask.for-SUBJN
    'The woman wants uncle to ask for cassava.'

    OR: Sona   manpi-ka kutsu   fari-sa   munara-e.
        woman uncle-ACC cassava ask.for-SUBJN want-DECL

38. Unila munara-n   sona   manpi-ka neya-sa.
    man   want-INTERROG woman uncle-ACC seek-SUBJN
    'Does the man want the woman to look for uncle?'

    OR: Unila sona-ka   manpi-ka neya-sa   munara-n.
        man   woman-ACC   uncle-ACC seek-SUBJN want-INTERROG

Continued

Dataset 282 continued:

39. Sona   miya-ka   ti   fi-sa   munara-n.
    woman chief-ACC what eat-SUBJN want-INTERROG
    'What does the woman want the chief to eat?'

    *Sona   munara-n   miya ti fi-sa.
     woman want-INTERROG   chief what eat-SUBJN

40. Manpi na-ka   ha-sa   munara-e.
    uncle child-ACC come-SUBJN want-DECL
    'Uncle wants the child to come.'

41. Miya mo-ka   hi-sa   munara-n.
    chief who-ACC go-SUBJN want-INTERROG
    'Who does the chief want to go?'

42. Fari-nun-ka   mira-e.
    ask.for-PTCPL-ACC know-DECL
    '(S/he$_i$ knows s/he$_j$ asked for (it).'

43. Miya fi-nun-ka   mira-e.
    chief eat-PTCPL-ACC know-decl
    '(S/he) knows the chief ate (it).'

44. Unila mira-e   na   watsa fari-nun-ka.
    man   know-DECL child fish ask.for-PTCPL-ACC
    'The man knows the child asked for fish.'

    *Unila na-ka   watsa fari-nun-ka   mira-e.
     man   child-ACC fish   ask.for-PTCPL-ACC know-DECL

45. Sona   mira-e   manpi mo-ka   neya-nun-ka.
    woman know-DECL uncle who-ACC seek-PTCPL-ACC
    'The woman knows for whom uncle looked.'

    *Sona   manpi-ka mo-ka   neya-nun-ka   mira-e.
     woman uncle-ACC who-ACC seek-PTCPL-ACC know-DECL

46. Mo   miya ha-nun-ka   mira-n.
    who chief came-PTCPL-ACC know-INTERROG
    'Who knows the chief came?'

47. Manpi mo hi-nun-ka   mira-n.
    uncle who go-PTCPL-ACC know-INTERROG
    'Does uncle know who went?'

48. Miya mira-e   sona   mo-ka   tsatsika fi-sa   munara-nun-ka.
    chief know-DECL woman who-ACC meat   eat-SUBJN want-PTCPL-ACC
    'The chief knows who the woman wants to eat the meat.'

    *Miya mira-e   sona   munara-nun-ka   mo tsatsika fi-sa.
     chief know-DECL woman want-PTCPL-ACC who meat   eat-SUBJN

49. Unila mira-n   na   kutsu   fi-no   munara-nun-ka.
    man   know-INTERROG child cassava eat-INF want-PTCPL-ACC
    'Does the man know the child wants to eat cassava?'

Dataset 283. Huixtec Tzotzil (Mexico)

1. tʃbát.
   3.IMPF.go
   'He will go.'

2. Tálem   ti-vínik.
   3.PRF.come   the-man
   'The man has come.'

3. Bátem   ti-vákaʃ.
   3.PRF.go the-cow
   'The cow has gone.'

4. Véʔem   ti-Mariána.
   3.PRF.stay   marian
   'Marian has stayed.'

5. tʃvéʔ   ti-Mariána ti-tálem.
   3.IMPF.stay the-marian the-3.PRF.come
   'Marian, who has come, will stay.'

   *tʃvéʔ   ti-tálem.
    3.IMPF.stay   the-3.PRF.come
    'He who has come, will stay.'

6. Véʔem   ti-vákaʃ ti-láx   smán.
   3.PRF.stay   the-cow the-CMPL 3.buy.3
   'The cow which he bought has stayed.'

7. Tálem   ti-kárta ti-láx   aták.
   3.PRF.come the-letter the-CMPL 2.send.3
   'The letter which you sent has come.'

8. Kʔótem   ti-láx   akʔámbun.
   3.PRF.arrive the-CMPL 2.ask.for.3.1
   'That which you asked me for has arrived.'

9. Kʔótem   ti-xún   ti-láx   akʔámbun.
   3.PRF.arrive the-paper the-CMPL 2.ask.for.3.1
   'The paper which you asked me for has arrived.'

Dataset 284. Sierra Populuca (Mexico)

1. Miɲum.
   'He came.'

2. Seːtum heʔm pʌːʃiɲ.
   'The man returned.'

3. Nʌkpa hemʌk hoymʌ.
   'He goes there tomorrow.'

4. Yʌʔm miɲpa heʔm yoːmo.
   'Here comes the woman.'

5. Nʌkpa heʔm pʌːʃiɲ hemʌk.
   'There goes the man.'

6. Oyum Peːtoh matʌk hemʌk.
   'Peter went there and returned yesterday.'

7. Yʌʔm seːtpa heʔm pʌːʃiɲ hoymʌ.
   'The man returns here tomorrow.'

8. Nʌkum matʌk heʔm yoːmo.
   'The woman went yesterday.'

9. Miɲum heʔm pʌːʃiɲ yʌʔm matʌk.
   'The man came here yesterday.'

10. Hemʌk seːtum heʔm pʌːʃiɲ heʔm miɲwʌʌp.
    'The man who came returned there.'

11. Hemʌk seːtum heʔm miɲwʌʌp.
    'The one who came returned there.'

12. Seːtum heʔm miɲpaap yʌʔm.
    'The one who comes here returned.'

13. Yʌʔm miɲum heʔm nʌkpaap.
    'The one who goes came here.'

14. Nʌkum hemʌk heʔm miɲpaap hoymʌ.
    'The one who comes tomorrow went there.'

15. Nʌkpa hemʌk hoymʌ heʔm oywʌʌp matʌk hemʌk.
    'The one who went there and returned yesterday, goes there tomorrow.'

16. Seːtpa hoymʌ heʔm nʌkwʌʌp hemʌk matʌk.
    'The one who went there yesterday will return tomorrow.'

Problen 285. English

1. I drove it.

2. You threw the ball.

3. He threw the board and balls.

4. I hid the bikes, ball, ..., and chairs.

5. You drove the chairs behind it.

6. He took the board under them.

7. I threw it over the bikes.

8. You hid them behind the balls.

9. I took the balls over the boards and bikes.

10. He drove it under them.

11. You threw the chairs, bike, and balls behind the board.

12. He hid the ball, ..., and chairs under the bikes, ..., and boards.

Dataset 286. Spanish

Stress explicitly marked beyond normal orthographic convention.

1. Él tóma.	'He drinks.'
2. Ustéd quiére água.	'You want water.'
3. Élla tóma cáldo y café.	'She drinks broth and coffee.'
4. Él quiére cáldo, léche, y água.	'He wants broth, milk, and water.'
5. Ustéd tóma café, cáldo, sópa, y atóle.	You drink coffee, broth, soup, and gruel.
6. Élla quiére atóle, café, água, léche, y sópa.	She wants gruel, coffee, water, milk, and soup.

Laboratory Manual for Morphology and Syntax

Dataset 287. Northern Puebla Totonac (Mexico)

1. ʃiwaːn staːʔ stapuːn.   'John sells beans.'

2. Pedro tamaːwa laːʃaʃ.   'Peter buys oranges.'

3. ʃiwaːn waʔ kinit laːʔ qaʔlwat.   'John eats meat and eggs.'

4. Pedro staːʔ laːʃaʃ laːʔ kinit.   'Peter sells oranges and meat.'

5. ʃiwaːn tamaːwa qaʔlwat laːʔ kinit laːʔ stapuːn.
   'John buys eggs, meat, and beans.'

6. Pedro waʔ stapuːn laːʔ kinit laːʔ laːʃaʃ laːʔ qaʔlwat laːʔ ...
   'Peter eats beans, meat, oranges, eggs, ...'

Dataset 288. Amharic (Ethiopia)

1. Yohannɨs təkʼəmmətʼə.
   John   sat.down
   'John sat down.'

2. Zare Markʼos məttʼa.
   today Mark   came
   'Mark came today.'

3. Tɨlantɨnna Mammo dərrəsə.
   yesterday Mammo arrived
   'Mammo arrived yesterday.'

4. Mammo məttʼanna Markʼos təkʼəmmətʼə.
   Mammo came.and   Mark   sat.down
   'Mammo came and Mark sat down.'

5. Tɨlantɨnna Mammo məttʼanna zare   Yohannɨs hedə.
   yesterday Mammo came.and today John   went
   'Mammo came yesterday and John went today.'

6. Zare Yohannɨs dərrəsə Markʼosɨm dərrəsə.
   today John   arrived Mark.and   arrived
   'John and Mark arrived today.'

7. Mammo hedə Yohannɨsɨm hedənna Markʼos təkʼəmmətʼə.
   Mammo went John.and   went.and Mark   sat.down
   'Mammo and John went, and Mark sat down.'

8. Zare Markʼos muz gəzzanna   Yohannɨs dabbo gəzza.
   today Mark   banana bought.and John   bread bought
   'Today Mark bought bananas and John bought bread.'

9. Tɨlantɨnna Mammo muz   gəzza dabbom gəzza.
   yesterday Mammo banana bought bread.and bought
   'Yesterday Mammo bought bananas and bread.'

Laboratory Manual for Morphology and Syntax

Dataset 289. Amharic (Ethiopia)

1. Markʾos məttʾa.
   'Mark came.'

2. Aster hedətʃ.
   'Esther went.'

3. Ɨrbɨkʾa məttʾatʃ.
   'Rebecca came.'

4. Mammo hedə.
   'Mamo went.'

5. Bɨrhane hedətʃ.
   'Birhane went.'

6. Yohannɨs məttʾa.
   'John came.'

7. Yohannɨsɨnna Markʾos hedu.
   'John and Mark went.'

8. Asterɨnna Mammo məttʾu.
   'Esther and Mamo came.'

9. Mammonna Markʾos hedu.
   'Mamo and Mark went.'

10. Bɨrhanenna Ɨrbɨkʾa hedu.
    'Birhane and Rebecca went.'

11. Ɨrbɨkʾanna Mammo Markʾosɨm hedu.
    'Rebecca, Mamo, and Mark went.'

12. Markʾosɨnna Yohannɨs Asterɨm məttʾu.
    'Mark, John, and Esther came.'

13. Asterɨnna Markʾos Bɨrhane Mammom hedu.
    'Esther, Mark, Birhane, and Mamo went.'

14. Yohannɨsɨnna Aster Mammo Bɨrhane Ɨrbɨkʾam hedu.
    'John, Esther, Mamo, Birhane, and Rebecca went.'

Dataset 290. Kunimaipa (Papua New Guinea)

1. Sohopuho noho.   'I went and then ate.'

2. Sata noho.   'I went and ate (same time).'

3. Seŋipuho neŋi.   'You went and then ate.'

4. Sata neŋi.   'You went and ate (same time).'

5. Sahapuho naha.   'He went and then ate.'

6. Sata naha.   'He went and ate (same time).'

7. Hehopuho soho.   'I stayed and then went.'

8. Heta soho.   'I stayed and went (same time).'

9. Hehana soho.   'He stayed and then I went.'

10. Sahana noho.   'He went and then I ate.'

11. Sahana neŋi.   'He went and then you ate.'

12. Hemapuho soma.   'I will stay and then go.'

13. Heta soma.   'I will stay and go (same time).'

14. Hekepuho seke.   'You will stay and then go.'

15. Heta seke.   'You will stay and go (same time).'

16. Hepanepuho sapane.   'He will stay and then go.'

17. Heta sapane.   'He will stay and go (same time).'

18. Hemana seke.   'I will stay and then you will go.'

19. Hekena soma.   'You will stay and then I will go.'

20. Hepanena seke.   'He will stay and then you will go.'

Dataset 291. Colorado (Ecuador)

1. Miya wanbi ha-e.
   chief later came-DECL
   'The chief came later.'

2. Unila fari-to   hi-e.
   man   request-PTCPL went-DECL
   'Having made the request, the man departed.'

3. Sona   kutsu   kisin   fi-to   hi-e.
   woman cassava yesterday eat-PTCPL went-DECL
   'Having eaten the cassava yesterday, the woman went.' OR
   'The woman ate the cassava yesterday and left.'

4. Unila sona-ka   neya-to   na-ka   neya-e.
   man   woman-ACC seek-PTCPL child-ACC sought-DECL
   'The man, having looked for the woman, looked for the child.'

5. Sona   kutsu   fi-to   hi-e.
   woman cassava eat-PTCPL went-DECL
   'Having eaten the cassava, the woman went.'

6. Na   unila-ka kisin   neya-e.
   child man-ACC yesterday sought-DECL
   'The child looked for the man yesterday.'

7. Unila tsatsika munara-to   ha-e.
   man   meat   want-PTCPL came-DECL
   'The man came desiring meat.' OR
   'The man came because he wanted meat.'

8. Miya kutsu   fi-nan   sona   hi-e.
   chief cassava eat-PTCPL woman went-DECL
   'When the chief had eaten the cassava, the woman left.'

9. Miya tsatsika fi-nan   manpi kutsu   fi-e.
   chief meat   ate-PTCPL uncle cassava ate-DECL
   'Since the chief had eaten the meat, uncle ate the cassava.'

Laboratory Manual for Morphology and Syntax

Dataset 292. Palantla Chinantec (Mexico)

Appositive elements are the focus of this material. Do not attempt detailed analysis.

1. Dsa^2 ŋioh^{12} ma^{2}ŋii^{12} jóg^3 hio^{13},   hi^2 cáih^1-dsa ja^3 jenh^1 gug^2 =dsa.
   3   male   provides dress woman, that wear 3   when join hand 3
   'The groom provides his wife's dress, the one she will wear at the wedding.'

2. hniú^{12} quián^2 jnieh^3 guiag^{13} jnieh^3
   house of   1x   REFL   1x
   'our own house'

3. gog^{12} quiah^{12} =dsa jøng^2
   trunk of   3   that
   'that trunk of his/hers/theirs'

4. Ha^{1}chii^2 jøng^2 jái^{12} =jni, he^2 lán^{12} dsa^2 héi^2.
   not   that see 1s what BE   3   that
   'I don't know, what that fellow is.'

5. Ja^{3}ŋiúh^3=dsa, dsa^2 ŋøa^{12} ta^3 hnai^{12} lio^{13}, ha^{1}chian^2 dsa^2 chian^2
   son   3   3   walk work sell   goods not   3   BE
   'Her son, the travelling saleman, he is not here.'

6. Jøng^2 ca^{1}ŋii^{3}jan^3 =dsa tøa^{12}-møa^{12}, dsa^2 jmo^{12} hí^3 lo^3 dsa^2 héi^2.
   so   went.see 3   doctor   3   do   care da-in-law 3   that
   'So she went to see the doctor, the one who would take care of said person's daughter-in-law.'

7. Jøng^2 báh^3 neng^{12} ni^3 jein^3 ja^{3}ná^3, ja^3 jmo^{12} =dsa má^1.
   so   AFF sit   on shelf there, where do   3   food
   'So it sits there on the shelf, where she prepares the meals.'

8. He^2 ho^{3}ra dság^{12} =dsa dsø^{2}quiín^2 =dsa hi^2 jøng^2.
   what hour go   3   go.get   3   REL that
   'What time does she go to fetch that stuff?'

9. quianh^{13} tsih^2 jian^{12} =dsa, tsih^2 mǿ^2
   with   youth fellow 3   youth female
   'with her young female friends'

Continued

Dataset 292 continued:

10. dsǿa¹² dsa² héi², dsa² hniu³
    heart 3 that 3 house
    'that person's heart, the man of the house'

11. jǿg³ ha²láh² ca¹løa¹, ha²láh² ca¹ŋii¹ŋé² hio¹³
    word how happened how experienced woman
    'the account of how it happened, of what the woman experienced'

12. Mi³chie¹ ti³ŋieh¹ =jni
    mother father 1s
    'my parents'

13. Ŋíh⁴ ku²ba¹³ ku²ma¹³?
    you.sit? cofather comother
    'Are you home, cofather and comother?'

14. ju³ná³ meh² dsa² ŋioh¹², ju³ná³ meh² mǿ² ca¹láh¹, ...
    if small 3 male if small female again
    'if the boy is young, or if again the girl is young, ...'

15. hi² cøh²-gǿah¹²-jni
    thing chew-eat 1s
    'my food'

16. ja³ hiá¹ ja³ hiég¹
    at tomorrow at day.after.tomorrow
    'in the future'

17. dsa² tiogh³ hniu³, dsa² tiogh³ dsii²néi² quiah¹²
    3 occupy house 3 occupy inside of
    'the family (who lives together)'

18. Ha²láh² løa¹² ja³ ŋiíh³ =hning, ha²láh² løa¹²?
    how BE where live 2s how BE
    'How are things at your house, how are they?'

19. He² má¹ cøh² =hning, he² má¹?
    what food eat 2s what food
    'What do you eat, what?'

Dataset 293. Sierra Popoluca (Mexico)

1. Tuːm pʌʃiɲ ipaʔtne ikawah.
   one man   3s.horse
   'A man has found his horse.'

2. Heʔm ʃiwan dʲa ikoʔtsgakum heʔm ikawah.
   that John not   that 3s.horse
   'John did not hit his horse again.'

3. Tuːm pʌːʃiɲ nʌkne playa
   one man   beach
   'A man has gone to the beach.'

4. Tsaːm yagats heʔm tuŋ.
   very long that road
   'The road is very long.'

5. Odoy nʌːkʌ.
   not
   'Don't go!'

6. Odoy nʌːkʌ hoymʌ.
   not   tomorrow
   'Don't go tomorrow!

7. Nʌkne playa kawahyukmʌ
          beach on.horse
   'He has gone to the beach on a horse.'

8. Dʲa miŋgakum.
   not
   'He did not come again.'

9. Iwatpa ikaːma   heʔm pʌːʃiɲ yʌʔm.
             3s.cornfield that man   here
   'The man will make his cornfield here.'

10. Hesʌk witʲpa tuːm ʃiʃ   tuŋhoːm.
    then   one cow on.road
    'Then a cow will walk on the road.'

11. Tsaːm mʌh heʔm kaːma.
    very big that cornfield
    'The cornfield is very big.'

12. Okmʌ heʔm kawah ikuʔtne haʔyaŋ mok.
    later that horse   much corn
    'Later the horse has eaten much corn.'

Continued

Dataset 293 continued:

13. Kootsʌ' heʔm kawah.
            that   horse
    'Hit the horse!'

14. Hesʌk ʌtʃ anʌkpa   ka:mho:m   hoymʌ   kawahyukmʌ.
    then   1s   in.cornfield   tomorrow on.horse
    'Then I will go to the cornfield tomorrow on horseback.'

15. Dʲa miɲpa tʌkkʌʌm sa:bʌy.
    not   at.house   later
    'He will not come to the house later.'

16. Witʲ me:sahyukmʌ hemʌk.
          on.table   there
    'He walked on the table there.'

17. Okmʌ mimiɲpa mitʃ iŋka:mho:m.
    later   2s   in.your.cornfield
    'Later you will come from your cornfield.'

18. Mitʃ iɲtʲʌŋ iŋka:ma   matʌk   a:tʃahmʌ.
    2s   2s.cornfield yesterday with.axe
    'You cut your cornfield yesterday with an axe.'

19. Kuutʌ tu:m a:ɲi.
           one tortilla
    'Eat a tortilla!'

20. Tʌ:ŋʌ iŋka:ma   sa:bʌy.
          your.cornfield later
    'Cut your cornfield later!'

21. Aŋwatgakum tu:m tʌk.
                one house
    'I made my house again.'

22. Dʲa ipaʔt.
    not
    'He did not find it.'

23. Hesʌ:k heʔm kawah tʌgʌygakum itʲʌkho:m.
    then   that horse   in.3s.house
    'Then the horse entered his house again.'

24. Tsa:m wʌ: heʔm playa.
    very good that beach
    'The beach is very good.'

25. Ikoʔts.
    'He hit it.'

Continued

Dataset 293 continued:

26. Miɲum haʔyaŋ aŋkawah.
        much   1s.horse
    'Many of my horses came.'

27. Amiɲɲe ʌtʃ aːtebet   ʃiʃyukmʌ.
        1s Soteapan on.cow
    'I have come from Soteapan on a cow.'

28. Wʌtʲi heʔm aːtebet.
    wide that   Soteapan
    'Soteapan is big.'

29. Heʔm ʃiwan oy huumʌ   matʌk.
    that John   far.away yesterday
    'John went far away and came back yesterday.'

30. Dʲa wʌː heʔm itʲʌk.
    not good that   3s.house
    'His house is not good.'

31. Hesʌk oygak heʔm peːtoh itʲʌkkʌʌm.
    then   that Peter at.3s.house
    'Then Peter went to his house and came back again.'

32. Ʌtʃ aoy mawʌʃki   hemʌk.
    1s   day.before.yesterday there
    'I went there and came back day before yesterday.'

33. Awitʲne.
    'I have walked.'

34. Antʌŋne tuːm kuy ʌtʃ maːtʃitʲmʌ.
            one tree 1s machete
    'I have chopped a tree with a machete.'

35. Okmʌ dʲa mioyɲe peːtohkʌʌm.
    later not   at.Peter
    'Later you have not gone to Peter's place and returned.'

36. Miːɲʌ kawahyukmʌ yʌʔm.
         on.horse   here
    'Come here on a horse!'

37. Mʌh heʔm aŋkawah.
    big that 1s.horse
    'My horse is large.'

38. Miɲʌkpa kaːmkʌʌm.
         at.cornfield
    'You will go near the cornfield.'

Continued

Dataset 293 continued:

39. Atʌgʌyɲe hʌmɲoːm.
               in.mountains
    'I have entered the mountains.'

40. Tʌgʌːyʌ.
    'Enter!'

41. Odoy kootsʌ heʔm pʌːʃiɲ kuymʌ.
    not   that man with.tree
    'Don't hit the man with a stick!'

42. tsaːm pʌːmi heʔm peːtoh.
    very strong that Peter
    'Peter is very strong.'

43. Hesʌk miwitʲum.
    then
    'Then you walked.'

44. Mitʲʌgʌypa iɲtʲʌkhoːm.
              in.2s.house
    'You will enter your house.'

45. Dʲa yʌk heʔm iɲʃiʃ.
    not black that 2s.cow
    'Your cow is not black.'

46. Aoyum aŋkawahkʌʌm matʌk.
           at.1s.horse   yesterday
    'I went to where my horse was yesterday and returned.'

47. Itʲʌŋgakpa ikaːma   hoymʌ.
           3s.cornfield tomorrow
    'He will cut his cornfield again tomorrow.'

48. Dʲa tsaːm mʌh heʔm ikaːma.
    not very big that 3s.cornfield
    'His cornfield is not very big.'

49. Hesʌk iwatum heʔm tuŋ ikaːmkʌʌm.
    then   that road at.3s.cornfield
    'Then he made the road near his cornfield.'

50. Hesʌk dʲa miɲʌkpa mitʃ kaːmhoːm ʃiʃyukmʌ hoymʌ.
    then not   2s in.cornfield on.cow tomorrow
    'Then you will not go to the cornfield tomorrow on a cow.'

51. Oy iʃiʃkʌʌm.
      at.3s.cow
    'He went to where his cow was and returned.'

Continued

Dataset 293 continued:

52. Wiːtʲʌ.
    'Walk!'

53. Nʌk heʔm ʃiwan.
          that John
    'John went.'

54. Ikoʔts ikawah   meːsahmʌ.
          3s.horse with.table
    'He hit his horse with a table.'

55. Odoy tʌgʌːyʌ tʌkhoːm.
    not   in.house
    'Don't enter the house!'

56. tsaːm wʌtyi heʔm hʌmɲi.
    very wide that mountains
    'The mountains are very big.'

57. Odoy waːtʌ itʲʌk   yʌʔm hoymʌ.
    not   3s.house here tomorrow
    'Don't build his house here tomorrow!'

58. Nʌknegak heʔm ʃiwan.
             that John
    'John has gone again.'

59. Ampaʔtnegak aɲʃiʃ matʌk   ʃiwankʌʌm.
              1s.cow yesterday at.John
    'I have found my cow yesterday at John's place again.'

60. Ipaʔtum tʌkhoːm mawaʃki.
            in.house day.before.yesterday
    'He found it in the house the day before yesterday.'

61. Iŋkuʔtne haʔyaŋ aːɲi   mitʃ.
            much tortillas 2s
    'You have eaten many tortillas.'

62. Paatʌ tuːm tuŋ.
          one road
    'Find a road!'

63. tsaːm huumʌ   heʔm aːtebet.
    very far.away that Soteapan
    'Soteapan is very far away.'

64. Nʌːkʌ.
    'Go!'

Continued

Dataset 293 continued:

65. Waːtʌ.
    'Make it!'

66. Impaʔtpa heʔm peːtoh saːbʌy.
                 that Peter later
    'You will find Peter later.'

67. Odoy miːɲʌ.
    not
    'Don't come!'

68. Kuutʌ.
    'Eat it!'

69. Wʌː heʔm mok.
    good that corn
    'The corn is good.'

70. Nʌːka hemʌk saːbʌy iŋkawahyukmʌ.
             there   later on.2s.horse
    'Go there later on your horse!'

71. Dʲa huumʌ   heʔm iŋkaːma.
    not far.away that 2s.cornfield
    'Your cornfield is not far away.'

72. Antʌŋpa ʌtʃ ammaːtʃitʲmʌ   hoymʌ.
             1s with.1s.machete tomorrow
    'I will cut it tomorrow with my machete.'

73. Tʌːŋʌ hoymʌ   ʃiwankʌʌm.
             tomorrow at.John
    'Cut it tomorrow at John's place!'

74. Wʌː heʔm aːtʃah.
    good that axe
    'The axe is good.'

75. Tʌːŋʌ heʔm kuy hoymʌ   maːtʃitʲmʌ.
           that   tree tomorrow with.machete
    'Chop the tree tomorrow with a machete!

Laboratory Manual for Morphology and Syntax

Dataset 294. Min Nan Chinese (Taiwan)

Phonemic tone is not indicated.

			ONE. . .	TWO. . .
1.	laŋ	'man'	tsit e laŋ	nəŋ e laŋ
2.	tsu	'book'	tsip pun tsu	nəŋ pun tsu
3.	kau	'dog'	tsit tsia kau	nəŋ tsia kau
4.	niau	'cat'	tsit tsia niau	nəŋ tsia niau
5.	eŋ pit	'pencil'	tsik ki eŋ pit	nəŋ ki eŋ pit
6.	tsʼiu	'arm'	tsik ki tsʼiu	nəŋ ki tsʼiu
7.	tsiŋ tʼao a	'finger'	tsik ki tsiŋ tʼao a	nəŋ ki tsiŋ tʼao a
8.	pit	'pen'	tsik ki pit	nəŋ ki pit
9.	kʼo tua	'belt'	tsit tiao kʼo tua	nəŋ tiao kʼo tua
10.	so a	'wire	tsit tiao so a	nəŋ tiao so a
11.	nia tua	'tie'	tsit tiao nia tua	nəŋ tiao nia tua
12.	lo	'path'	tsit tiao lo	nəŋ tiao lo
13.	tsʼio tʼau	'stone'	tsit tiap tsʼio tʼau	nəŋ tiap tsʼio tʼau
14.	tsʼĩ	'star'	tsit tiap tsʼĩ	nəŋ tiap tsʼĩ
15.	nəŋ	'egg'	tsit tiap nəŋ	nəŋ tiap nəŋ
16.	tsʼu	'house'	tsik kieŋ tsʼu	nəŋ kieŋ tsʼu
17.	to su kuaŋ	'library'	tsik kieŋ to su kuaŋ	nəŋ kieŋ to su kuaŋ

Dataset 295. Tabasco Chontal (Mexico)

1.	unkʔe wah	'one tortilla'	31.	tʃʌn kʔe wah	'four tortillas'
2.	unkʔe hun	'one paper'	32.	tʃʌnkʔe hun	'four papers'
3.	unkʔe yopo	'one leaf'	33.	tʃʌnkʔe yopo	'four leaves'
4.	umpʔe hun	'one book'	34.	tʃʌmpʔe hun	'four books'
5.	umpʔe pop	'one mat'	35.	tʃʌmpʔe pop	'four mats'
6.	untu mut	'one bird'	36.	tʃʌntu mut	'four birds'
7.	untu tʃitam	'one pig'	37.	tʃʌntu tʃitam	'four pigs
8.	untu winik	'one man'	38.	tʃʌntu winik	'four men'
9.	untsʔit tʃan	'one snake'	39.	tʃʌntsʔit tʃan	'four snakes'
10.	untsʔit ʌhin	'one alligator'	40.	tʃʌntsʔit ʌhin	'four alligators'
11.	tʃakʔe wah	'two tortillas'	41.	ho kʔe wah	'five tortillas'
12.	tʃakʔe hun	'two papers'	42.	hokʔe hun	'five papers'
13.	tʃakʔe yopo	'two leaves'	43.	hokʔe yopo	'five leaves'
14.	tʃapʔe hun	'two books'	44.	hopʔe hun	'five books'
15.	tʃapʔe pop	'two mats'	45.	hopʔe pop	'five mats'
16.	tʃaʔtu mut	'two birds'	46.	hoʔtu mut	'five birds'
17.	tʃaʔtu tʃitam	'two pigs'	47.	hoʔtu tʃitam	'five pigs'
18.	tʃaʔtu winik	'two men'	48.	hoʔtu winik	'five men'
19.	tʃatsʔit tʃan	'two snakes'	49.	hotsʔit tʃan	'five snakes'
20.	tʃatsʔit ʌhin	'two alligators'	50.	hotsʔit ʌhin	'five alligators'
21.	uʃkʔe wah	'three tortillas'	51.	wʌ kʔe wah	'six tortillas'
22.	uʃkʔe hun	'three papers'	52.	wʌkʔe hun	'six papers'
23.	uʃkʔe yopo	'three leaves'	53.	wʌkʔe yopo	'six leaves'
24.	uʃpʔe hun	'three books'	54.	wʌpʔe hun	'six books'
25.	uʃpʔe pop	'three mats'	55.	wʌpʔe pop	'six mats'
26.	uʃtu mut	'three birds'	56.	wʌtu mut	'six birds'
27.	uʃtu tʃitam	'three pigs'	57.	wʌtu tʃitam	'six pigs'
28.	uʃtu winik	'three men'	58.	wʌtu winik	'six men'
29.	uʃtsʔit tʃan	'three snakes'	59.	wʌtsʔit tʃan	'six snakes'
30.	uʃtsʔit ʌhin	'three alligators'	60.	wʌtsʔit ʌhin	'six alligators'

Laboratory Manual for Morphology and Syntax

Dataset 296. Kiowa (USA)

Acute accent indicates high tone; low tone is unmarked. All verb prefixes indicate first person singular subject. The verb stem is ɔ́ 'gave'.

1. Tsenbó: gyaɔ́.   'I gave a cow.'
2. Tsenbó: nɛ̃nɔ́.   'I gave two cows.'
3. Tsenbó:gɔ déɔ́.   'I gave (three or more) cows.'
4. Ayp'íʔegɔ déɔ́.   'I gave a potato.'
5. Ayp'íʔe nɛ̃nɔ́.   'I gave two potatoes.'
6. Ayp'íʔe gyatɔ́.   'I gave (three or more) potatoes.'
7. Álɔgɔ déɔ́.   'I gave an apple.'
8. Álɔ nɛ̃nɔ́.   'I gave two apples.'
9. Álɔgɔ déɔ́.   'I gave (three or more) apples.'
10. Tsɛ́ gyaɔ́.   'I gave a horse.'
11. Tsɛ́ nɛ̃nɔ́.   'I gave two horses.'
12. Tsɛ́gɔ déɔ́.   'I gave (three or more) horses.'
13. Ts'ó: gyaɔ́.   'I gave a stone.'
14. Ts'ó: nɛ̃nɔ́.   'I gave two stones.'
15. Ts'ó: gyatɔ́.   'I gave (three or more) stones.'
16. Yáypɔ́ gyaɔ́.   'I gave a rope.'
17. Yáypɔ́ nɛ̃nɔ́.   'I gave two ropes.'
18. Yáypɔ gyatɔ́.   'I gave (three or more) ropes.'
19. Áydɛ̃gɔ déɔ́.   'I gave a leaf.'
20. Áydɛ̃ nɛ̃nɔ́.   'I gave two leaves.'
21. Áydɛ̃ gyatɔ́.   'I gave (three or more) leaves.'
22. Sanéʔegɔ déɔ́.   'I gave a blackberry.'
23. Sanéʔe nɛ̃nɔ́.   'I gave two blackberries.'
24. Sanéʔegɔ déɔ́.   'I gave (three or more) blackberries.

Dataset 297. Northern Tepehuán (Mexico)
Phonemic tone is not indicated.

1. Umoiɲdagu ʌsai   umoko tʌligi.
   once   plants one   wheat
   'Once upon a time a certain man planted wheat.'

2. Dai ali   ʌʌʃidi toʃi.
   and very steals rabbit
   'And rabbit kept stealing it.'

3. Muidu mamaradʌ ʌgai   makʌ ʌsai   tʌligi.
   many 3s.sons   that.one who   plants wheat
   'Now that man who planted the wheat had many sons.'

4. Dai otoi ʃiʌgi   vʌʃia gʌdokʌdʌ sobidana toʃi.
   and sent older.brother most big.one   spy   rabbit
   'So he sent the oldest of the brothers to spy on rabbit.'

5. Dai i   ʌgai   Dai mʌʌ vaʃi   sobidamu toʃi.
   and went that.one and there exactly will.spy   rabbit
   'And so he went to spy on rabbit right there (some distance away).'

6. Dai mʌʌ moskoi   dai maiʃobi.
   and there just.slept and not.spied
   'But some distance away he just went to sleep, and did not spy.'

7. Dai vʌʃkʌrʌ divia toʃi   daidi au   tʌligi.
   and still   came rabbit and   was.eating wheat
   'So rabbit continued to come and eat the wheat.'

8. Dai ʃiadi   ʌpan divia dai maivua   gʌtoʃi.
   and dawn.time again came and not.brought that.rabbit
   The next morning he returned without the rabbit.'

9. Dai tʌkaxa ogadʌ   gimmara sobipʌʃi   api gʌtoʃi.
   and asked Po.father 1s.son   PST.2s.spy? 2s that.rabbit
   'His father asked him, "My son, did you spy on the rabbit?"'

10. ʧu giɲoga   maiʃobi anʌ astʌtʌdai.
    no 1s.father not.spied 1s was.telling
    ' "No, father, I did not spy," he said.'

11. Daidi tʌkaxa ogadʌ   koipʌʃi   api.
    and   asked Po.father PST.2s.sleep? 2s
    'And his father asked him, "Did you go to sleep?"'

12. ʌxʌ astʌtʌdai   koienta.
    yes was.telling 1s.slept
    ' "Yes," he said, "I went to sleep."

Continued

Laboratory Manual for Morphology and Syntax

Dataset 297 continued:

13. Tukarʌ   otoi gokʌli   ʌpʌ   goka mamara.
    nighttime sent the.man other two sons
    'At night the man sent two other sons.'

14. Imʌkai sobidamu toʃi.
    Pl.went will.spy   rabbit
    'They went to spy on rabbit.'

15. Agʌ kokoi   ʌpʌ.
    3p Pl.slept also
    'They also went to sleep.'

16. ʃiadi   dada   kiirʌ   ʌpamo.
    dawn.time Pl.came at.house again
    'The next morning they returned home.'

17. Daidi tʌkaxa ogadʌ   ʌga koimʌʃi apimu ʌpʌ.
    and   asked Po.father those 2p.slept? 2p   also
    'And their father asked them, "Did you also go to sleep?"'

18. Koietʌta.
    1p.slept
    "We went to sleep."

19. Tʌʌmʌʃi apimu toʃi   tʌkaxa ogadʌ   ʌga.
    2p.saw? 2p   rabbit asked Po.father those
    'Did you see rabbit?" their father asked them.'

20. Daidi tʌkaxa sukuli   tʌʌtʌʃi   atʌmʌ toʃi.
    and   asked younger.brother 1p.saw? 1p   rabbit
    'And the younger brother asked, "Did we see the rabbit?"'

21. Tʌʌetʌta dai maibʌi   astʌtʌdai ʃiʌgidʌ.
    1p.saw   and not.grabbed was.telling 3s.older.brother
    ' "We saw it but did not catch it," his older brother said.'

22. Tʌkaxa sukuli   tʌʌɲʃi anʌ.
    asked   younger.brother 1s.saw? 1s
    'The younger brother asked, "Did I see it?"'

23. Tʌʌepʌta.
    2s.saw
    "You saw it."

24. Ogadʌ   otoi vaʃia sukuli.
    Po.father sent most younger.brother
    'Their father sent the youngest of all the brothers.'

25. Alidukʌdʌ tai   latʃi sera dai dui umo mono.
    little.one   asked.for little wax and made one doll
    'The little one asked for a small amount of wax and he made a doll.'

Continued

Dataset 297 continued:

26. Dai mʌʌ ʃiavapakʌi   toʃi   voogʌdʌrʌ kʌi.
    and there where.entered rabbit in.3s.road   stood
    'And he stood it up over there where rabbit entered his trail.'

27. Dai divia toʃi   tukarʌ.
    and came rabbit nighttime
    'So at night rabbit came.'

28. Kʌkivaɲi askaiti aba   daivuskui anʌ.
    move!   said   there pass   1s
    "Move!" he said, "That's where I always pass."

29. Dai maikʌkiva mono.
    and not.moved doll
    'But the doll did not move.'

30. Iʃmaikʌkiva api gʌmuamu   anʌ.
    if.not.move   2s   2s.will.kill 1s
    "If you do not move, I'll kill you."

31. Vʌʃkʌrʌ moskʌka dai maiɲiokai.
    still   just.stood and not.speaking
    'It still just stood there, and did not speak.'

32. Kaitukata.
    struck
    'He hit it.'

33. Aba vaʃi   sai   novidʌ.
    there exactly stuck 3s.hand
    'And his hand stuck right there.'

34. Iɲoogiʃa padʌrʌ amumuai   anʌ.
    1s.left   from   am.killing 1s
    "I kill with my left hand."

35. Kaituka oogiʃa padʌrʌ.
    struck   left   from
    'He hit it with his left hand.'

36. Aba sai   ʌpʌ   novidʌ.
    there stuck other 3s.hand
    'His other hand stuck there.'

37. Dai gokirʌ kuituka toʃi   mono.
    and after   kicked rabbit doll
    'So then rabbit kicked the doll.'

38. Dai aba vaʃi   sai   ʌpʌ   taradʌ.
    and there exactly stuck other 3s.foot
    'And his other foot stuck right there.'

Continued

Laboratory Manual for Morphology and Syntax

Dataset 297 continued:

39. Daidi akʌi dai aba vaʃi sai tʌɲidʌ.
    and bit and there exactly stuck 3s.mouth
    'So he bit it and his mouth stuck right there.'

40. Aba vaʃi kavuli daxa toʃi monoaba.
    there exactly bunched sits rabbit on.doll
    'Right there was rabbit all bunched up on the doll.'

41. ʃiadi vaɲi ʌgai makʌ niukadai.
    dawn.time arose that.one who is.watching
    'In the morning the one who was watching got up.'

42. Bʌi dai bʌida gʌoga.
    grabbed and took that.father
    'He grabbed it and took it to his father.'

43. Dai divia umo ʃiʌgi.
    and came one older.brother
    'Then one of the older brothers came.'

44. Dai tʌkaxa ogadʌ tʌʌʃi ʌgai.
    and asked Po.father saw? that.one
    'And asked his father, "Did that one see it?"'

45. Tʌʌeta astʌtʌdai ogadʌ.
    saw was.telling Po.father
    '"He saw it," his father said.'

46. Gokirʌ tʌʌ gʌsukuli dai tʌkaxa tʌʌpʌʃi.
    after saw that.younger.brother and asked 2s.saw?
    'Then he saw his younger brother and asked him "Did you see it?"'

47. Tʌʌenta dai tan daxa astʌtʌdai.
    1s.saw and here sits was.saying
    '"I saw it and here it is," he said.'

Dataset 297: Stage two:

48. Sobidamu ʌgai api.   'He will spy on you.'
49. Gʌsobidamu ʌgai api.   'He will spy on you.'
50. Gʌgʌ anʌ gʌʃiʌgi.   'I hit your older brother.'
51. Gʌgʌgʌ atʌmʌ toʃi.   'We hit rabbit.'
52. Sosobimʌʃi ʌga gotoʃi.   'Did they spy on the rabbit?'
53. Giɲʃosobimʌʃi apimu.   'Did you (pl) spy on me?'
54. Maiʃobipʌʃi api ʌga.   'Didn't you spy on them?'
55. Maiʃosobimʌʃi ʌga apimu.   'Didn't they spy on you (pl)?'

Continued

Dataset 297 continued:

56. Maiʃobidaimʌʃi ʌga gʌrʃiʃiʌgi.   'Aren't they spying on our older brothers?'

57. Gʌbʌkamuʃi.   'Will he grab you?'

58. Oxotosamumʌʃi.   'Will you (pl) send it?'

59. Tʌʌenta ʃiagʌgʌ gouʃi.
    1s.saw where.hit this.tree
    'I saw where he hit the tree.'

60. ʃiadaxa api gʌtʌʌenta anʌ.
    where.sit 2s 1s.saw.2s 1s
    'I saw where you were sitting.'

61. Sobidai anʌ gokʌli makʌ aba koso.
    am.spying 1s this.man who there sleeps
    'I am spying on the man who is sleeping there.'

62. Tukarʌ imʌkai gʌtotoʃi ʃiaʌiepʌta api tʌligi.
    nighttime Pl.went those.rabbits where.2s.planted 2s wheat
    'At night the rabbits went where you planted wheat.'

63. Dai ʃiagʌotoi gʌoga api kʌsana api gʌbʌidamu anʌ.
    and where.sent.2s 2s.father 2s stand 2s will.take.2s 1s
    'And I shall take you where your father sent you to stand it.'

64. Aba daraxa vʌʌ vaika kʌkʌli ʌga makʌ gʌgʌgʌ goaali takavo.
    there sit all three men 3p who Pl.hit these.children yesterday
    'There sit those three men who hit the children yesterday.'

65. Gʌntʌʌenta apimu gouʃirʌ.
    1s.saw.2p 2p in.this.tree
    'I saw you (pl) up in the tree.'

66. Kokosoi gʌtataiʃoli uʃi uta.
    Pl.sleep 2s.pigs trees under
    'Your pigs sleep under the trees.'

67. Giɲʃiʌgi daxa gouʃirʌ gʌdokʌdʌ.
    1s.older.brother sits in.this.tree big.one
    'My older brother is up in the big tree.'

68. Tan vaʃi atʌtʌmʌ ʌxʌi tʌligi.
    here exactly 1p planted wheat
    'Right here is where we planted wheat.'

69. Takavo kiiaba koi gotaiʃoli.
    yesterday against.house slept this.pig
    'The pig slept against the house yesterday.'

Continued

Dataset 297 continued:

70. Anan gʌgʌ gokʌli makʌ divia takavo.
    1s   hit   this.man who came yesterday
    It was I who hit the man who came yesterday.'

71. Gʌkʌli   makʌ mʌʌ kʌka giɲʃobidai.
    that.man who there stands is.spying.1s
    The man who is standing way over there is spying on me.'

72. Gʌgʌvamu anʌ iʃʃobidana api gʌtotoʃi.
    will.hit.2s 1s if.spy   2s those.rabbits
    'I shall hit you if you spy on the rabbits.'

73. Gʌbʌkamu   anʌ iʃgʌvana giɲoga.
    will.grab.you 1s if.hit   1s.father
    'I shall grab you if you hit my father.'

74. Askaiti sobidana anʌ goaali.
    said   spy   1s these.children
    'He said I should spy on the children.'

75. Giɲotoi gʌvana vʌʌ goka ʃiʃiʌgi.
    sent.1s hit   all two older.brothers
    'He sent me to hit both of his older brothers.'

76. Gʌotosamu   gʌvana vʌʌ goka susukuli.
    will.send.2s hit   all two younger.brothers
    'He will send you to hit both of his younger.brothers.'

77. Askaitiʃi giɲoga   gʌsobidana anʌ.
    said?   1s.father spy.2s   1s
    'Did my father say that I should spy on you?'

78. Askaitiʃi ʌgai   muana api.
    said?   that.one kill 2s
    'He said that you should kill it?'

79. Askaitiʃi ʌgai maigʌrgʌgʌvana apimu.
    said?   3s   not.hit.1p   2p
    'Did he say that you (pl) should not hit us?'

80. Askaiti ʌgai mosdaxana kiiana.
    said   3s   just.sit   at.home
    'He said to just stay home.'

81. Askaitiʃi ʌgai giɲgʌvana gʌkʌli   anʌ.
    said?   3s   hit.1s   that.man 1s
    'Did he say that that man should hit me?'

82. Otoi api kʌsana api gomono kiiana.
    sent 2s stand 2s this.doll at.house
    'He sent you to stand the doll at home.'

Continued

Dataset 297 continued:

83. Maikʌkivamu anʌ iʃgʌvana gʌkʌli   anʌ.
    not.move   1s if.hits   that.man 1s
    'I shall not move if that man hits me.'

84. Gʌotosamu anʌ daxana api kiiana   iʃʌʌʃidana api gʌtʌligi.
    will.send.2s 1s sit   2s at.house if.steal 2s that.wheat
    'I shall send you to sit at home if you steal the wheat.'

85. Dada vaika totoʃi   aalidukʌdʌ.
    came three rabbits little.ones
    'Three little rabbits came.'

86. Dai dada   goka ʃiʃiʌgi.
    and Pl.came two older.brothers
    'And two older brothers came.'

87. Dada   vʌʌ goka mamara.
    Pl.came all two   sons
    'Both sons came.'

88. Tʌʌeta gʌrʃiʃiʌgi   tuvuʃtama tataiʃoli giʌkʌdʌ.
    saw   1p.older.brothers nine   pigs   fat.ones
    'Our older brothers saw nine fat pigs.'

89. Tʌʌeta ʌga vʌʌ makova tataiʃoli gagakiɲikʌdʌ ʌpʌ.
    saw   3p all four   pigs   skinny.ones also
    'They saw the four skinny pigs also.'

90. Daidi tʌʌemʌta apimu ʌpʌ   vaika tataiʃoli gagakiɲikʌdʌ.
    and   Pl.saw   you.Pl other three pigs   skinny.ones
    'But you (Pl) saw three other skinny pigs.'

91. Ʌpan gʌgʌ anʌ gotoʃi.
    again hit 1s this.rabbit
    'I hit the rabbit again.'

92. Apapi ʌpʌ   gʌgʌ gotoʃi.
    2s   other hit this.rabbit
    'You also hit the rabbit.'

93. Daidi gʌgʌ anʌ gotoʃi   ʌpamo.
    and   hit 1s this.rabbit again
    'Then I hit the rabbit again.'

94. Daidi gʌgʌ api gotaiʃoli ʌpʌ.
    and   hit 2s this.pig   also
    'Then you hit the pig too.'

95. Tʌʌeta ʌga vʌʃi gʌtʌligi.
    saw   they all that.wheat
    'They saw all the wheat.'

Continued

Dataset 297 Stage three:

96. GʌGʌ anʌ vaʃi gototoʃi.
    hit   1s all these.rabbits
    'I hit all the rabbits.'

97. Sobidai anʌ gʌmara vaʃia tʌvʌdʌkʌdʌ.
    spy   1s 2s.son most tall.one
    'I'm spying on your tallest son.'

98. Ali   tʌvʌdʌ gotova.
    very tall   this.turkey
    'The turkey is very tall.'

99. Tuku gotaiʃoli.
    black this.pig
    'The pig is black.'

100. Ali   kʌgado gouʃi.
     very fine   this.tree
     'The tree is very fine.'

101. Ali   kʌkʌgado vʌʌ tuvuʃtama tataiʃoli.
     very good   all nine   pigs
     'The nine pigs are very fine.'

102. Tʌtʌvʌdʌ vʌʌ vaika tutukukʌdʌ.
     tall   all three black.ones
     'The three black ones are tall.'

103. Ali   tʌvʌdʌ gotaiʃoli tukukʌdʌ.
     very tall   this.pig black.one
     'The black pig is very tall.'

104. Ali   tuku gotaiʃoli tʌvʌdʌkʌdʌ.
     very black this.pig tall.one
     'The tall pig is very black.'

105. Ali   tutuku vʌʌ vaika tataiʃoli kʌkʌgadokʌdʌ.
     very black all three pigs   good.ones
     'The three good pigs are very black.'

106. Ali   kʌgado gotova   alidukʌdʌ.
     very good   this.turkey little.one
     'The little turkey is very fine.'

107. Tuku gʌtova   tʌvʌdʌkʌdʌ.
     black that.turkey tall.one
     'The tall turkey is black.'

108. Ali   aalidu vʌʌ tuvuʃtama tataiʃoli tutukukʌdʌ.
     very little all nine   pigs   black.ones
     'The nine black pigs are very little.'

Continued

Dataset 297 continued:

109. Ali   alidu gouʃi   kʌgadokʌdʌ.
     very little this.tree good.ones
     'The fine tree is very little.'

110. Ali   tʌtʌvʌdʌ vʌʌ vaika uʃi.
     very tall   all three trees
     'The three trees are very tall.'

111. Ali   alidu gotukukʌdʌ.
     very little this.black.one
     'The black one is very little.'

112. Tuku   gotʌvʌdʌkʌdʌ.
     black this.tall.one
     'The tall one is black.'

113. Ali   tuku   goalidukʌdʌ.
     very black this.little.one
     'The little one is very black.'

114. Ali   kʌkʌgado vʌʌ tuvuʃtamatai.
     very good   all nine
     'The nine of them are very good.'

115. Ali   tʌvʌdʌ gotukukʌdʌ   kʌgadokʌdʌ.
     very tall   this.black.one good.one
     'The good black one is very tall.'

116. Ali   kʌkʌgado vʌʌ tuvuʃtama tʌtʌvʌdʌkʌdʌ.
     very good   all nine   tall.ones
     'The nine tall ones are very good.'

117. Ali   tuku   giɲtaiʃoli.
     very black 1s.pig
     'My pig is very black.'

118. Ali   muidu   gʌrtataiʃoli.
     very many   1p.pigs
     'We have very many pigs.'

119. Gʌgʌrʌ vʌʃi gʌrvʌpʌgikʌdʌ.
     big   all 1p.red.ones
     'All our red ones are big.'

120. Ali   gʌgʌrʌ vʌʌ gʌvaikatai.
     very big   all 2s.three
     'All three of yours are very big.'

121. Ali   gʌdo   vʌgikʌdʌdʌ.
     very big   3s.red.one
     'His red one is very big.'

Continued

Laboratory Manual for Morphology and Syntax

Dataset 297 continued:

122.	Ali ʃon koi anʌ.	'I slept very well.'
123.	Vʌʃkʌrʌ ʃon daxa anʌ.	'I continued to be happy.'
124.	Takavo kavuli koi anʌ.	'I slept all bunched up yesterday.'
125.	Ali kavami gʌvamu anʌ ʌgai.	'I'll really hit him hard.'
126.	I ʌgai vʌʃkʌrʌ.	'He continued to go.'
127.	Maiʃobipʌʃi api anʌ aba takavo.	'Didn't you spy on me there yesterday?'
128.	Koipʌʃi api ʌpʌ.	'Did you go to sleep again?'
129.	Dai gokirʌ kavami gʌgʌvamuʃi ʌgai.	'And afterwards will he hit you hard?'
130.	Giɲgʌvaɲi.	'Hit me!
131.	Gʌvaɲi.	'Hit him!
132.	Gʌvaɲi api maradʌ.	'Hit his son!
133.	Sobidaɲi gʌkʌkʌli.	'Spy on those men!
134.	Giɲgʌgʌvavurai.	'(You.Pl) hit me!
135.	Gʌgʌvavurai apimu.	'(You.Pl) hit him/them!
136.	Gʌrgʌgʌvavurai.	'(You.Pl) hit us!
137.	Maigʌgʌɲi api.	'Don't hit him!
138.	Muaɲi ʌgai.	'Kill him!
139.	Takavo anan ʌi tʌligi.	'I planted wheat yesterday.'
140.	Gʌrsosobi apimu atʌmʌ.	'You (Pl) spied on us.'
141.	Giɲʃosobi apimu anʌ.	'You (Pl) spied on me.'
142.	Giɲʃobi api.	'You spied on me.'
143.	Gʌrsobi api.	'You spied on us.'
144.	Gʌgʌ giɲʃukuli.	'He hit my younger brother.'
145.	Gʌgʌgʌgʌ.	'They hit you.'
146.	Gʌgʌgʌvamu atʌmʌ.	'We will hit you.'
147.	Gʌrgʌvai atʌmʌ.	'He is hitting us.'
148.	Gʌgʌvai giɲoga.	'They are hitting my father.'
149.	Mosgiɲvuapai.	'He is just bringing it to me.'
150.	Maigʌgʌgʌ ʌgai.	'He didn't hit you.'
151.	Gʌnsobietʌta.	'We spied on you (Pl).

Dataset 298. Pocomchí (Guatemala)

1. Re tinamit wilik ʧik mas pat.
   town   much house
   'The town already has many houses.'

2. ʃelik ew   pan   tinamit.
          yesterday stomach town
   'He/they left town yesterday.'

3. Ew iʃ ʔox Maria pan   kʔaybal.
   Yesterday Mary stomach market
   'Yesterday Mary went to the market.'

4. Ar   ʃiyew xinax tulul.
   there   one   banana
   'He gave one banana there.'

5. Re riʃim   Dominga ma naxt ta ruːkʔ kʔaybal.
       3s.corn Dominga   far   market
   'Dominga's corn is near the market.'

6. Qʔan   iʃim.
   yellow corn
   'The corn is yellow.'

7. Re Beta   re ritut   taniʃ.
          Bertha   3s.mother Tanish
   'Bertha is Tanish's mother.'

8. Re rasbes   Dominga.
       3s.older.sibling Dominga
   'Dominga is his/her older sister.'

9. Kaq riʃim   taniʃ.
   red 3s.corn Tanish
   'Tanish's corn is red.'

10. Wilik ma kʔisin ta ritsʔiʔ Hwan taniʃ.
               little   3s.dog John Tanish
    'Tanish has John's big dog.'

11. Re hwan ʃokik yuʔnak pan   ripat.
        John   now   stomach 3s.house
    'John now entered his house.'

12. Re Beta   maʃta wilik ʧik ratsʔam Dominga.
         Bertha   3s.salt Dominga
    'Bertha no longer has Dominga's salt.'

13. Ne nikʔuʃ ritulul.
               3s.banana
    'I will eat his banana.'

Continued

Dataset 298 continued:

14. Xewo eqal   iʃoq   nel kikʼuʃ kinaqʼ.
    also   tomorrow woman   beans
    'Also the women will eat beans tomorrow.'

15. Re nitut   ar.
        1s.mother there
    'There is my mother.'

16. Re qatut   Beta.
        1p.mother Bertha
    'Bertha is our mother.'

17. Re tumin   watʃ meʃa.
        money   table
    'The money is on the table.'

18. Re re.
        he
    'It is he.'

19. Atob hat.
    good you
    'You are good.'

20. Qʼan   qapat.
    yellow 1p.house
    'Our house is yellow.'

21. Qʼan   qatsʼam.
    yellow 1p.salt
    'Our salt is yellow.'

22. Re hat ʃayew awiʃim   wiluʔ.
        2s   2s.corn   over.there
    'You gave your corn over there.'

23. Ew   ʃoxʔox
    yesterday 1p.went
    'We went yesterday.'

24. Xewo ʃoxʔox tʃik hox naxt tʃiriːx pat.
    Also   1p far   house
    'Also we already went way behind the house.'

25. Re Hwan wilik mas   qʼeq qʼotʃ.
        John   much black crow
    'John has a very black crow.'

26. Suq   atulul.
    sweet 2s.banana
    'Your bananas are sweet.'

Continued

Dataset 298 continued:

27. Re Maria re wanab.
       Mary   1s.younger.sister
    'Mary is my younger sister.'

28. Kʔisin qʔotʃ.
    little   crow
    'Crows are little.'

29. Re ritumin iʃoq pan pat ar.
        3s.money woman stomach house there
    'The woman's money is there in the house.'

30. Re xinax winaq nel inokik ruːkʔ Hwan
        one man
    'A man will enter with John.'

31. Mas atob winaq.
    much good man
    'The man is very good.'

32. Re ke wiluʔ.
       they over.there
    'They are over there.'

33. Ma re ta tʃiriːx tʃeʔ.
       he   tree
    'He is not behind the tree.'

34. Mas saq ratsʔam.
    much white 3s.salt
    'His salt is very white.'

35. Re rasbes awiʃqʔun.
       3s.older.sibling 2s.daughter
    'Your daughter is his/her older sister.'

36. Re iʃoq maʃta wilik atumin watʃ meʃa ar.
       woman   2s.money   table there
    'The woman does not have your money there on the table.'

37. Xewo iʃ kikʔuʃ iʃim.
    also   corn
    'Also they ate corn.'

38. ʃiyew riʃim wiluʔ.
    3s.corn   over.there
    'He gave his corn over there.'

39. Wilik kiʔib kakʔun tʃiriːx ripat rehkʔen Pablo.
        two 3p.son   3s.house 3s.wife Paul
    'Paul's wife has two sons behind her house.'

Continued

Dataset 298 continued:

40. Re hin ʃinʔox pan   tinamit.
        1s   stomach town
    'I went to town.'

41. Re hox maʃta wilik katsʼam tʃiːrx tʃeʔ.
        1p   3p.salt   tree
    'We do not have their salt behind the tree.'

42. Nel kibehik iʃib   winaq eqal   kibil.
                 three man   tomorrow
    'Tomorrow the three men will walk alone.'

43. Re Hwan naxt tʃiːrx pat.
        John   far   house
    'John is far behind the house.'

44. Qʼeq kikinaqʼ.
    black 3p.beans
    'Their beans are black.'

45. Re nitʃaqʼ   ruʃ   Dominga.
        1s.younger.brother 3s.younger.brother Dominga
    'Dominga's younger brother is my younger brother.'

46. Re hin Hwan.
        1s John
    'I am John.'

47. Saq   atsʼam.
    white salt
    'The salt is white.'

48. Re qatsʼiʔ fidel.
        1p.dog Fidel
    'Fidel is our dog.'

49. Ew   reh kʼen ʃikʼay tulul   pan   kʼaybal.
    yesterday 3s.wife   banana stomach market
    'His wife sold bananas in the market yesterday.'

50. Wilik xinax ritʃaqʼ   Hwan.
        one   3s.younger.brother John
    'John has one younger brother.'

51. Re iʃib   iʃoq   iʃ kiloqʼ tsʼiʔ.
        three woman   dog
    'The three women bought a dog.'

52. Wilik tʃik.
    'There already is/are.'

Continued

Dataset 298 continued:

53. ʃiʔox.
    'They went.'

54. Wilik.
    'There is/are.'

55. Nel kinʔox hin wibil.
    'I will go alone.'

56. Maʃta wilik.
    'There is/are none.'

57. ʃiʔox tʃik.
    'They already went.'

58. Ma nel ta kelik tʃiqiːx.
    'They will not leave after us.'

59. Xewo ma nel ta tokik.
    'Also you will not enter.'

60. Maʃta wilik tʃik.
    'There no longer are any.'

61. ʃatokik tʃik ew.
    'You already entered yesterday.'

62. ʃinelik tʃik ruːkʼ.
    'I already left with him.'

63. Ma ʃatnitow ta.
    'I did not help you.'

64. Xewo yuʔnak hat ʃakox atumin   ar.
    also   now   2s   2s.money there
    'Also you put your money there now.'

65. Re ribahil   Hwana atʃaqʼ.
        3s.husband Jane   2s.younger.brother
    'Jane's husband is your younger brother.'

66. Nim rikinaqʼ.
    big   3s.beans
    'His beans are big.'

67. Re ripat   Maria.
        3s.house Mary
    'It is Mary's house.'

68. Wilik nitʃaqʼ   ke.
         1s.younger.brother they
    'They have my younger brother.'

Continued

Dataset 298 continued:

69. Re Maria inʔox tʃik ruːm Dominga.
    Mary   Dominga
    'Dominga is already making Mary go.'

70. Re hat waxaw.
    2s 1s.father
    'You are my father.'

71. Re saq atsʼam pan   pat.
    white salt   stomach house
    'The white salt is in the house.'

72. Kinʔox yuʔnak kuːkʼ.
           now
    'I go now with them.'

73. Wilik mas tumin iʃib awasbes.
       much money three 2s.older.sibling
    'Your three older siblings have a lot of momey.'

74. Kʼisin re.
    little   he
    'He is little.'

75. Yuʔnak iʃ nikox qatumin   pan   pat.
    now   1p.money stomach house
    'I put our money in the house now.'

76. Re re naxt ruːkʼ pat.
      he far   house
    'He is far from the house.'

77. Re Pablo wilik ma mas ta nim pat.
      Paul   much   big house
    'Paul does not have a very big house.'

78. Ew   ʃikʼay tʃik tulul.
    yesterday   banana
    'He already sold bananas yesterday.'

79. Mas suq tulul.
    much sweet banana
    'The bananas are very sweet.'

80. Yuʔnak qoʔox awuːkʼ.
    now
    'We go now with you.'

81. Re rakʼun Beta awakʼun.
        3s.son Bertha 2s.son
    'Your son is Bertha's son.'

Continued

Dataset 298 continued:

82. Ma re ta Taniʃ.
   he Tanish
 'He is not Tanish.'

83. Ne rikʼay rikinaqʼ rehkʼen atʃaqʼ   eqal.
   3s.beans 3s.wife 2s.younger.brother tomorrow
 'Your younger brother's wife will sell her beans tomorrow.'

84. Nel kinelik hin.
      1s
 'I will leave.'

85. Mas nitulul.
 much 1s.banana
 'My bananas are many.'

86. Re Dominga wilik xinax ritʃaqʼ.
   Dominga one 3s.younger.sister
 'Dominga has one younger sister.'

87. Re Hwan wilik xinax ripat.
   John   one 3s.house
 'John has a house.'

88. Xewo hin i nikʼuʃ kinaqʼ.
 also 1s   beans
 'Also I eat beans.'

89. Mas suq kiʃim.
 much sweet 3p.corn
 'Their corn is very sweet.'

90. Pan kʼaybal nel tibehik quːm.
 stomach market
 'We will make you walk to the market.'

91. Ma re ta Hwan tʃiriːx tʃeʔ.
    John   tree
 'It is not John behind the tree.'

92. Maʃta wilik rasbes   Hwan.
   3s.older.sibling John
 'John does not have an older brother or sister.'

93. Mas watsʼam.
 much 1s.salt
 'My salt is plentiful.'

94. Ma hat ta tʃiriːx kʼaybal.
   2s   market
 'It is not you behind the market.'

Continued

Dataset 298 continued:

95. Yuʔnak kiʔib wanab   kokik.
     now   two   1s.younger.sister
     'My two younger sisters enter now.'

96. Re mas   tumin   ʃiyew atob winaq yuʔnak ar.
         much money   good man   now   there
     'The good man gave a lot of money there now.'

97. Mas   awiʃim.
     much 2s.corn
     'Your corn is plentiful.'

98. Xewo ʃatbehik ew.
     also   yesterday
     'Also you walked yesterday.'

99. Re Maria ʃiyokʔ ribahil.
         Mary   her.husband
     'Mary cut her husband.'

100. Re nim pat   ma naxt ta ruːkʔ be.
         big house   far   road
      'The big house is near the road.'

101. Re Taniʃ   wilik ranab.
         Tanish   3s.younger.sister
      'Tanish has a younger sister.'

102. Maʃta wilik mas   nim pat   Taniʃ.
                much big   house Tanish
      'Tanish does not have a very big house.'

103. Ma mas   ta suq   kinaqʔ.
         much   sweet beans
      'The beans are not very good.'

104. Naxt ruːkʔ pat   kiʔib riʃqʔun   Beta   ʃinkisakʔ hin.
      far   house two   3s.daughter Bertha   1s
      'Far away from the house Bertha's two daughters hit me.'

105. Re iʃoq   re atut.
         woman   2s.mother
      'Your mother is a woman.'

106. Maʃta wilik rakʔun.
                3s.son
      'He has no son.'

107. Re kʔaybal ma mas   ta naxt ruːkʔ pat.
         market   much   far   house
      'The market is not very far from the house.'

Continued

Dataset 298 continued:

108. Nel kinokik pan ripat Pablo.
               stomach 3s.house Paul
    'I will enter Paul's house.'

109. Re ke nel kawil hat.
        they   you
    'You will see them.'

110. Re tulul tʃiriːx ripat Hwan.
        banana   3s.house John
    'The bananas are behind John's house.'

111. Re tʃintʃel tinamit iʃ kitsʼap kipat ew.
        all   town   3p.house yesterday
    'The whole town closed their houses yesterday.'

112. Xewo hat telik awibil.
    also you
    'Also you leave alone (by yourself).'

113. Re Maria wilik iʃib riʃqʼun.
        Mary   three 3s.daughter
    'Mary has three daughters.'

114. Ma mas ta kʼisin hin.
        much   little 1s
    'I am not very little.'

115. Wilik kinaqʼ.
        beans
    'There are beans.'

116. Re kikinaqʼ iʃ kikʼuʃ tʃik kiʔib winaq tʃiriːx kʼaybal.
        3p.beans   two man   market
    'The two men already ate their beans behind the market.'

117. ʃatokik hat ew pan nipat wuːkʼ.
        2s yesterday stomach 1s.house
    'You entered my house with me yesterday.'

118. Mero qʼeq atulul.
    slightly black 2s.bananas
    'Your bananas are a little black.'

119. Maʃta wilik qanab ar.
               2s.younger.sister there
    'We do not have a younger sister there.'

120. Re hox nel qokik eqal.
        1p   tomorrow
    'We will enter tomorrow.'

Continued

Laboratory Manual for Morphology and Syntax

Dataset 298 continued:

121. Wilik q'eq iʃim.
             black corn
     'There is black corn.'

122. Re kiʔib rak'un Beta   maʃta wilik kehk'en.
          two   3s.son Bertha   3p.wives
     'Bertha's two sons do not have wives.'

123. Re saq   iʃim ar.
          white corn there
     'The white corn is there.'

124. Mero   kaq wiʃim.
     slightly red 1s.corn
     'My corn is a little red.'

125. Iʃ wil ripat   waxaw   hin.
             3s.house 1s.father 1s
     'I saw my father's house.'

126. Wilik tʃintʃel qatumin   wiluʔ   Beta.
            all   1p.money over.there Bertha
     'Bertha has all our money over there.'

127. Re hat Pablo.
           2s Paul
     'You are Paul.'

128. Re n i m pat   naxt ruːk' be.
          big   house far   road
     'The big house is far from the road.'

129. Xewo tiqil hat yuʔnak.
     also   2s   now
     'Also we now see you.'

130. Ma nim ta nipat.
         big   1s.house
     'My house is small.'

131. Wilik kaq tulul   rehk'en.
            red banana 3s.wife
     'His wife has a red banana.'

132. Maʃta wilik tumin.
                  money
     'There is no money.'

133. Xewo ar   q'otʃ kibehik.
     also   there crow
     'Also the crows walk there.'

Continued

Dataset 298 continued:

134. Re kinaqʼ tʃiriːx pat wiluʔ.
    beans   house over.there
    'The beans are over there behind the house.'

135. Ma saq ta ripat Dominga.
    white   3s.house Dominga
    'Dominga's house is not white.'

136. ʃinbehik wiluʔ.
        over.there
    'I walked over there.'

137. Re Maria wilik ritumin pan pat.
    Mary   3s.money stomach house
    'Mary has her money in the house.'

138. Re nim tulul iʃ qakʼay ar.
    big banana   there
    'There we sold big bananas.'

139. Mas naxt ripat Pablo.
    much far 3s.house Paul
    'Paul's house is very far away.'

140. Re rasbes Dominga wilik tʃik rakʼun pan tinamit.
    3s.older.sibling Dominga   3s.son stomach town
    'Dominga's older brother already has a son in town.'

141. Re ruʃ Dominga rasbes Maria.
    3s.younger.brother Dominga 3s.older.sibling Mary
    'Dominga's younger brother is Mary's older brother.'

142. tʃiriːx nim tʃeʔ kiʔib ruʃ Beta iʃ kil mas atsʼam.
    big tree two 3s.younger.brother Bertha   much salt
    'Bertha's two younger brothers saw a lot of salt behind a big tree.'

143. Xewo inʔox rehkʼen Pablo.
    also   3s.wife Paul
    'Also Paul's wife goes.'

144. Ma Taniʃ ta pan kʼaybal.
    Tanish   stomach market
    'It is not Tanish in the market.'

145. Re Dominga wilik tʃik riyiʔab pan kʼaybal.
    Dominga   3s.place stomach market
    'Dominga already has her place in the market.'

146. Re kiʃqʼun wilik iʃib tulul.
    3p.daughter   three banana
    'Their daughter has three bananas.'

Continued

Dataset 298 continued:

147. Xewo pan   pat   ʃakox atsˀam.
     also stomach house   salt
     'Also you put the salt in the house.'

148. Re qatsˀiʔ maʃta wilik pan   tinamit.
     1p.dog   stomach town
     'Our dog is not in town.'

149. Re re ritʃaqˀ   Dominga.
     3s 3s.younger.sister Dominga
     'She is Dominga's younger sister.'

150. Re hox rasbes   Maria.
     1p 3s.older.sibling Mary
     'We are Mary's older brothers and sisters.'

151. Re Dominga maʃta wilik tʃiriːx ripat.
     Dominga   3s.house
     'Dominga is not behind her house.'

152. Ma ew   ta iʃ kikox tumin pan   pat   wiluʔ.
     yesterday   money stomach house over.there
     'It was not yesterday that they put money over there in the house.'

153. Wiluʔ in kikitow yuʔnak.
     'They help them over there now.'

154. Iʃ behik waxaw tʃiriːx tʃeʔ quːkˀ
     'My father walked with us behind the tree.'

155. Ma mas ta tumin.
     'There is little money.'

156. Ma atob ta Dominga.
     'Dominga is evil.'

157. Re kinaqˀ wiluʔ.
     'The beans are over there.'

158. Wilik qayiʔab.
     'We have a place.'

159. Re apat in atsˀap tʃik yuʔnak.
     'You already close your house now.'

160. Ma qˀan ta riʃim winaq.
     'The man's corn is not yellow.'

161. Wilik iʃib wiʃqˀun.
     'I have three daughters.'

162. Ma tulul ta watʃ meʃa.
     'It is not bananas on the table.'

Continued

Dataset 298 continued:

163. Wilik tulul ma naxt ta ruːkʼ ripat.
    'There are bananas near his house.'

164. Re nitʃaqʼ nel inelik tʃawiːx.
    'My younger brother will leave after you.'

165. Eqal wanab nel kiwil.
    'Tomorrow I will see my younger sisters.'

166. Maʃta wilik qʼan ripat awakʼun.
    'Your son doesn't have a yellow house.'

167. Ma ew ta ʃokik.
    'It was not yesterday that he/they entered.'

168. Ma kʼisin ta hat.
    'You are big.'

169. Ma ar ta iʃ nisakʼ tʃeʔ.
    'It was not there that I hit the tree.'

170. Mas nim pat.
    'The house is very big.'

171. Maʃta wilik hat pan pat.
    'You are not in the house.'

172. Mas nim ripat Hwan.
    'John's house is very big.'

173. Xewo ma nel ta qayew tulul.
    'Also we will not give bananas.'

174. Ma yuʔnak ta kinʔox hin.
    'It is not now that I go.'

175. Suq kinaqʼ.
    'The beans are sweet.'

176. Re winaq pan tinamit.
    'The man is in town.'

177. Wilik xinax ranab Taniʃ.
    'Tanish has one younger sister.'

Continued

Dataset 298 continued:

Partial paradigm of the Pocomchí verb 'help':

	PRESENT	PAST	FUTURE
178. 'I ... you.'	tinitow	ʃatnitow	nel tinitow
179. 'I ... him.'	initow	iʃ nitow	nel initow
180. 'I ... them.'	kinitow	ʃinitow	nel kinitow
181. 'You ... me.'	kinatow	ʃinatow	nel kinatow
182. 'You ... him.'	inatow	ʃatow	nel inatow
183. 'You ... us.'	qoxatow	ʃoxatow	nel qoxatow
184. 'You ... them.'	katow	ʃatow	nel katow
185. 'He ... me.'	kiritow	ʃiritow	nel kiritow
186. 'He ... you.'	tiritow	ʃatritow	nel tiritow
187. 'He ... him.'	iritow	ʃitow	nel iritow
188. 'He ... us.'	qoxritow	ʃoxritow	nel qoxritow
189. 'He ... them.'	kiritow	ʃiritow	nel kiritow
190. 'We ... you.'	tiqatow	ʃatqatow	nel tiqatow
191. 'We ... him.'	inqatow	iʃ qatow	nel inqatow
192. 'We ... them.'	kiqatow	ʃiqatow	nel kiqatow
193. 'They ... me.'	kinkitow	ʃinkitow	nel kinkitow
194. 'They ... you.'	tikitow	ʃatkitow	nel tikitow
195. 'They ... him.'	inkitow	iʃ kitow	nel inkitow
196. 'They ... us.'	qoxkitow	ʃoxkitow	nel qoxkitow
197. 'They ... them.'	kikitow	ʃikitow	nel kikitow
198. 'I ... the dog.'	i nitow tsʔiʔ	iʃ nitow tsʔiʔ	ne nitow tsʔiʔ
199. 'You ... the dog.'	in atow tsʔiʔ	ʃatow tsʔiʔ	nel atow tsʔiʔ
200. 'He ... the dog.'	i ritow tsʔiʔ	ʃitow tsʔiʔ	ne ritow tsʔiʔ
201. 'We ... the dog.'	in qatow tsʔiʔ	iʃ qatow tsʔiʔ	nel qatow tsʔiʔ
202. 'They ... the dog.'	in kitow tsʔiʔ	iʃ kitow tsʔiʔ	nel kitow tsʔiʔ

Continued

Dataset 298 continued:

Partial paradigm of the Pocomchí verb 'see':

	PRESENT	PAST	FUTURE
203. 'I ... you.'	tiwil	ʃatwil	nel tiwil
204. 'I ... him.'	inwil	iʃwil	nel inwil
205. 'I ... them.'	kiwil	ʃiwil	nel kiwil
206. 'You ... me.'	kinawil	ʃinawil	nel kinawil
207. 'You ... him.'	inawil	ʃawil	nel inawil
208. 'You ... us.'	qawil	ʃoxawil	nel qawil
209. 'You ... them.'	kawil	ʃawil	nel kawil
210. 'He ... me.'	kiril	ʃiril	nel kiril
211. 'He ... you.'	tiril	ʃatril	nel tiril
212. 'He ... him.'	iril	ʃil	nel iril
213. 'He ... us.'	qoxril	ʃoxril	nel qoxril
214. 'He ... them.'	kiril	ʃiril	nel kiril
215. 'We ... you.'	tiqil	ʃatqil	nel tiqil
216. 'We ... him.'	inqil	iʃ qil	nel inqil
217. 'We ... them.'	kiqil	ʃiqil	nel kiqil
218. 'They ... me.'	kinkil	ʃinkil	nel kinkil
219. 'They ... you.'	tikil	ʃatkil	nel tikil
220. 'They ... him.'	inkil	iʃ kil	nel inkil
221. 'They ... us.'	qoxkil	ʃoxkil	nel qoxkil
222. 'They ... them.'	kikil	ʃikil	nel kikil
223. 'I ... the dog.'	in wil tsʔiʔ	iʃ wil tsʔiʔ	nel wil tsʔiʔ
224. 'You ... the dog.'	in awil tsʔiʔ	ʃawil tsʔiʔ	nel awil tsʔiʔ
225. 'He ... the dog.'	i ril tsʔiʔ	ʃil tsʔiʔ	ne ril tsʔiʔ
226. 'We ... the dog.'	in qil tsʔiʔ	iʃ qil tsʔiʔ	nel qil tsʔiʔ
227. 'They ... the dog.'	in kil tsʔiʔ	iʃ kil tsʔiʔ	nel kil tsʔiʔ

CPSIA information can be obtained
at www.ICGtesting.com
Printed in the USA
BVOW04s1156120817
491730BV00017B/56/P

9 781556 71